How to Do
*Everything*™

W9-BPK-884

# iCloud®

Jason R. Rich

New York  Chicago  San Francisco  Lisbon
London  Madrid  Mexico City  Milan  New Delhi
San Juan  Seoul  Singapore  Sydney  Toronto

**The McGraw·Hill Companies**

**Library of Congress Cataloging-in-Publication Data**

Rich, Jason.
　　How to do everything. iCloud / Jason Rich.
　　　　p.　　cm.
　　ISBN 978-0-07-179017-8 (alk. paper)
　　1. Cloud computing.　2. iCloud.　3. Apple computer.　4. iOS (Electronic resource)
5. Mac OS.　I. Title.　II. Title: iCloud.
　　QA76.585.R43　　2012
　　004.6782—dc23

2011052627

McGraw-Hill books are available at special quantity discounts to use as premiums and sales promotions, or for use in corporate training programs. To contact a representative, please e-mail us at bulksales@mcgraw-hill.com.

# How to Do Everything™: iCloud®

Cover image courtesy of Apple, Inc.
iCloud is a registered trademark and the iCloud logo is trademark of Apple, Inc. in the U.S. and/or other countries.

Model image from Thayer Allison Gowdy, used with permission and © 2011

Model image courtesy of Level III Modeling & Talent

MacBook photos used by permission and © 2011 Doug Rosa

iPhone and iPad photos used by permission and © 2011 Frederick Lieberath

34567890　DOC DOC　1098765432

ISBN　　978-0-07-179017-8
MHID　　0-07-179017-9

| | | |
|---|---|---|
| **Sponsoring Editor**<br>Megg Morin | **Technical Editor**<br>Donald Bell | **Production Supervisor**<br>James Kussow |
| **Editorial Supervisor**<br>Jody McKenzie | **Copy Editor**<br>Lisa Theobald | **Composition**<br>Cenveo Publisher Services |
| **Project Manager**<br>Vastavikta Sharma,<br>Cenveo Publisher Services | **Proofreader**<br>Claire Splan | **Illustration**<br>Cenveo Publisher Services |
| | **Indexer**<br>Jack Lewis | **Art Director, Cover**<br>Jeff Weeks |
| **Acquisitions Coordinator**<br>Stephanie Evans | | |

*This book is dedicated to Steve Jobs (1955–2011). He was an amazing man, a true visionary, and Apple's fearless leader. He changed the world forever.*

# About the Author

**Jason R. Rich** (www.JasonRich.com) is the bestselling author of more than 48 books covering a wide range of topics. His books include *How To Do Everything: Digital Photography* (McGraw-Hill Professional, 2011), *How To Do Everything: Kindle Fire* (McGraw-Hill Professional, to be released in 2012), *Your iPad 2 at Work* (Que), *Using iPhone: iOS 5 Edition* (Que), *iPad & iPhone Tips & Tricks* (Que), and *Blogging for Fame & Fortune* (Entrepreneur Press).

To read more than 50 feature-length, how-to articles about the iPhone and iPad, visit www.iOSArticles.com. Jason's work also appears in a wide range of other national magazines, major daily newspapers, and popular web sites. You can follow Jason R. Rich on Twitter (@JasonRich7).

## About the Technical Editor

**Donald Bell** is a senior editor for CNET.com, covering portable media players and tablets. He is the writer responsible for CNET's official iPad review and regularly publishes tutorials for CNET's iPad Atlas blog. You can also hear him each week on CNET's Crave podcast. When he's not testing the latest gadgets, he enjoys playing guitar, listening to old records, and being a dad.

# Contents at a Glance

**Part I**  **Learn About Online File Sharing and Apple's iCloud**

　　1　Learn About Cloud-Based Online File Sharing Services . . . . . . . . . . . .　3
　　2　How Mac Users Can Utilize iCloud . . . . . . . . . . . . . . . . . . . . . . . . .　17
　　3　How iPhone, iPad, and iPod touch Users Can Utilize iCloud . . . . . . . . .　29
　　4　Migrate from Apple MobileMe to iCloud . . . . . . . . . . . . . . . . . . . . .　39

**Part II**  **Manage Your Music and Photos in the Cloud**

　　5　Manage Your Digital Music Library with iCloud . . . . . . . . . . . . . . . . .　59
　　6　Use the Premium iTunes Match Service . . . . . . . . . . . . . . . . . . . . . .　81
　　7　Use iCloud to Store and Manage Your Digital Photos . . . . . . . . . . . . .　95

**Part III**  **Share Documents, Music, Data, and More via iCloud and Other Services**

　　8　Share Documents and Files with iCloud . . . . . . . . . . . . . . . . . . . . .　117
　　9　Cloud-Based File/Document Sharing Alternatives to iCloud . . . . . . . .　139
　　10　Cloud-Based Music Service Alternatives to iCloud . . . . . . . . . . . . . .　157
　　11　The Microsoft 365 and Google Docs Alternatives to iCloud . . . . . . . . .　175

**Part IV**  **Use iCloud with Your iPhone and iPad Running iOS 5**

　　12　Manage Apps, App-Related Data, and eBooks with iCloud . . . . . . . . . .　187
　　13　Back Up Your iPhone and iPad with iCloud . . . . . . . . . . . . . . . . . . .　209
　　14　iCloud and Apple TV: The Perfect Entertainment Combination . . . . . .　225
　　A　Troubleshoot iCloud-Related Problems . . . . . . . . . . . . . . . . . . . . . .　241

　　Index . . . . . . . . . . . . . . . . . . . . . . . . . . . . . . . . . . . . . . . . . . .　245

# Contents

Acknowledgments . . . . . . . . . . . . . . . . . . . . . . . . . . . . . . . . . . . . . . . .  xiii
Introduction . . . . . . . . . . . . . . . . . . . . . . . . . . . . . . . . . . . . . . . . . .  xv

## PART I  Learn About Online File Sharing and Apple's iCloud

### CHAPTER 1  Learn About Cloud-Based Online File Sharing Services . . . . . . . .  3
What Is a Cloud-Based File Sharing Service Anyway? . . . . . . . . . . . . . . .  5
What Apple's iCloud Can Do for You . . . . . . . . . . . . . . . . . . . . . . . . . . .  6
What Using a Cloud-Based File Sharing Service Costs . . . . . . . . . . . . . . .  9
What You'll Need to Start Using iCloud with a Mac . . . . . . . . . . . . . . . . .  10
   Find a Lost or Stolen Mac, iPhone, or iPad . . . . . . . . . . . . . . . . . . . . .  11
What You'll Need to Start Using iCloud with an iPhone or iPad . . . . . . . . .  13
Let's Get Started... . . . . . . . . . . . . . . . . . . . . . . . . . . . . . . . . . . . . . . .  14

### CHAPTER 2  How Mac Users Can Utilize iCloud . . . . . . . . . . . . . . . . . . . .  17
Use the Find Your Mac Feature via iCloud . . . . . . . . . . . . . . . . . . . . . . .  21
Share Files Using the Back to My Mac Feature . . . . . . . . . . . . . . . . . . . .  24
Use iCloud as a Virtual Drop Box for Cloud-Based File Sharing . . . . . . . . .  26
Additional iCloud Functionality for Your Mac . . . . . . . . . . . . . . . . . . . . .  28

### CHAPTER 3  How iPhone, iPad, and iPod touch Users Can Utilize iCloud . . . . .  29
What an iOS Device User Can Do with iCloud . . . . . . . . . . . . . . . . . . . . .  29
Setting up Your iOS Devices to Work with iCloud . . . . . . . . . . . . . . . . . . .  30
   How to Check for iOS 5 Updates . . . . . . . . . . . . . . . . . . . . . . . . . . . . .  31
   Turn on iCloud Functionality on Your iOS Devices . . . . . . . . . . . . . . . . .  33
Sharing Content With and Without iCloud . . . . . . . . . . . . . . . . . . . . . . . .  36

### CHAPTER 4  Migrate from Apple MobileMe to iCloud . . . . . . . . . . . . . . . . .  39
Making the Switch from MobileMe to iCloud . . . . . . . . . . . . . . . . . . . . . .  41
   What You'll Need to Make the MobileMe-to-iCloud Transition . . . . . . . . . .  42
   Initiate the MobileMe-to-iCloud Conversion . . . . . . . . . . . . . . . . . . . . .  43

**vii**

**PART II   Manage Your Music and Photos in the Cloud**

**CHAPTER 5   Manage Your Digital Music Library with iCloud** . . . . . . . . . . . . . **59**

Shop for Music from the iTunes Store . . . . . . . . . . . . . . . . . . . . . . . . 62
  Learn More About Music Before Purchasing It . . . . . . . . . . . . . . . . . . . . 64
  Browse the iTunes Store for Music by Genre . . . . . . . . . . . . . . . . . . . . 66
  Save Money Using iTunes' Complete My Album Feature . . . . . . . . . . . . . 66
Apple ID Required . . . . . . . . . . . . . . . . . . . . . . . . . . . . . . . . . . . . . 68
Install and Set Up iTunes to Acquire and Manage Your Music Library . . . . . . . . 69
  First, Get iTunes Running on Your Mac or PC . . . . . . . . . . . . . . . . . . . . 70
How Digital Music Becomes Accessible from iCloud . . . . . . . . . . . . . . . . . 73
  Access and Download Past iTunes Purchases from Your PC or Mac . . . . . . 75
  Access and Download Past iTunes Purchases from Your iPhone,
    iPad, or iPod touch . . . . . . . . . . . . . . . . . . . . . . . . . . . . . . . . . . 77

**CHAPTER 6   Use the Premium iTunes Match Service** . . . . . . . . . . . . . . . . . **81**

Signing up for iTunes Match . . . . . . . . . . . . . . . . . . . . . . . . . . . . . . . 82
Cancel Your Auto-Renewing iTunes Match Subscription . . . . . . . . . . . . . . . 86
Activate iTunes Match on Your iPhone or iPod Touch . . . . . . . . . . . . . . . . . 87
Activate iTunes Match on Your iPad . . . . . . . . . . . . . . . . . . . . . . . . . . . 89
Activate iTunes Match on Another Computer . . . . . . . . . . . . . . . . . . . . . . 91
Keeping Your Music Library up to Date on iCloud . . . . . . . . . . . . . . . . . . . 93

**CHAPTER 7   Use iCloud to Store and Manage Your Digital Photos** . . . . . . . . . **95**

Turn on the Photo Stream Feature . . . . . . . . . . . . . . . . . . . . . . . . . . . . 97
  Turn on Photo Stream on Your Mac . . . . . . . . . . . . . . . . . . . . . . . . . 98
  Turn on Photo Stream on Your PC . . . . . . . . . . . . . . . . . . . . . . . . . . 102
  Turn on Photo Stream on Your iPhone, iPad, or iPod touch . . . . . . . . . . . 102
How to View Your Photo Stream Images . . . . . . . . . . . . . . . . . . . . . . . . 103
  View Photo Stream Images on a Mac . . . . . . . . . . . . . . . . . . . . . . . . . 104
  View Photo Stream Images on Any iOS Device . . . . . . . . . . . . . . . . . . . 104
  View Photo Stream Images on Your PC . . . . . . . . . . . . . . . . . . . . . . . 106
  View Photo Stream Images on Your HD Television . . . . . . . . . . . . . . . . . 107
Manually Add Images to Your Photo Stream from Your Computer . . . . . . . . . . 108
Edit Photos in Your Photo Stream . . . . . . . . . . . . . . . . . . . . . . . . . . . . 108
Delete Your Entire Photo Stream . . . . . . . . . . . . . . . . . . . . . . . . . . . . . 110
  Remove Photo Stream Images from Your iOS Device . . . . . . . . . . . . . . . 111
  Remove Photo Stream Images from iPhoto '11 on Your Mac . . . . . . . . . . . 112
  Remove Photo Stream Images from Your PC . . . . . . . . . . . . . . . . . . . . 112
Turn off Photo Stream Without Deleting Photos on Your Mac . . . . . . . . . . . . 113
Share Images Among Computers and Devices . . . . . . . . . . . . . . . . . . . . . 113

**PART III   Share Documents, Music, Data, and More via iCloud and Other Services**

**CHAPTER 8   Share Documents and Files with iCloud** . . . . . . . . . . . . . . . **117**

Set up a Free iWork.com Account . . . . . . . . . . . . . . . . . . . . . . . 117

Transfer Office and iWork Documents to iWork.com . . . . . . . . . . . . . . . . 119

Use a Mac to Password-Protect a File Being Uploaded to iWork.Com . . . . 120

Use an iOS Device to Password-Protect a File Being Uploaded
to iWork.Com . . . . . . . . . . . . . . . . . . . . . . . . . . . . . . . 121

E-mail Yourself Office Documents or Files from Your Computer . . . . . . . 124

Transfer iWork for Mac Files to iWork.com and iCloud . . . . . . . . . . . . . . 125

Share iWork for iOS Files on Your iPhone or iPad
with Other Computers/Devices . . . . . . . . . . . . . . . . . . . . . . . . . 126

Turn on iCloud Functionality for iWork Apps on an iOS Device . . . . . . . 126

Use iWork for iOS Apps with iCloud . . . . . . . . . . . . . . . . . . . . 129

Manually Export a Document from an iWork App on an iOS Device . . . . . 131

Other Third-Party Apps with iCloud Compatibility . . . . . . . . . . . . . . . . 136

**CHAPTER 9   Cloud-Based File/Document Sharing Alternatives to iCloud** . . . **139**

Introduction to Dropbox . . . . . . . . . . . . . . . . . . . . . . . . . . . . . 141

Get Started Using Dropbox . . . . . . . . . . . . . . . . . . . . . . . . . 142

Create Dropbox Folders Using Your Mac . . . . . . . . . . . . . . . . . . 145

Use Dropbox with Your iPhone or iPad . . . . . . . . . . . . . . . . . . . 146

Transfer a Word Document to Your iPad via Dropbox . . . . . . . . . . . . 147

Manage Files Directly from Dropbox.com . . . . . . . . . . . . . . . . . . 151

Dropbox vs. iCloud: Similarities and Differences . . . . . . . . . . . . . . 152

Introduction to WebDAV . . . . . . . . . . . . . . . . . . . . . . . . . . . . . 153

Copy a File or Document from Your Primary Computer
to Your iPhone or iPad . . . . . . . . . . . . . . . . . . . . . . . . . . . 154

Transfer and Share a File or Document from Your iPhone or iPad
to WebDAV . . . . . . . . . . . . . . . . . . . . . . . . . . . . . . . . . 156

**CHAPTER 10   Cloud-Based Music Service Alternatives to iCloud** . . . . . . . . **157**

The Benefits of Keeping Your Music in the Cloud . . . . . . . . . . . . . . . . 159

Amazon.com Cloud-Based Services . . . . . . . . . . . . . . . . . . . . . . . 159

What Amazon.com's Cloud Drive Offers . . . . . . . . . . . . . . . . . . . 160

Managing Your Amazon Cloud Drive Account . . . . . . . . . . . . . . . . 162

Using Amazon Cloud Player . . . . . . . . . . . . . . . . . . . . . . . . . 165

Acquiring Music from the Amazon MP3 Store . . . . . . . . . . . . . . . . 167

Amazon's Cloud-Based Offerings vs. iCloud Offerings . . . . . . . . . . . . 167

Google Music Cloud-Based Music Management . . . . . . . . . . . . . . . . . 169

Other Music-Oriented Cloud Services . . . . . . . . . . . . . . . . . . . . . . 172

Spotify Music Streaming Option . . . . . . . . . . . . . . . . . . . . . . . 172

Music Unlimited Cloud-Based Music Service . . . . . . . . . . . . . . . . . 173

More Options . . . . . . . . . . . . . . . . . . . . . . . . . . . . . . . . . . . 174

**x** Contents

CHAPTER 11  **The Microsoft 365 and Google Docs Alternatives to iCloud** ... **175**

Microsoft Takes to the Cloud with Office 365 ........................... 176
Google Docs: Another Cloud-Based Application Option ................... 182
Do Browser-Based Apps Make Sense for You? .......................... 184

**PART IV  Use iCloud with Your iPhone and iPad Running iOS 5**

CHAPTER 12  **Manage Apps, App-Related Data, and eBooks with iCloud** .... **187**

Set up Your iCloud-Specific E-mail Account ........................... 189
  Syncing the Notes App on Your iOS Device with iCloud .............. 194
Configure Your iOS Device's Contacts, Calendars, and Reminders Apps
  to Work with iCloud ........................................... 196
  Using the Contacts App with iCloud .............................. 196
  Using the Calendar and Reminders App with iCloud ................ 198
Access Contacts, Calendars, and Reminders via Address Book and iCal
  on Your Mac ................................................... 200
Set up Your PC to Access and Use Contacts, Calendars,
  and Reminders via Outlook ..................................... 200
Configure Your iOS Device's Safari App to Work with iCloud ........... 201
  Set up Your Computer to Use Safari Bookmarks and Reading List Data ... 202
Configure iCloud to Synchronize Music, Apps, and eBooks Among Devices .... 203
  Manually Install Purchased Apps from the App Store ............... 203
  Manually Access Past iTunes Store Purchases via iTunes ............ 203
  Manually Access Past iBookstore Purchases ........................ 204
  Set up Automatic App, eBook, and Music Synchronization ........... 205
The Benefits of Syncing App-Related Data via iCloud ................. 207

CHAPTER 13  **Back Up Your iPhone and iPad with iCloud** .............. **209**

Back Up Your iOS Device to iCloud ................................... 210
  Use iCloud to Back up App-Related Documents, Files, and Data ........ 217
Restore Your iOS Device from an iCloud Backup ....................... 218
Create an iTunes Sync Backup from Your iOS Device ................... 220
Create a Wireless iTunes Sync Backup from Your iOS Device ........... 221
Use iTunes Sync and iCloud Together ................................. 222

CHAPTER 14  **iCloud and Apple TV:
            The Perfect Entertainment Combination** .............. **225**

What Is Apple TV and How Does It Work? .............................. 226
Using Apple TV to Access iTunes Content via iCloud ................... 230
  Access Movies Rented on iTunes Using Another Computer or Device .... 231
  Use AirPlay to Stream Content from an iOS Device to Apple TV ........ 232
  Access Purchased TV Shows from iCloud to Watch via Apple TV ........ 233

Using Apple TV to Access Your iCloud Photo Stream  . . . . . . . . . . . . . . . . . . . . . 236
  View Individual Photo Stream Images
    on Your Television Set via Apple TV  . . . . . . . . . . . . . . . . . . . . . . . . . 238
  Set up the Screen Saver to Display Photo Stream Images  . . . . . . . . . . . . 238
iCloud's Evolution Continues...  . . . . . . . . . . . . . . . . . . . . . . . . . . . . . . . . . . . 240

**APPENDIX A  Troubleshoot iCloud-Related Problems**  . . . . . . . . . . . . . . . . **241**
What to Do if iCloud Doesn't Work as Expected  . . . . . . . . . . . . . . . . . . . . . . 241
Avoid Accidently Overwriting One File Version with Another  . . . . . . . . . . . . . 242
What to Do if You Forget Your iCloud Account Information  . . . . . . . . . . . . . . . 243

**Index**  . . . . . . . . . . . . . . . . . . . . . . . . . . . . . . . . . . . . . . . . . . . . . . . . **245**

# Acknowledgments

Thanks to Megg Morin at McGraw-Hill for inviting me to work on this book. Thanks also to Stephanie Evans, Donald Bell, and everyone else who contributed their talents and publishing know-how as this book was being created.

I'd also like to thank everyone at Apple who helped to create iCloud, as well as the iPhone, iPad, iMac, MacBook, Apple TV, and the other computers and devices I spend so much of my days using.

Thanks also to my friends and family for their endless support and encouragement.

For their help with the book cover, the publisher would like to thank Sue Carroll and Selena Seldiver at Apple as well as Renee Roquet at Thayer Photographs, Joyce Mills at Exposure NY, and Emmanuel Tanner at Marek and Associates.

# Introduction

The concept of "cloud-based computing" is nothing new or revolutionary. However, as Apple was developing iCloud, it took the concept beyond online-based file sharing and dramatically improved upon it for its Mac, iOS device, and Apple TV users.

Once iCloud is set up (which you'll learn how to do from this book), you'll discover that it's never been easier to transfer and sync data, documents, files, photos, music, and other content between your computers and iOS devices (including your iPhone and/or iPad). In fact, much of the synchronization happens automatically and behind the scenes.

As you're using your iPad 2 to create or edit a document using the Pages word processor, for example, as soon as you're done working with the file, it automatically becomes accessible from your other computers and iOS devices via iCloud. Or, if you're out and about, and you update an event within the Calendar app on your iPhone, that new or modified appointment information will automatically synchronize with your schedule maintained on your primary computer and on your other iOS devices. Thanks to iCloud, your files and data will always be up to date.

iCloud is designed primarily for Apple users. It works with all Mac-based computers running the OS X Lion operating system. It's also designed to work in conjunction with Apple TV and all versions of the iPhone and iPad, as well as the more recent models of the iPod touch. As long as each computer or device has Internet connectivity and is linked to the same iCloud account, all of the various iCloud-related features and functions take traditional cloud-based computing and online file sharing to a new level of sophistication and convenience (especially when it comes to transferring information among your computers and iOS devices).

In addition to the functionality iCloud offers, you can begin using it within minutes, and it's free. Once you set up a free iCloud account, it comes with 5GB of online storage space, an e-mail account, plus as much additional online storage space as is necessary to store your iTunes Store, iBookstore, and App Store content purchases (music, TV show episodes, movies, audiobooks, apps, eBooks, and so on). As soon as your personal iCloud account is set up, everything you've ever purchased from the iTunes Store, iBookstore, and/or the App Store becomes instantly available on all of your computers and iOS devices that are linked to the same iCloud account, without your ever having to repurchase any content.

# What's in this Book?

This book covers all you need to know to get the most out of Apple's iCloud service. The book contains 14 chapters divided into four parts.

## Part I: Learn About Online File Sharing and Apple's iCloud

- Chapter 1, "Learn About Cloud-Based Online File Sharing Service," explains the basics of what cloud-based computing offers and provides an overview of the unique features of Apple's iCloud service.
- Chapter 2, "How Mac Users Can Utilize iCloud," explains the core features of iCloud that can be used by Mac (and in some cases Windows-based PC) users.
- Chapter 3, "How iPhone, iPad, and iPod touch Users Can Utilize iCloud," explains the core features of iCloud that can be used by iOS device users.
- Chapter 4, "Migrate from Apple MobileMe to iCloud," shows you how to convert your existing MobileMe account into a free iCloud account.

## Part II: Manage Your Music and Photos in the Cloud

- Chapter 5, "Manage Your Digital Music Library with iCloud," focuses on how to access all of your iTunes music purchases from any computer or device that's linked to the same iCloud account.
- Chapter 6, "Use the Premium iTunes Match Service," shows you how to use this fee-based service to access your entire digital music collection (not just iTunes Store purchases) from all of your computers and iOS devices.
- Chapter 7, "Use iCloud to Store and Manage Your Digital Photos," explains how to use iCloud's Photo Stream feature.

## Part III: Share Documents, Music, Data, and More via iCloud and Other Services

- Chapter 8, "Share Documents and Files with iCloud," explains how to sync files and documents among computers and iOS devices via iCloud.
- Chapter 9, "Cloud-Based File/Document Sharing Alternatives to iCloud," introduces you to other online-based services you can use instead of or in addition to iCloud.
- Chapter 10, "Cloud-Based Music Service Alternatives to iCloud," explains how to shop for music from services other than iTunes Store and share that music among your computers and mobile devices.
- Chapter 11, "The Microsoft 365 and Google Docs Alternatives to iCloud," shows you how to use some of iCloud's competing services to manage your files and documents in the cloud.

### Part IV:  Use iCloud with Your iPhone and iPad Running iOS 5

- Chapter 12, "Manage Apps, App-Related Data, and eBooks with iCloud," explains show to sync and share apps and app-related data among iOS devices via iCloud.
- Chapter 13, "Back Up Your iPhone and iPad with iCloud," introduces you to the iCloud Backup option that's used to create and maintain a remote backup of your iOS device.
- Chapter 14, "iCloud and Apple TV: The Perfect Entertainment Combination," shows you how to use your iOS device in conjunction with Apple TV to stream content to your HD television set or home theater system.
- Appendix A, "Troubleshoot iCloud-Related Problems," helps you diagnose and solve problems you might encounter when setting up or using iCloud.

## Conventions Used in this Book

To help you better understand some of the more complex or technical aspects of using iCloud, plus to focus your attention on particularly useful iCloud-related features and functions, you'll discover Note, Tip, and Caution paragraphs throughout this book that highlight specific tidbits of useful information.

Plus, throughout this book, you'll discover "How To..." and "Did You Know?" sidebars that provide additional topic-related information and advice that pertains to the issues covered within the chapter you're reading.

# PART I

Learn About Online File Sharing and Apple's iCloud

# 1

# Learn About Cloud-Based Online File Sharing Services

## HOW TO...

- Learn about the iCloud cloud-based file-sharing service and its uses.
- Determine whether you want or need to use a cloud-based file sharing service, such as iCloud.
- Determine what equipment you'll need to use iCloud or a similar file sharing service.
- Learn how much using the iCloud file sharing service costs.

If you have recently upgraded to the Mac OS X Lion operating system or you've upgraded your Apple iPhone or iPad to the iOS 5 operating system, you have no doubt discovered hundreds of new features and functions. Among new features offered by Apple in conjunction with these major operating system upgrades is a new way to share, back up, and synchronize data and files using iCloud.

As its core, Apple's iCloud is an online (cloud-based) file sharing service. What this means and how it can be useful to you is explained in this chapter. Although access to this type of service might be new to you, its technology and functionality have been around for a while. Apple has taken the cloud-based file sharing concept, vastly improved upon it, added features, and created a service that works seamlessly with its Mac desktop and laptop computers, as well as iPhones, iPad tablets, iPod touch, and Apple TV devices.

iCloud is one of many cloud-based file sharing services available, and while the specific focus of this book is on Apple's new iCloud service, you'll learn about some of the other useful cloud-based file sharing services as well. This information will help you choose the best services to meet your needs.

 Keep in mind that iCloud was designed primarily for everyday computer users, not for business applications. If you're operating a midsize to large business, and you want to tap into what cloud-based computing offers, another cloud-based file sharing service will probably be more appropriate.

**You Must Have Internet Access to Use iCloud**

To use iCloud, or any cloud-based file sharing service, your computer or device must have access to the Internet. If you're using iCloud with an iOS device, such as an iPhone or iPad, some of iCloud's functions will work using a 3G Internet connection. However, to use all of iCloud's functionality for file sharing, data backup, and synchronizing data, a Wi-Fi Internet connection is necessary.

Once iCloud is set up to work with your computer and/or iOS mobile device (such as your iPhone or iPad), most of its functionality works automatically in the background. Your computer or device will upload and download relevant data or files to and from iCloud as needed. For example, if you're using your iPhone and create a new entry using the Contacts app while you're on the go, as soon as that new entry is created, it will be uploaded to iCloud (assuming an Internet connection is available) and then immediately synchronized with the contact management software running on your primary computer(s) and other iOS devices.

Likewise, if you update the Calendar app on your iPad with a new appointment, that new entry will immediately be uploaded to iCloud and synchronized with the scheduling software running on your primary computer(s) and other iOS devices. Or if you snap a photo on your iPad and have iCloud's Photo Stream feature set up (which will be explained in Chapter 7), that image will automatically be uploaded to iCloud and then shared with your other computer(s) and devices, including your Apple TV device.

The latest versions of Pages, Numbers, and Keynote (Apple's iWork suite of applications for word processing, spreadsheet management, and digital slideshow presentations, respectively) are also fully iCloud-compatible. So when you create or update a document within Pages, the latest version of that document can be automatically set to upload to iCloud, so you'll have almost immediate access to that file on your other computer(s) and devices—complete with the latest round of revisions. You never need to worry about which version of a document you're working with, or whether the document you're viewing is the latest one. iCloud now handles this for you automatically.

**Did You Know?** **You Can Pick and Choose Which iCloud Features to Utilize**

Most people will not want or need to use all the functionality that iCloud offers. At least initially, you can choose which features will be most useful to you, and then customize those features. You can turn off the features you're not interested in using. Options for personalizing and/or turning on and off individual iCloud features are discussed throughout this book.

Described here are just a few of the services iCloud offers to Mac and iOS device users. Many more ways to use this cloud-based file sharing service will be revealed in this chapter and others.

# What Is a Cloud-Based File Sharing Service Anyway?

You can think of iCloud and other cloud-based file sharing services as an external hard drive for your computer or a device that's located somewhere in cyberspace, as opposed to being installed within your computer (or device) or directly connected to it via a cable. So when your computer or device is connected to the Web, files and data can be uploaded, either automatically or manually, to the cloud-based service. At the same time, your computer or device can download files and data from the cloud-based service as needed. Easily sharing and synchronizing files, documents, and data is what cloud-based computing is all about.

 Many cloud-based file sharing services are available to consumers. Dropbox, for example, can be used for sharing general files and/or documents. Amazon Cloud Drive is more specialized and allows you to store and access Amazon music purchases while managing your digital music library. Chapters 10 and 11 focus on these competing services and also include cloud-based file sharing services from Google and Microsoft.

In its most basic form, a cloud-based file sharing service allows you to create and maintain a remote backup or copy of your data and files. So if your computer or device gets damaged, lost, or stolen, for example, a copy of your important information is always safely stored and password-protected on a web-based server in cyberspace (that is, in the "cloud").

As you'll soon discover, cloud-based file sharing services, particularly Apple iCloud, offer a handful of features and functions that are designed to make much of what you do on your Mac, iPhone, or iPad more efficient and easier, because they let you easily share files, data, and other information among computers and devices.

 In Chapter 3, you'll learn specifically how iCloud can be used with a Mac-based desktop or laptop computer. Chapter 4 focuses on using iCloud in conjunction with your iPhone, iPad, or iPod touch.

Although cloud-based file sharing services are not new, in conjunction with the release of the iOS X Lion and iOS 5 operating system upgrades, Apple has introduced many new ways that everyday computer users can easily use cloud-based computing without having to pay a fortune or becoming more computer savvy than they already are. After all, using iCloud requires no programming knowledge whatsoever.

# What Apple's iCloud Can Do for You

You might be thinking, I've been using a computer for years, and using a cloud-based file sharing service has never been necessary, so why start using it now? Or perhaps you're perfectly content manually connecting your iPhone or iPad to your primary computer via the supplied USB cable to synchronize and back up its data. But once you discover all of the ways iCloud can be used to automate many tasks that previously required effort and time on your part, plus how it can be used to safeguard your data and important files automatically, and make that data and those files available wherever and whenever they're needed, chances are you'll understand iCloud's benefits and will want to begin using this new service in conjunction with your computer and/or mobile device.

Over time, Apple will continue to improve the iCloud service by adding new features, while third-party software developers will continue to find innovative new ways to tap into its functionality to make popular software and apps even more useful. Here's a quick summary of the core features and functions that have initially been built into iCloud.

iCloud stores your music, photos, apps, calendars, documents, and other important data and files, and then makes them available on all of your computers and Apple mobile devices. You'll no longer need to copy files manually from one device to another or use a USB thumb drive or e-mail, for example, to transfer a file or data from one computer or device to another.

iCloud allows you to access your iTunes purchases (including music, eBooks, apps, and video) from any compatible device or computer. All purchases from iTunes, iBookstore, the App Store, and Apple's Newsstand, for example, are automatically stored within your free iCloud account. From your iPad, for example, you can access iTunes and tap the Purchased icon at the bottom of the screen (shown in Figure 1-1) to access all of the music you've purchased to date from iTunes, and then download any of those songs directly to your tablet without having to repurchase them.

If you upgrade to iCloud's premium iTunes Match service for an annual fee, your entire digital music library (including music not purchased through iTunes) can be made available to you via iCloud.

iCloud also allows you to create and maintain a Photo Stream; you can synchronize and share up to 1000 digital images at a time among your computer(s), iOS mobile device(s), and Apple TV device. You can also maintain a complete database of all your digital images on your primary computer's hard drive. This feature works with both Macs and PCs.

Using iCloud, you can automatically share important documents and files among your devices and keep file versions synchronized. So if you update a file on one computer or device, that updated file will become available almost immediately on all of the other devices and computers that are linked to your secure iCloud account. This feature works flawlessly with a growing selection of software (and apps), including Apple's own Pages (a Microsoft Word–compatible word processor), Numbers (an Excel-compatible spreadsheet manager), and Keynote (a PowerPoint-compatible digital slide presentation tool).

**FIGURE 1-1**   From iTunes, access previously purchased content and download it to the device you're currently using.

In conjunction with your iPhone, iPad, or iPod touch, all of your apps, eBooks, and data associated with Contacts, Calendar, and Safari, for example, will automatically be synchronized and backed up onto iCloud (and accessible from other computers or devices linked to the same iCloud account). Thus, as you surf the Web using Safari on your iPhone, for example, if you save a bookmark for a web site you like, that same bookmark will automatically and almost instantly appear within your compatible web browser's bookmark listing on other linked computers and devices.

If the Backup feature is turned on, and your iPhone or iPad, for example, has access to a Wi-Fi Internet connection, iOS 5 will automatically maintain a daily (wireless) backup of your mobile device on the iCloud service, replacing the need to sync the device to your primary computer using a USB cable (although this option is still available). This includes storing a remote backup of all purchased music, apps, and eBooks; all photos and videos stored in the Camera Roll (associated with the Camera and Photos apps); all personalized device settings and app data; your Lock Screen and Home Screen customizations; an archive of all text and Multimedia Message Service (MMS) messages; plus all custom ringtones. From the remote backup on iCloud, you can later wirelessly restore your device or specific content.

iCloud comes with a free e-mail account that can be managed and accessed from any web-based device. As you send and receive e-mails, changes to the account are stored on iCloud and remain synchronized among all of your computers and devices. The free *[username]@me.com* e-mail account is set up at the same time you create your free iCloud account, or it can be transferred from your existing MobileMe account. Whether or not you set up a free e-mail account through iCloud is optional, and whether you choose to set it up or not, all incoming e-mails can easily be forwarded to your primary (preexisting) e-mail address.

Whether you use a Mac computer, an iPhone, and/or an iPad, all of your important contacts and calendar data, as well as e-mails sent and received from your free iCloud e-mail account, are automatically synchronized between all of your compatible computers and devices that are linked to the same iCloud account. This synchronization happens in real time, so when a change is made on one device, it's reflected on all devices almost instantly (as long as all of the devices are connected to the Internet).

Your iCloud account is accessed via your free Apple ID, which is password-protected. Thus, unauthorized users don't have access to your data, files, and information that are stored on the iCloud servers. However, all of the computers and devices you own or use that are linked to the same iCloud account will automatically and securely be able to share information, data, and files.

iCloud offers the free Find My iPhone, Find My iPad, and Find My Mac features, which allow you to pinpoint the exact location of your computer or device on a map if it gets lost or stolen, and then either retrieve the hardware, send a message to it, erase its contents, or remotely lock the device (as long as it's connected to the Internet).

Each of iCloud's core features and functions are customizable and can be turned on or off, so you can use iCloud only in ways that will be helpful to you. Once you've set up most individual features or functions, however, they will automatically work in the background, so you won't have to give any thought to backing up, copying, or transferring important data or files, for example.

Unlike other cloud-based file sharing services (several of which will be covered within this book), iCloud has been fully integrated into the OS X Lion and iOS 5 operating systems.

**Did You Know?** **iCloud Has Replaced Apple's MobileMe Service**

MobileMe is an online service offered by Apple that uses some cloud-based computing functionality, although the services offered via MobileMe are primitive when compared to those offered by iCloud. This is why MobileMe is being discontinued as of June 2012 and being replaced by iCloud.

# What Using a Cloud-Based File Sharing Service Costs

In addition to offering many different features and uses that have now been fully integrated into your Mac or iOS device's operating system, as well as popular software or apps you're probably already using, Apple has made getting started with iCloud extremely inexpensive. In fact, it's free!

When you set up a free iCloud account, you're given immediate access to 5GB of online storage space, plus an unlimited amount of extra online storage space for all of your iTunes, iBookstore, App Store, and Apple Newsstand purchases. All the music, TV show episodes, movies, audio books, podcasts, eBooks, and digital publications that you've purchased and/or downloaded from iTunes or one of Apple's other online ventures will automatically be stored and made available to you via your iCloud account.

Not only does this provide you with an automatic backup of the content you purchase and/or download from Apple, but it also makes that content available to all of your Mac computers and iOS devices (including your iPhone and iPad), as well as your Apple TV device, for no additional charge. Thus, if you purchase an app for your iPhone and it's a hybrid app (meaning it will also run on an iPad), you will be able to download and install that same app for free to your tablet. If you've purchased a song from iTunes, you'll be able to download and listen to that song on your Mac, iPhone, iPad, or other iOS device (such as Apple TV) at any time; the storage space necessary to keep this content readily accessible on iCloud will not be counted against your primary 5GB of online storage.

Sharing music and apps among computers and devices is only one of the features built into iCloud. You'll soon discover that having an iCloud account also makes it easy to transfer and share digital photos among various computers and devices. Plus, iCloud works as a powerful documents and data file sharing service.

For most people, the features and functionality offered using a free iCloud account will be more than adequate. However, if your online storage needs go beyond 5GB, you can purchase additional online storage space for an annual fee. An additional 10GB of online storage costs $20 per year (giving you 15GB of online storage space total). You can purchase 20GB of extra storage space for $40 per year, or 50GB of extra storage space for $100 per year directly from your iPhone, iPad, or Mac.

To upgrade your online storage capacity from an iPhone or iPad, for example, launch the Settings app from the Home Screen, and then, from the main Settings menu, tap the iCloud option. When the Storage & Backup screen appears (as shown in Figure 1-2), tap the Buy More Storage option. Then, from the Buy More Storage window, tap the amount of storage you want. Your in-app purchase will be charged directly to the credit card associated with your Apple ID, and the additional storage space will instantly become available to you.

If you want to make your entire digital music collection available to all of your computers and devices (including content that was not purchased through iTunes), you can upgrade to the iTunes Match service for $24.99 per year. You'll learn more about the iTunes Match service in Chapter 6.

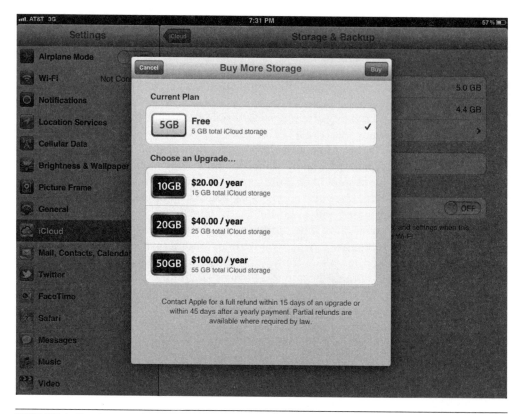

**FIGURE 1-2** At any time, you can increase the amount of online storage space available to you on iCloud for an annual fee (shown here on the iPad 2).

# What You'll Need to Start Using iCloud with a Mac

What will be required to begin using iCloud will depend in part on how you'll be using it. If you're a Mac user, you'll first need to upgrade to iOS X Lion, which is available from the Mac App Store for $29.99. If you have multiple Macs registered under the same Apple ID account, you'll need to pay for this operating system upgrade only once. In addition, you'll need to upgrade some of your Mac's software to the latest versions. You can do this by clicking the Apple logo icon that's displayed in the upper-left corner of your Mac's screen, and then clicking the Software Update option.

To use iCloud, you'll also need to upgrade to the most recent version of iTunes. iTunes should automatically upgrade when you install OS X Lion on your Mac or when you choose the Software Update command.

Beyond upgrading your Mac's operating system and iTunes, if you'll be using iCloud to create a Photo Stream and to share photos among computers or iOS mobile devices, you'll need to upgrade to the latest version of iPhoto '11. Meanwhile, if you want to use iCloud to keep your iWork files and documents synchronized and easily share those files and documents with your other Macs or iOS devices, upgrading to the latest versions of Pages, Numbers, and Keynote will also be necessary, on both your Mac and your iOS devices.

Many third-party software developers are also making their applications iCloud-compatible. Thus, it will be necessary to upgrade to the latest version of those software packages as well.

The good news is that beyond paying for the OS X Lion operating system upgrade, the updates to all of Apple's other software, including those applications that are part of iLife '11 and iWork '11 (such as iPhoto '11, Pages, Numbers, and Keynote) will be free. However, these software updates are necessary to use much of the new functionality built into iCloud.

If you're already a subscriber to Apple's MobileMe service, you'll need to make the transition to iCloud before June 2012, since Apple has announced that the MobileMe service will be discontinued and ultimately taken offline. Most of the services and features offered through MobileMe, including your free e-mail account, can be transferred to iCloud for free. How to do this is explained within Chapter 4.

Just as MobileMe was used to synchronize and back up certain data on your Mac, such as your Calendar and Contacts databases, as well as your Safari bookmarks, the new iCloud service will take over these backup and synchronization functions, as you'll soon discover.

Finally, to use all the features available from the iCloud service with your Mac(s), each computer will need access to the Internet, preferably via a constant high-speed connection. After all, iCloud is an online-based service. If your computer can't access the Web (and iCloud's servers) when necessary, the features and functions that iCloud offers will not be available to your computer(s).

# Find a Lost or Stolen Mac, iPhone, or iPad

In addition to keeping your data and important files safe on a remote server, the popular and powerful Find My iPhone (or Find My iPad) feature, which was introduced as part of MobileMe and is now part of iCloud, has been expanded. There's now a Find My Mac feature as well. It allows you to pinpoint the exact location of your MacBook, for example, if it gets lost or stolen. For this feature to work, the free Find My iPhone/iPad/Mac feature must be set up in advance (before it gets lost or stolen), and the computer or device must have access to the Internet.

## How to...

# Track the Location of Your Mac or iOS Mobile Device Using iCloud

To pinpoint the location of your lost or stolen iPhone, iPad, or Mac, from any web-enabled device, visit www.iCloud.com/find, and then sign in using your Apple ID and password. Within a few seconds, once your computer or device is located, its precise location will be displayed on a detailed Google Map (as shown next). You can then either have the computer or device play a sound and display a message, lock down the device, or erase the entire contents of the distant device remotely.

This optional feature is explained in greater detail in Chapter 2; you should definitely turn on and set up this service so you'll be able to take advantage of it when and if it ever becomes necessary.

**Tip** After the service is activated, using any computer or device that connects to the Web, visit www.iCloud.com/find to access the Find My iPhone/iPad/Mac service. Then you'll be able to pinpoint the exact location of your device or computer on a map.

**Did You Know?** **You Can Use Find My Friends to Track Your Friends and Family Members**

Using the free Find My Friends app for iPhone and iPad, you can keep tabs on the whereabouts of your friends, coworkers, and family members (with their permission), and they can track your location in real time as well. Locations can be displayed on a detailed map, making it easy to meet up with people when you're out and about.

# What You'll Need to Start Using iCloud with an iPhone or iPad

Your Apple iPhone, iPad, or iPod touch operates using Apple's cutting-edge iOS operating system, which is among the most powerful and robust operating systems available for any mobile devices. In October 2011, iOS 5 was released, providing iPhone, iPad, and iPod touch users with the most significant upgrade to the iOS operating system yet. Literally hundreds of new features, including seamless integration with iCloud, along with a handful of new preinstalled apps, are part of iOS 5.

For Apple's iPhone 3Gs, iPhone 4, iPhone 4S, iPad, and iPad 2 users, the iOS 5 upgrade is free of charge and necessary if you want to begin using iCloud in conjunction with your mobile device. You can upgrade the iOS of your device using the familiar iTunes sync process. However, once iOS 5 is installed and operational on your device, all new iOS updates, as well as app updates, can then occur wirelessly.

 If you purchased your iPhone, iPad, or iPod touch after the release of iOS 5, the new operating system will be preinstalled on your device. However, if iOS 5.1 (or later) has since been released, your device will notify you that an update is available. To update your iOS from iOS 5 to the latest version, launch the Settings app from your device's Home Screen, tap the General menu option, and then tap Software Update.

When you begin using iOS 5, you will be prompted to set up a free iCloud account or to link your existing iCloud account with your device using your Apple ID. However, to use some of iCloud's features, you'll need to adjust settings on your iPhone, iPad, or iPod touch, plus make sure the apps that are compatible with iCloud (such as Pages, Numbers, and Keynote) also get updated to the most current versions.

 To use the iPhone or iPad version of Pages, Keynote, or Numbers with iCloud, make sure you have version 1.5 or later of these popular iWork apps.

### On an iOS Mobile Device, Some iCloud Features Require Wi-Fi

To use iCloud with your iPhone or iPad, for example, the device must have access to the Internet (via a 3G or Wi-Fi connection). Keep in mind that some of iCloud's features (such as the iPhone or iPad Backup feature) require a Wi-Fi connection. None of these features will work, however, if the device is turned off or placed in Airplane mode.

You can update the apps stored on your iOS device wirelessly (from your device) or from your primary computer using iTunes. From an iOS device that's connected to the Internet, launch the App Store app from the Home Screen, and then tap the Updates icon that's displayed at the bottom of the screen. If any of your existing apps require updates, you'll be prompted to download and install them for free.

Once you have the latest versions of iOS 5 and all iCloud-compatible apps running on your iPhone, iPad, or iPod touch, you'll need to adjust certain settings manually using the Settings app to turn on and begin using many of iCloud's features and functions. Chapter 3 outlines all the ways you can use iCloud in conjunction with your iOS device.

# Let's Get Started...

Just reading about the various features offered by iCloud may already have set off a light bulb in your mind, as you contemplate the various ways this service will soon be helpful to you. Although you'll find plenty of other cloud-based file sharing services out there, none have been integrated into the core operating system of your computer or device, and none have ever offered the vast selection of features and functions offered by iCloud. Apple has managed to keep the service easy to use and extremely customizable based on how you personally use your computer, iPhone, or iPad.

If you're a Mac user, Chapter 2 will introduce you to some of the ways iCloud now works in conjunction with your iMac or MacBook. But even if you're a loyal PC user who runs the latest version of Windows, you can still use iCloud in conjunction with that computer and your iPhone, iPad, and/or iPod touch. This functionality is explained in Chapter 3.

When set up and used correctly, iCloud can provide a secure and reliable remote backup option for your most important data and files, plus ensure that the data and files you need are readily available to you on whatever iCloud-compatible device you are using. Plus, iCloud will ensure you can always listen to or watch your iTunes purchased content on any compatible device, as long as a web connection is present.

Welcome to the world of cloud-based computing, where your important files, documents, content, and data are remotely stored on an online-based server via the Internet, and accessible from multiple computers or devices linked to the same iCloud account.

 As you will discover, access to iCloud, as well as your iTunes, iBookstore, and Apple Newsstand purchases, and your FaceTime and iMessage usernames, are all associated with your Apple ID (which you must link with a major credit or debit card to make online or in-app purchases). Your Apple ID is also used in conjunction with the Find My iPhone/iPad/Mac feature. Thus, it is essential that you keep the password associated with your Apple ID confidential. Otherwise, someone could access your private files stored on iCloud, make online purchases, and even track your exact whereabouts in real time.

# 2

## How Mac Users Can Utilize iCloud

**HOW TO...**

- Use the Find My Mac feature of iCloud.
- Set up your Mac(s) to work with iCloud using OS X Lion.
- Activate the Back to My Mac feature of iCloud.
- Share data, files, and documents between Macs (such as an iMac and MacBook).

In the process of developing the latest OS X Lion operating system for the Mac, Apple began incorporating iCloud functionality into this operating system. Much of the publicity surrounding iCloud focuses on how this cloud-based file sharing service can be used by iPhone, iPad, and iPod touch users to share documents, data, and files; back up their device; and even locate their iOS mobile device if it gets lost or stolen.

For people who enjoy music, iCloud also makes it extremely easy to share all of your iTunes music purchases among all of the computers and/or mobile devices that are linked to the same iCloud account, without your having to repurchase the same songs multiple times. In Chapter 5, you'll discover that all your past iTunes music purchases are immediately accessible via iCloud (and the Internet) to all of your computers and iOS devices. You can see your purchases (as shown in Figure 2-1) when accessing the iTunes Store using the iTunes software on your Mac or the iTunes app on your iOS device.

You can also set up your Mac(s) so that any time you purchase new music from iTunes, on any computer or iOS mobile device, it will immediately be downloaded and stored on each of your Macs or iOS devices. By default, iCloud can be used to synchronize and share your iTunes music purchases automatically. However, if you invest $24.99 per year to subscribe to the iTunes Match service through iCloud, all of your music, including songs and albums not purchased from iTunes, can be stored on iCloud and made available on all of your computers and iOS devices.

 Chapter 6 shows you how to use the iTunes Match service.

**FIGURE 2-1** You can access all past iTunes music and content purchases, even if the music or content was initially purchased on another computer or device linked to the same iCloud account.

In addition to music that's been purchased from iTunes, using iCloud, you can access any other content that you've previously purchased from iTunes, such as TV show episodes or movies. This includes purchases made on other computers or devices using the same Apple ID used to create your iCloud account.

As a Mac user, you can also benefit from iCloud by using its Photo Stream feature, which allows you to share up to 1000 of your most recently shot or imported digital photos, via the Internet (and iCloud), among your various Mac and PC computers, Apple TV, and/or your iOS mobile devices.

**Note** You'll discover in Chapter 7 how to use iCloud's Photo Stream feature to share digital photos automatically among Macs, PCs, and your iPhone, iPad, and/or iPod touch.

By default, if you're an iPhone, iPad, or iPod touch user who also uses a Mac, you can benefit from being able to synchronize data from the Calendar and Contacts apps wirelessly on your mobile device and share it with iCal and/or Address Book on your Mac, for example. In the past, this was possible using the iTunes Sync process. With iCloud, you can do this wirelessly via the Web, so your computer and iOS device(s) never need to be physically connected using a USB cable to synchronize data or exchange information.

## How to... **Access Past iTunes Purchases on Your Mac**

To access past iTunes purchases from a Mac, launch the latest version of the iTunes software (version 10.5 or later) and click the iTunes Store option that's displayed on the left side of the screen under the Store heading. Then, under the Quick Links heading on the right side of the iTunes screen, shown here, click the Purchased option.

When the Purchased screen is displayed, near the top of the screen select the type of purchased content you want to find and download, such as Music, TV Shows, Apps, or Books. If you click TV Shows, for example, on the left side of the Purchased screen, the names of each TV series that you've purchased will be displayed. Click a TV series name to reveal individual episodes that you've already purchased. On the right side of the screen, click the TV series icon to reveal individual episode listings (shown next) that you can download.

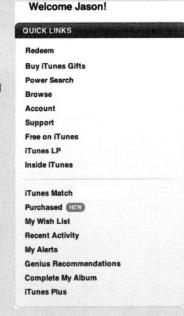

**Welcome Jason!**

QUICK LINKS

Redeem
Buy iTunes Gifts
Power Search
Browse
Account
Support
Free on iTunes
iTunes LP
Inside iTunes

iTunes Match
Purchased (NEW)
My Wish List
Recent Activity
My Alerts
Genius Recommendations
Complete My Album
iTunes Plus

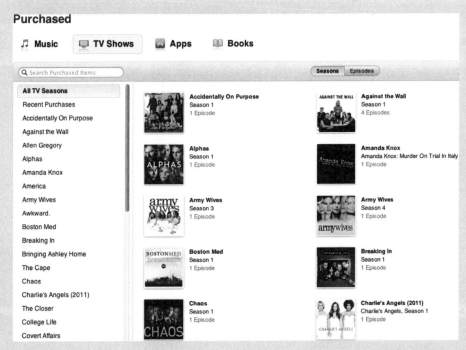

**Purchased**

♫ Music    🖥 TV Shows    🗔 Apps    📖 Books

Q Search Purchased Items                              Seasons | Episodes

| All TV Seasons |
| Recent Purchases |
| Accidentally On Purpose |
| Against the Wall |
| Allen Gregory |
| Alphas |
| Amanda Knox |
| America |
| Army Wives |
| Awkward. |
| Boston Med |
| Breaking In |
| Bringing Ashley Home |
| The Cape |
| Chaos |
| Charlie's Angels (2011) |
| The Closer |
| College Life |
| Covert Affairs |

**Accidentally On Purpose** — Season 1, 1 Episode
**Against the Wall** — Season 1, 4 Episodes
**Alphas** — Season 1, 1 Episode
**Amanda Knox** — Amanda Knox: Murder On Trial In Italy, 1 Episode
**Army Wives** — Season 3, 1 Episode
**Army Wives** — Season 4, 1 Episode
**Boston Med** — Season 1, 1 Episode
**Breaking In** — Season 1, 1 Episode
**Chaos** — Season 1, 1 Episode
**Charlie's Angels (2011)** — Charlie's Angels, Season 1, 1 Episode

*(Continued)*

If the episode is not already stored on your Mac, to the right of each episode listing will be an iCloud icon (shown next). Click it to download that specific episode. Once downloaded, the episode will be added to your iTunes library on the Mac you're using, so you can watch that content. Keep in mind that the TV show file will be saved on your Mac's hard drive and will be accessible from the computer you're using until you manually delete the file.

 **Note** Data synchronization between your Mac and iOS device using iCloud is the focus of Chapter 8.

Much of iCloud's functionality is designed to make wireless communication between your Macs and iOS mobile devices more efficient, since it lets you exchange data, documents, and files via the Web, rather than using the iTunes Sync process. If you're a Mac user but have not yet invested in an iPhone, iPad, or iPod touch, you can still use iCloud for a variety of tasks, some of which are described in this chapter.

From any computer or mobile device that's connected to the Internet, you can access your Contacts, Calendar, iCloud Mail account, or iWork.com files simply by pointing your web browser to www.iCloud.com. Online-based applications, such as or similar to iCal (Mac), Address Book (Mac), Calendar (iOS), and Contacts (iOS),

**Did You Know?**

## Windows PC Users Can Also Use iCloud

First and foremost, Apple's iCloud service was designed for Apple Macs (including iMacs and MacBooks) as well as Apple's iOS mobile devices. As a Windows PC user, you can download the free iCloud Control Panel software to take advantage of iCloud's ability to synchronize data between your computer and iPhone, iPad, and/or iPod touch.

Plus, you can access your iTunes music purchases from iCloud on your Windows-based PC and access your Photo Stream, for example. However, if you're a Windows PC user who is not also an Apple iOS mobile device user, plenty of other cloud-based file sharing services might be more suitable to your needs. Throughout this book, you'll learn how Windows PC users can use various iCloud features.

grant you access to your web-based data and files that are stored on iCloud, even if the computer or mobile device you're currently using to surf the Web is not linked to your iCloud account.

# Use the Find Your Mac Feature via iCloud

If your iPhone or iPad gets lost or stolen, and you've preactivated iCloud's Find My iPhone or Find My iPad feature, from any computer or device that's connected to the Internet, you can visit the iCloud web site (www.iCloud.com/find) and pinpoint the exact location of your iOS mobile device. At the same time iCloud was launched, Apple introduced the Find My Mac feature, which works in conjunction with Find My iPhone and Find My iPad. As long as your iMac or MacBook is connected to the Internet via Wi-Fi, you can pinpoint its exact location on a map via the iCloud web site, and then perform a handful of tasks remotely to retrieve your lost or stolen computer or, at the very least, protect the data stored on that computer.

 In the future, the Find My Mac feature will most likely be adapted to work with any Internet connection, not just a Wi-Fi connection.

Obviously, the Find My Mac feature will be more useful for locating a MacBook that's extremely mobile, as opposed to an iMac that probably sits on a desk in your home or office. However, this feature works with any Mac computer that's running the latest version of OS X Lion.

 If you also use an iPhone or iPad, download the free Find My iPhone app from the App Store, which can also be used to pinpoint the location of your Mac, as long as your iOS device and Mac has access to the Internet. This is useful if you want to track the location of your Mac as it's being moved or as you're moving.

**How to...** # Activate and Use the Find My Mac Feature

For the Find My Mac feature to work, you must first activate it on each of your Macs. Then, to pinpoint the location of your computer(s), the computer must be connected to the Internet via a wireless network or Wi-Fi connection and be turned on. (An Ethernet Internet connection will not currently work.)

To turn on the Find My Mac feature, which you need to do only once, launch System Preferences from your Mac's Dock or from the Applications folder. Then, from the System Preferences window, click the iCloud icon.

When the iCloud window (within System Preferences) is displayed, if prompted to do so, log into your iCloud account using your Apple ID and password. Then, within the iCloud window, use the mouse to add a checkmark next to the Find My Mac option.

Click the red dot displayed in the upper-left corner of the iCloud window to exit System Preferences. Or, from the System Preferences pull-down menu displayed near the top-left corner of the Mac's screen, select the Quit System Preferences option to save your changes and exit System Preferences.

Be sure to turn on the Find My Mac feature on each of your iMac or MacBook computers separately, after each is linked to your iCloud account.

When you access www.iCloud.com/find (shown in the accompanying illustration) from any computer or mobile device that's connected to the Internet, and then log into your iCloud account using your Apple ID and password, the Find My Mac feature will pinpoint and display the exact geographic location of your Mac on a detailed map.

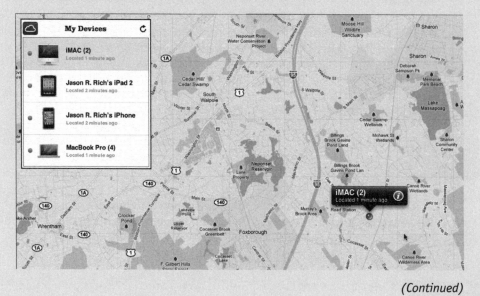

*(Continued)*

As you're looking at the map, click or tap the Zoom In or Zoom Out icons displayed in the upper-right corner of the iCloud map screen to see more or less detail, respectively, on the map. The next illustration shows a Satellite view map after the Zoom In feature has been used to display more detail. You can also click or tap the Standard, Satellite, or Hybrid map view to change the map's appearance.

Once the Find My Mac feature locates your Mac, tap the blue-and-white Info ("i") icon on the map that's displayed in conjunction with your Mac's location. An Info pop-up window will appear that allows you to play a sound or send a message to your remote Mac, password-protect your Mac remotely, or erase all of the data from your Mac remotely (shown in the next illustration).

# Share Files Using the Back to My Mac Feature

The Back to My Mac feature was included with the now defunct MobileMe online service. It allows you to transfer documents and files between Macs over the Internet or control a Mac from a remote location using another Mac. This useful feature is now offered through iCloud.

 When you use the Back to My Mac feature to share files, documents, or data, you must do so manually. It will not automatically sync files between two machines.

For this feature to work, you'll need to activate it on each of your Macs. Once it's activated, whenever you access the Finder on your Mac, you'll see a Shared heading displayed on the left side of the Finder window (shown in Figure 2-2). Below that Shared heading is a listing for the Macs that are accessible wirelessly using the Back to My Mac feature.

You can then manually drag-and-drop or copy files between the Mac you're using and any other wirelessly connected Mac that's listed under the Shared heading within the Finder window. Basically, the folder displayed in the Finder for other Macs with

**FIGURE 2-2** Once the feature is activated, you can access a Mac remotely by clicking its listing under the Shared heading in the Finder window of the Mac you're currently using.

which you're sharing acts like an external hard drive or thumb drive. As you copy files to the folder, however, they're accessible on the other machine (and vice versa).

To activate the Back to My Mac feature on each of your Macs, follow these steps:

1. Launch System Preferences from the Mac's Dock or Applications folder.
2. From the main System Preferences window, click the iCloud icon.
3. When the iCloud window (within System Preferences) becomes available, log into your iCloud account if you're prompted to do so.
4. Using the mouse, place a virtual checkmark next to the Back to My Mac option displayed within the iCloud window within System Preferences (shown in Figure 2-3).

 It might be necessary to make adjustments on your wireless Internet router to use the Back to My Mac feature with the maximum possible file transfer speeds. This feature requires a router that supports NAT Port Mapping Protocol (NAT-PMP) or Universal Plug and Play (UPnP).

5. Exit System Preferences to save your changes.
6. Repeat this step on each of your Macs.

 For the Back to My Mac feature to function properly, all Macs must be using the same version of the OS X Lion operating system (version 10.7.2 or later), and they need to be linked to the same iCloud account.

**FIGURE 2-3**    Add a checkmark to the Back to My Mac option within the iCloud window of System Preferences to turn on this feature.

# Use iCloud as a Virtual Drop Box for Cloud-Based File Sharing

In Chapter 8, you'll learn all about how you can use iCloud's "Documents in the Cloud" feature to share documents and files created using Apple's iWork software on your Mac with other computers or your iOS devices using iWork.com, which links to your iCloud account. When you use this feature, your documents and files are automatically synchronized. There's no need to copy or drag-and-drop files manually, as you must do with the Back to My Mac feature.

iWork for Mac comprises three software packages: Pages, Numbers, and Keynote. Pages is a word processor that is compatible with Microsoft Word. Numbers is a spreadsheet management program that's compatible with Microsoft Excel, and Keynote is a digital slide presentation tool that's compatible with Microsoft PowerPoint.

From your Mac, you can import a Microsoft Word file into Pages, for example, and then automatically share it with other computers and/or iOS mobile devices via iWork.com (iCloud). As you use the Pages, Numbers, and/or Keynote software, you'll discover a Share pull-down menu displayed near the top of each program's screen. One of the options available from this pull-down menu is Share via iWork. com (shown in Figure 2-4).

Once you set up a free iWork.com account (using the same log in information you used for your iCloud account), your iWork.com account integrates with iCloud

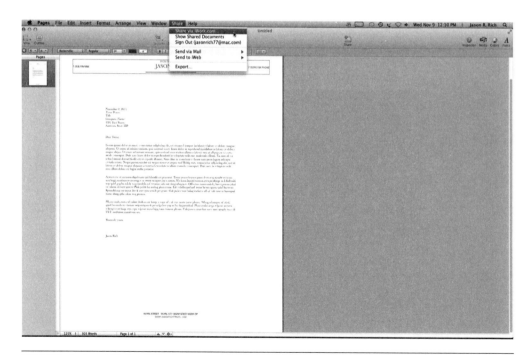

**FIGURE 2-4**   All the iWork programs for Mac have a Share pull-down menu and offer the same Share via iWork.com option. Shown here is Pages running on a Mac.

and becomes accessible from www.iCloud.com and/or www.iWork.com, for example. (This is all explained in greater detail within Chapter 8.)

One feature that Apple didn't officially release in conjunction with iCloud (when the online file sharing service was launched in October 2011), but that nevertheless works on most newer Macs in conjunction with any iCloud account, is the ability to use iCloud to share and synchronize Mac files and documents created using non-iWork software. This functionality goes beyond what Apple advertises as "Documents in the Cloud," which allows for iWork for Mac and iWork for iOS files and documents to be automatically synchronized and shared via iCloud.

Using this Drop Box feature (which should not be confused with the Dropbox file-sharing service described in Chapter 9), you can transfer or sync files and documents between Macs that are linked to the same iCloud account. This makes it easier to transfer other types of files wirelessly, via the Web, between your iMac and MacBook, for example, that are in separate locations.

 The Drop Box functionality will most likely be formally introduced in a future revision of iCloud and/or iWork.com. However, this "short cut" will work now on any Mac or MacBook that has the built-in AirDrop feature.

According to Apple, AirDrop is built into the following Mac and MacBook models: MacBook Pro (late-2008 or newer), MacBook Air (late-2010 or newer), MacBook (late-2008 or newer), iMac (early-2009 or newer), Mac Mini (mid-2010 or newer), and Mac Pro (early-2009 with AirPort Extreme card, or mid-2010).

To use the Drop Box feature of iCloud, you'll still need to create a free iCloud account and free iWork.com account. After you do this and activate them on each of your computers, also make sure the Documents & Data option is turned on, which is available from the iCloud window within System Preferences.

To turn on iCloud's Documents & Data option on each of your Macs, follow these steps:

1. Launch System Preferences from the Mac's Dock or Applications folder.
2. From the main System Preferences window, click the iCloud icon.
3. When the iCloud window (within System Preferences) becomes available, log into your iCloud account, if you're prompted to do so.
4. Using the mouse, place a virtual checkmark next to the Documents & Data option displayed within the iCloud window within System Preferences.
5. Using any iWork for Mac or iWork for iOS program, create a file and upload it to your iWork.com account, and then download (transfer) it to your Mac from iWork.com.

After these steps are completed once, you can then manually drag-and-drop or copy and paste files and documents from any folder stored on your Mac to the /Library/ Mobile Documents folder that's used by iCloud/iWork.com to sync iWork files. To make this easier, you can create an alias for this folder by dragging it within the sidebar of your Finder window or to your Dock. Files placed into this folder will be automatically copied and synchronized with all the computers and iOS devices linked to your iCloud/ iWork accounts.

## Find the /Library/Mobile Documents Folder

To pinpoint the location of the /Library/Mobile Documents folder on your Mac, first click the Finder icon that's displayed in the lower-right corner of the Mac's screen (on your Dock). When the Finder window opens, access the Go pull-down menu that's displayed at the top of the screen, and select the Go To Folder... option. When the Go to the Folder field appears, enter **/Library/Mobile Documents** (as shown in the illustration). Then click Go. You can create an easy-to-access alias for this folder by dragging it to the left side of the Finder screen or to the Mac's Dock.

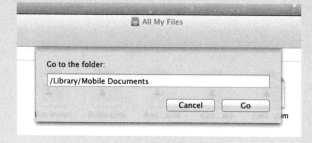

# Additional iCloud Functionality for Your Mac

Third-party software developers are beginning to make their applications compatible with iCloud, so you'll be able to transfer and sync files, documents, and data with ease via the Web.

Using the iWork.com functionality that works in conjunction with iCloud, one potentially useful feature is the ability to embed a Keynote digital slide presentation (including animations, audio, and video) into a web site or blog. When you do this, the person visiting the web site or blog is given access to a series of on-screen controls for playing, pausing, fast-forwarding, or rewinding the presentation as it's being viewed.

**Note**   For information on how to embed a Keynote presentation into a web site or blog using the iWork.com (iCloud) service, go to http://help.apple.com/iworkcom/index.html#iwc72fa5d6c.

Over time, Apple and a variety of third-party software developers will begin to introduce new features and functionality that can be used on your Mac in conjunction with iCloud to handle a wide range of new tasks. As time passes, Apple will better integrate iWork.com with iCloud, making the file and document sharing and syncing process of iWork-related files a more seamless and automated process.

# 3

## How iPhone, iPad, and iPod touch Users Can Utilize iCloud

**HOW TO...**

- Discover what iCloud can do in conjunction with your iOS devices.
- Turn on iCloud functionality on your iOS devices.

When you combine iCloud's functionality with the power and portability of your iPhone, iPad, or iPod touch, you gain the ability to access your own data, music, files, documents, photos, and other content instantly, any time, and from anywhere with an Internet connection. Plus, once iCloud is set up on your computers and iOS devices, your contacts database and schedule can be perfectly synced between your other computer(s) and iOS device(s), which makes it easy to stay in touch with people and consult your schedule.

## What an iOS Device User Can Do with iCloud

iCloud, when used in conjunction with your iOS device(s), can handle a variety of tasks, including the following:

- iCloud gives you instant access to all your iTunes music purchases (via the iTunes and Music apps preinstalled with iOS 5). Music you own can be downloaded to your iPhone, iPad, or iPod touch if that music was not originally purchased on that iOS device or isn't currently stored on it. You'll discover how to access your iTunes-purchased music and other content via iCloud from Chapter 5.
- iCloud grants you access to your entire digital music library, including non-iTunes purchases if you upgrade to the iTunes Match service for $24.99 per year. You'll learn about the iTunes Match service in Chapter 6.

- iCloud lets you access and update your iCloud-based Photo Stream. As you snap photos using the cameras built into your iOS device (or import photos into your iPhone, iPad, or iPod touch from other sources), your most recent images can automatically be added to your Photo Stream and then shared, almost immediately, with your other iOS devices and computers. You'll learn more about how to create and manage your iCloud Photo Stream from Chapter 7.

- Using iCloud's "Documents in the Cloud" functionality, you can create or edit documents and files using the iWork for iOS apps (or other iCloud-compatible apps), and then wirelessly and automatically sync them with your other computers or iOS devices that are linked to the same iCloud account. You'll learn more about "Documents in the Cloud" and how best to use this feature in Chapter 8.

- With iCloud, you can synchronize app-specific data related to Contacts, Calendars, Safari (Bookmarks), Mail (for your iCloud-related e-mail account only), eBooks, and the apps themselves that you purchase. This sync process is done wirelessly. Chapter 12 provides information about syncing app-related data.

- iCloud lets you wirelessly create and maintain a backup of your iOS device. This replaces the familiar iTunes Sync process. In Chapter 13, you'll discover the advantages of using iCloud Backup, as opposed to iTunes Sync, to maintain a backup of your iOS device(s). Your backup files are stored online (via iCloud), rather than on your primary computer's hard drive, so if it becomes necessary, you can perform a Restore from anywhere with an Internet connection.

As you'll discover throughout this book, after iCloud functionality is established, you can pick and choose which iCloud-related features and functions you want to use, and then customize that functionality so it best meets your needs.

# Setting up Your iOS Devices to Work with iCloud

If you're a Mac or PC user who also owns and uses an iOS device, your best bet is first to establish an iCloud account on your primary computer. You'll need to establish an iCloud account only once, and only one account is needed to connect all of your computers and iOS devices together via iCloud.

## Create Your iCloud Account from Your iOS Device (or Computer)

You can establish an iCloud account directly from your iOS device. However, only one iCloud account needs to be activated on each computer and iOS device that you want to be wirelessly linked together. Then the devices can share and synchronize data, files, documents, photos, and content.

If you're migrating from MobileMe to iCloud, this can be done from your primary computer. Follow the steps outlined in Chapter 4. If you currently have multiple MobileMe accounts to migrate, perform the MobileMe-to-iCloud migration process only once using the Apple ID and password you want to use with iCloud (the password used for your iTunes purchases, for example).

 After you've established an iCloud account, make sure each of your iOS devices has been upgraded to the most recent version of iOS 5. If you've already upgraded to iOS 5, check to see if a more recent update to the operating system has been released.

# How to Check for iOS 5 Updates

In October 2011, Apple released the iOS 5 operating system for the iPhone, iPad, and iPod touch. About a month later, the company released an update to the iOS, called iOS 5.01. By the time you're reading this, newer updates will have been released. Among other things, iOS 5.01 fixed bugs and issues relating to using iCloud with the "Documents in the Cloud" feature.

To make sure your iPhone, iPad, or iPod touch is running the latest version of its operating system, either use the iTunes software on your computer, or if you have a Wi-Fi connection, check for and install the iOS updates wirelessly directly from your iOS device. (Using the wireless iOS update feature works only if you're already running iOS 5.0 or later. Otherwise, you'll need to perform the iOS update using the iTunes software on your primary computer in conjunction with the iTunes Sync process.)

If you want to use the iTunes Sync process to check for iOS updates, connect your primary computer to your iOS device using the supplied USB cable, or set up the wireless iTunes Sync process.

Launch the iTunes software on your primary computer. Then, on the left side of the iTunes screen, under the Devices heading, click the name of your iOS device. Then click the Summary icon displayed near the top-center of the screen.

When the Summary screen is displayed, under the Version heading, click the Check For Updates icon (shown in Figure 3-1). If an update is required, follow the onscreen prompts to back up your iOS device, and then download and install the newest version of the operating system. This process could take between 5 and 30 minutes, depending on how much of your own data needs to be restored to the device after the operating system upgrade.

To check for an iOS upgrade from your iOS device, a Wi-Fi connection is required. From the Home Screen, launch the Settings app. Then, from the main Settings menu, select the General option. When the General menu is displayed within Settings, tap the Software Update option (shown in Figure 3-2). If an update is required, follow the onscreen prompts to download and automatically install it.

 Before you perform a wireless iOS update from your iPhone, iPad, or iPod touch, it's a good idea to use the iCloud Backup feature to create a backup of your device.

FIGURE 3-1 You can check for iOS updates when your iOS device is connected to your primary computer using the supplied USB cable.

FIGURE 3-2 You can check for, download, and install iOS updates wirelessly, directly from your iOS device, if you have access to a Wi-Fi Internet connection.

# Turn on iCloud Functionality on Your iOS Devices

Now that you've created an iCloud account and you have iOS 5 (or later) running on your iPhone, iPad, or iPod touch, you need to turn on iCloud functionality on each device separately. Then you'll need to choose which iCloud features and functions you want to activate and, in some cases, turn on iCloud functionality within specific apps.

To turn on iCloud functionality on an iOS device, follow these steps:

1. Launch the Settings app from the Home Screen.
2. From the main Settings menu, tap the iCloud option.
3. When the iCloud menu screen appears within Settings, tap the Account option that's displayed near the top of the screen.
4. Near the top of the Account screen, enter your Apple ID and password that was used to create the iCloud account (shown in Figure 3-3 on an iPhone). It's essential that you use the same Apple ID account on all devices you want to link together via iCloud.
5. Tap the Done icon after you've finished entering the account information. iCloud functionality is now activated on that device.
6. Return to the iCloud screen within Settings. Below the Account option (shown in Figure 3-4) are options for Mail, Contacts, Calendar, Reminders, Bookmarks,

**FIGURE 3-3**   Turn on iCloud functionality by entering your iCloud account information within the Settings app, shown here on an iPhone 4S.

**FIGURE 3-4**    Turn on the iCloud-related features you want to use on your iOS device, shown here on an iPhone 4S.

Notes, Photo Stream, Documents & Data, and Find My iPad (Find My iPhone). To the right of each of these options is a virtual on/off switch. Tap the virtual switch that corresponds to the iCloud features you want to turn on (or off).

7. Choose which iCloud features and functions you want to turn on and begin using on the iOS devices with which you're currently working. Each of these features is explored in future chapters in this book.

8. Repeat this process on each of your iOS devices.

**Did You Know?** **Once App-Specific Syncing Is Turned on, Your Data Will Automatically Be Synchronized**

As soon as you turn on an iCloud feature, such as Contacts, for example, your iOS device will immediately begin syncing your Contacts app-related data with iCloud. Any time you make changes to your Contacts database, and your iOS device has access to the Internet, those changes will be synced with iCloud. Once your Contacts data is stored on iCloud, it will be synced automatically with any other iOS devices or computers that are linked to that iCloud account. So any changes you made to your Contacts database on your computer or on another iOS device will be downloaded from iCloud and synced with the information on the device you're currently using. This all happens automatically and in the background once the feature is activated.

## How to... Turn on iCloud Functionality for Specific iOS Apps

If you turn on the Documents & Data feature, you will also need to turn on iCloud functionality related to the specific apps you want to use with this feature, such as Pages, Numbers, or Keynote.

To do this, return to the main Settings menu and scroll down to the Apps heading. Below the Apps heading, find the app(s) with which you want to use iCloud to sync data between your iOS device and iCloud.

For example, tap the Pages option (shown in the following illustration on an iPhone).

At the top of the Pages menu screen within iCloud, tap the virtual switch associated with the Use iCloud feature, and turn it on (shown next). Repeat this process for each app that's capable of syncing files or data with iCloud, including Numbers and Keynote.

**Did You Know?**

## Your iTunes Content Is Always Accessible via iCloud

After you establish your iCloud account, you can access any purchased iTunes content from a iOS device that you purchased in the past or that was purchased on another computer or device. This includes music, TV show episodes, movies, ringtones, and audiobooks, for example, as well as eBooks purchased from iBookstore and apps acquired from the App Store.

You'll learn later in this book that you can download any of this content to your iOS device at anytime. For music, a 3G Internet connection will work. However, to transfer TV show episodes, movies, or content with a file size greater than 20MB, a Wi-Fi connection is required.

On your iOS device, if you delete a song that was purchased from the iTunes Store, you can re-download it any time from iCloud to that iPhone, iPad, or iPod touch. However, remember that if you delete any of your own data that is being synchronized via iCloud, such as a contact entry from Contacts, an event from your calendar, a bookmark from Safari, a Pages document, a Numbers spreadsheet, or a Keynote presentation file, that data, document, or file will almost immediately be deleted from the device you're using and from the other computers and iOS devices that are linked to your iCloud account.

To retrieve that deleted file, you'll need to refer back to a recent backup (if one exists). Otherwise, that data or file could be lost forever. Before deleting data or files that are being synchronized with iCloud, make sure you won't need that information in the future on the device you're using, or on your other computers or iOS devices.

Your iOS device is now ready to begin utilizing the features and functions of iCloud. Keep in mind that all iCloud features require that your iOS device has access to the Internet via a 3G or Wi-Fi connection. However, to use the Photo Stream or iCloud Backup feature, you must have a Wi-Fi connection.

If you plan to use your iOS device in conjunction with Apple's AirPlay feature (to stream content between your iOS device and your Apple TV) or Apple's Home Sharing feature (to transfer data between your iOS device and primary computer), the two devices will need to be connected to the same wireless home network. How to do this is explained in greater detail in Chapter 14.

# Sharing Content With and Without iCloud

iCloud is designed to make it easy for you to share your own data, documents, files, photos, music, and content with your other computer(s) and iOS devices. It is not, however, useful for sharing this content with other people or with computers or devices that are not linked to your personal iCloud account.

That being said, to share iWork-related documents and files with other people via the Web (including Pages, Numbers, and Keynote documents and files), you can use Apple's iWork.com cloud-based file sharing service, which works in conjunction with iCloud (but requires that you set up a separate, free iWork.com account).

From any computer or device that has Internet access, you can also access your Contacts or Calendar data directly from www.iCloud.com, after you log into this service using your Apple ID. This grants you access to your own data from any computer or device, even if you don't have your Mac, PC, iPhone, iPad, or iPod touch with you. However, accessing iCloud.com does not allow you to share documents and data with other people.

If you want to share your personal documents, files, and data with others, take advantage of the Share menu options that are offered in many iOS 5 apps. Depending on the app, these options allow you to share data, files, content, or photos, for example, with other people via e-mail, Twitter, text message, or in some cases other online social networking or file sharing sites, such as Facebook or flickr.com (for sharing photos).

 Although you can receive e-mail attachments using the Mail app on your iPhone, iPad, or iPod touch, to send an e-mail with an app-specific attachment, you'll need to use the Share feature built into apps such as Photos and Pages.

Another option is to use a cloud-based file sharing service, such as Dropbox, that offers functionality for sharing specific files or documents (beyond those created using iWork) with someone else. You'll learn more about Dropbox in Chapter 9.

# 4

# Migrate from Apple MobileMe to iCloud

**HOW TO...**

- Transfer your existing Apple MobileMe Account to iCloud.
- Copy other MobileMe data to iCloud.

More than a decade before Apple launched its online-based iCloud service in October 2011, it offered the iTools online service, which ultimately evolved into .Mac (which was exclusively for Mac users). Over time, the .Mac service was transformed into the fee-based MobileMe online service, which in its last incarnation became a free service available to Mac and iOS device users. MobileMe, shown in Figure 4-1, will remain operational until June 30, 2012, at which time it will be taken offline, and everything stored on it (including your content and data) will be deleted forever.

 This chapter's focus is on converting your existing MobileMe account into a free iCloud account. If you're not currently a MobileMe user, you can skip this chapter.

The various features and online-based services offered by MobileMe includes the following:

- A free (.me or .Mac) e-mail account
- Online storage space to store document and data files (via iDisk)
- The ability to sync iCal (Mac) and Address Book (Mac) data, as well as Contacts (iOS) and Calendar (iOS) app data, Safari bookmarks, and Mac keychain-related data wirelessly
- An online-based web server to host and share online photo galleries (created by iPhoto) and personal web pages (created by iWeb)
- The Find My iPhone and Find My iPad services

**FIGURE 4-1** MobileMe main screen

As soon as iCloud was launched in October 2011, however, Apple's MobileMe service immediately became obsolete.

 If you have an existing MobileMe account, you'll need to make the transition to a free iCloud account and then transfer your relevant files and data, or this content will eventually be deleted from the MobileMe service and lost forever.

In addition, some files and data that were previously stored on MobileMe and that utilized iWeb, Gallery, and iDisk, for example, are not compatible with iCloud. Thus, you must transfer these files back to your primary computer or find a new online host for them. For example, you can manually transfer your online photos that are stored within online-based MobileMe Galleries to another online photo service, such as Flickr.com, SmugMug.com, or KodakGallery.com.

In conjunction with the launch of iCloud, the following MobileMe features can easily be transferred, for free, to iCloud:

- Mail
- Contacts
- Calendar
- Bookmarks
- Find My iPhone/iPad
- Back to My Mac

So, for example, if you already have a *me.com* or *mac.com* e-mail address that's associated with MobileMe, you'll be able to keep it, and it will continue to work fine using iCloud.

In addition to managing your MobileMe (soon to be iCloud-related) e-mail address from the Mail software on your Mac or the Mail app on your iOS device, you could manage this e-mail account online, using any web browser, by visiting www.MobileMe .com/mail. Once you make the transition to iCloud, you'll be able to access your iCloud-related e-mail account from the Mail software on a Mac, the Mail app on an iOS device, or by pointing your web browser to www.iCloud.com/mail. In fact, you'll also be able to access your Address Book/Contacts data online by pointing your web browser to www.iCloud.com/contacts, or you can access your iCal/Calendar data online by pointing your web browser to www.iCloud.com/calendar.

To pinpoint the exact location of your iPhone, iPad, or Mac using the Find My iPhone, Find My iPad, or Find My Mac feature that's built into iCloud, point your web browser to www.iCloud.com/find. Or you can use the free Find My iPhone app (available from the App Store) from any iOS device that's connected to the Internet.

To access iWork-related documents and files that are stored on iWork.com (which works in conjunction with iCloud and the Pages, Numbers, and Keynote Mac software and iOS apps), point your web browser to either www.iCloud.com/iwork or www.iWork .com after your free iCloud and iWork.com accounts are set up.

 At the time iCloud was launched, it was not yet possible to view your iCloud Photo Stream from the Web. However, as you'll discover in Chapter 7, you can visit www.iCloud.com to reset the Photo Stream feature of your iCloud account and delete all of the digital photos currently stored within your Photo Stream.

If you have photo Galleries stored on MobileMe, you'll need to transfer those images back to iPhoto '11 on your Mac (or to another online photo service) or otherwise make a backup of them before June 30, 2012. Likewise, you'll need to move any files stored on iDisk to your primary computer and find a new online hosting service for any of your web pages currently being hosted by MobileMe.

Although some of the functionality that was once offered by MobileMe is no longer available, as you'll discover from reading this book and exploring the iCloud service, iCloud offers an array of new and useful features that will appeal to Mac, Apple TV, and iOS mobile device users alike. And if you're someone who uses multiple Apple computers or devices, you'll find that iCloud offers easy solutions for automatically keeping files, data, documents, and content synchronized among all of your computers and devices.

# Making the Switch from MobileMe to iCloud

No matter how much you love using MobileMe, it's time to say goodbye to the past and embrace the future of cloud-based computing with iCloud. The good news is that the transition takes just a few minutes, it costs nothing, and you can keep your existing Apple ID (and password) as well as your .me or .Mac e-mail account.

Your e-mail access (for your .me or .Mac account), as well as all of your Contacts and Calendar synchronized data and your Safari Bookmarks will transfer over to iCloud in a matter of minutes after you initiate the transfer process.

Unlike MobileMe, iCloud does not offer "Family Accounts." So each member of your family who was using the same MobileMe account as you will ultimately need to create his or her own personal iCloud account.

## What You'll Need to Make the MobileMe-to-iCloud Transition

Before you make the transition from MobileMe to iCloud, make sure that you're running the most current version of OS X Lion (version 10.7.2 or later) on your Mac, as well as iOS 5 on your iPhone, iPad, and/or iPod touch. You'll also need to know the Apple ID and password you used to set up your MobileMe account. If you're an Apple TV user, make sure you download and install the latest operating system update for that device.

Ultimately, you can use one Apple ID for your iCloud account and a separate one to make purchases on the iTunes Store, App Store, or iBookstore. If you do this, however, it will get very confusing if and when you attempt to sync iTunes content, apps, eBooks, as well as other data between your computers and iOS devices. It's a much better strategy to use just one Apple ID and password for everything relating to all of your Apple computers, Apple online services (such as FaceTime and iMessage), iCloud, and iOS devices.

After the most current operating system is running on your Mac(s) and/or iOS device(s), back up your Address Book, iCal, and Safari Bookmark data on your Mac (using Time Machine, for example) and perform an iTunes Sync to back up your iOS devices.

Ultimately, iCloud will synchronize your contact and calendar database from the Address Book and iCal software, as well as the Contacts and Calendar apps. And it will synchronize your Safari bookmarks from Safari on your Mac(s) and iOS devices. No personal data will actually be transferred from MobileMe. Thus, you must have your entire Contacts database and/or Calendar database stored safely on your computer and/or iOS device(s) before proceeding.

If your Contacts or Calendars database is stored only online (on MobileMe) and not on your Mac and/or your iOS device(s), do not proceed with the MobileMe-to-iCloud transfer process until your data has been retrieved and stored on at least one computer or iOS device.

Once your iCloud account is set up, it will link to all of your Mac(s), Apple TV, and iOS devices, and, as appropriate, it will sync the Contacts, Calendar, and Safari-related data into databases that will be stored online within your iCloud account and continuously shared and synchronized with your Mac or PC computers and iOS devices via the Web.

 Prior to making the transition from MobileMe to iCloud, make sure that your MobileMe account was updated to use what Apple refers to as the "New MobileMe Calendar" feature. When you log into www.MobileMe.com, if you can view your current calendar data using the online-based Calendar app, you're in good shape. Otherwise, be sure to turn off Calendar syncing on your Macs and iOS devices, and choose to keep the Calendar data on your devices. If you do not do this, you can experience data loss during the conversion.

If you never upgraded to the "New MobileMe Calendar" feature to turn off Calendar syncing on your iOS device(s) before making the MobileMe-to-iCloud transition, follow these steps:

1. Launch the Settings app from the iPhone, iPad, or iPod touch's Home Screen.
2. From the main Settings menu, tap the Mail, Contacts, Calendars option.
3. From the Mail, Contacts, Calendars screen within Settings, tap the MobileMe option under Accounts, and then turn off the virtual switch associated with Calendars.
4. A pop-up window will appear that says, "Turn off Calendars. What would you like to do with the previously synced MobileMe calendars on your iPhone (iPad/iPod touch)?" Tap the Keep On My iPad (iPhone/iPod touch) icon.

 Once you begin using iCloud, it will no longer create a backup or synchronize your Mac's Keychain items, Dashboard widgets, or Dock items.

# Initiate the MobileMe-to-iCloud Conversion

As you begin the MobileMe-to-iCloud conversion process, keep in mind that you will need to use the e-mail address associated with your Apple ID to set up your iCloud account on each of your Macs, your Apple TV, and on all of your iOS devices. Even if you use your MobileMe (soon to be iCloud-related) e-mail account for no other purpose, it can be used to set up and manage your iCloud account.

To begin the account transition process, which will take just a few minutes, from your web browser, go to www.MobileMe.com/move. When prompted, as shown in Figure 4-2, enter your existing Apple ID and password (or your MobileMe account name and password). This process needs to be done only once from your primary computer. After you've created an iCloud account, you can sign into it from your other computers and devices when you turn on iCloud functionality.

Another way to initiate the MobileMe to iCloud transition is to launch System Preferences on your Mac and click the MobileMe option. When prompted, sign into your MobileMe account from within the MobileMe window of System Preferences.

**FIGURE 4-2**    Begin the transition process to iCloud by visiting www.MobileMe.com/ move and signing in to your MobileMe account.

Then click the Move To iCloud icon displayed near the bottom of the MobileMe window (shown in Figure 4-3). In the future, after you make the transition, if you try to access the MobileMe window within System Preferences, the iCloud window will automatically appear.

When the initial Move screen is displayed (Figure 4-4), click the Get Started button. MobileMe will begin the process by transferring your Mail and Calendars information from MobileMe to iCloud (Figure 4-5) and will automatically make the necessary adjustments on the computer you're currently using.

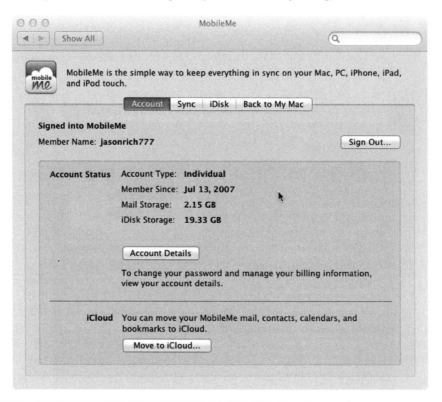

**FIGURE 4-3**    You can also initiate the transition to iCloud from within System Preferences on your Mac.

**FIGURE 4-4**    Click the Get Started button to begin the transition to iCloud.

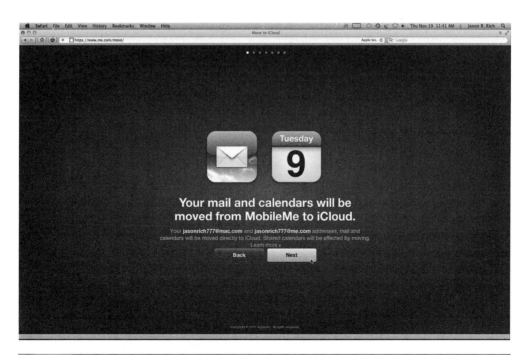

**FIGURE 4-5**    First, your Mail and Calendars data gets prepared for the transfer.

If you click the Learn More option from the screen shown in Figure 4-5, you'll discover that your privately shared calendars will be preserved as you make the transition between services, but the people with whom you're sharing your calendars with must also begin using iCloud to view them (as shown in Figure 4-6). Calendars that are publically shared will become "unpublished" when you make the service transition. Thus, you'll need to republish those calendars once you're an iCloud user.

To transfer your iDisk-related files to your Mac, visit www.me.com/idisk, sign in to your account, select the files you want to transfer, and then click the Download icon that's displayed near the top of the screen.

Click the close box to close the message, and then click Next to continue. From the next screen that appears during the transition process (shown in Figure 4-7), you'll be reminded that your photo galleries, files stored on iDisk, and web pages created using iWeb will remain functional (via MobileMe) until June 30, 2012, even after you transition to iCloud. Click Next to continue.

To transfer your photos out of your online-based galleries, copy your important files using iDisk and/or find a new hosting service to publish your web sites. Instead of waiting until the last minute (June 30, 2012), consider handling these tasks right away.

As you already know, some of MobileMe's features will no longer be supported by iCloud. Once again, you'll be reminded of which features are being discontinued (shown in Figure 4-8). Continue the transition process by clicking the Next icon.

Next, you'll need to confirm that you've already upgraded the operating system on your Mac to OS X Lion 10.7.2 (or later), the operating system on your iOS device to iOS 5 (or later), and/or the operating system on your Windows-based PC. If you're a PC user, be sure to download and install the iCloud Control Panel software before you continue the MobileMe-to-iCloud transition process.

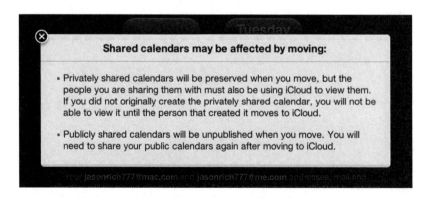

**FIGURE 4-6** On any screen associated with the MobileMe-to-iCloud transfer process, after you click the Learn More option you'll see information about that step of the transition.

**FIGURE 4-7**   Don't forget to find a new home for your photo galleries, files stored on iDisk, and your web pages hosted using iWeb.

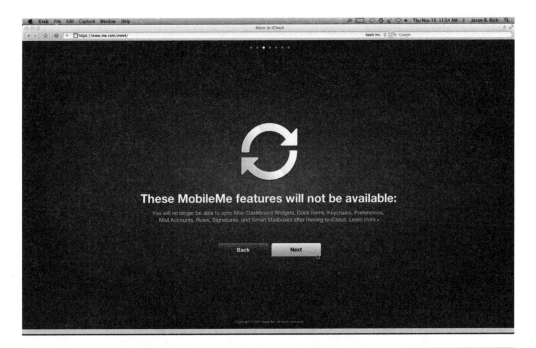

**FIGURE 4-8**   Some features and functions of MobileMe will no longer be supported.

## How to... Transfer Your MobileMe Galleries to iPhoto '11 on Your Mac

If you have created MobileMe photo galleries that are not also saved on your Mac, you should transfer the images from those online-based galleries to your Mac. To do this, access your MobileMe Galleries either by signing into www.MobileMe.com or by pointing your web browser to www.me.com/gallery.

From the main MobileMe Galleries screen, you'll see thumbnails depicting each of your galleries. Click one Gallery at a time to view thumbnails of the images stored within it. At the top of each Gallery screen, click the Album Settings icon. Make sure the Allow Downloading of Photos, Movies or Entire Album option is selected by placing a checkmark next to it. Click the Publish icon.

To the right of the Gallery command icons, you'll see the web site URL displayed for that Gallery. Click it. When the Gallery screen is shown, you'll see a Download command icon displayed near the top-center of the screen. Click it to create a compressed .ZIP file of your images, and download them to your computer's hard drive. When you click the Download icon, the image files will be compressed and downloaded to your Mac's Downloads folder as a single .ZIP file. They'll be decompressed automatically once they're downloaded, and the contents of each Gallery will now be contained in a separate folder on your Mac.

Repeat this process for each of your MobileMe galleries to move them from your online-based MobileMe account to your computer's hard drive. Once the .ZIP files are stored on your Mac, you can import the images into iPhoto '11, copy them to an external hard drive, or upload them to another online photo-sharing and archiving service.

If you're confident that you've made the necessary software upgrades to your computer(s) and iOS devices, click the checkbox that's associated with the All Of The Devices I Want To Use With iCloud Are Now Running The Required Software option (shown in Figure 4-9). Once a checkmark appears within the checkbox, click the Next icon to continue.

**Note** While you're thinking about updating the software on your computer in preparation to use iCloud, also be sure you download and install the latest version of the iTunes software (version 10.5 or later). This is necessary to use some of iCloud's features that relate to iTunes content.

You'll now be reminded to ensure that all of your contacts (from your Address Book database on your Mac and the Contacts app on your iOS device), as well as your Safari Bookmarks (from your Macs and/or iOS devices) are backed up and stored on their respective devices (shown in Figure 4-10). This is extremely important. Ultimately, your iCloud account will populate your new Contacts, Calendar, and Safari Bookmark database with data already stored on your Mac(s) and iOS device(s), not from data stored online within your existing MobileMe account.

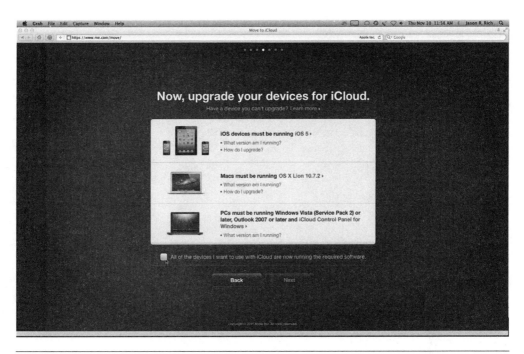

**FIGURE 4-9**    Before proceeding, make sure you've upgraded the operating system on your Mac and iOS devices.

**FIGURE 4-10**    Be sure to back up your Contacts and Calendar databases and Safari bookmarks before proceeding.

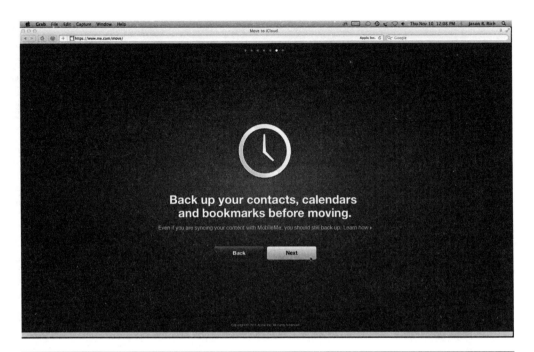

**FIGURE 4-11** If MobileMe was your primary backup method for archiving data and files, choose another option before proceeding with the MobileMe-to-iCloud transition.

Click the Next icon to continue. This second-to-last MobileMe-to-iCloud transition screen (shown in Figure 4-11) reminds you to back up your data. To back up your iOS device(s), use the iTunes Sync process, Wireless iTunes Sync process, or the iCloud Backup process.

**How to...** Manually Back up Your Contacts, Calendars, and Safari Bookmarks on Your Mac

To create a backup of your Address Book contacts database manually, launch the Address Book software on your Mac, and then choose File | Export | Address Book Archive option (shown in the next illustration). Select a storage location for the backup file, such as an external hard drive or a USB thumb drive. (Or you can create a folder on your Mac's primary hard drive.)

To create a backup of your iCal calendar database manually, launch the iCal app on your Mac. Choose File | Export | Export. Select a storage location for the backup file. If you manage multiple calendars from the iCal software, repeat this process for each separate Calendar database.

*(Continued)*

To back up your Safari Bookmarks manually, launch the Safari web browser on your Mac. Choose File | Export Bookmark. Select a storage location for the backup file, which will be called Safari Bookmarks.html.

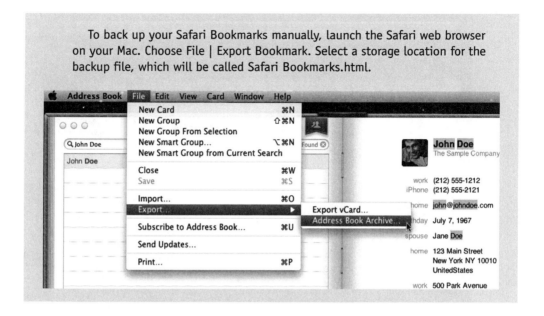

Click the Next icon (for the last time) to finish up the MobileMe-to-iCloud account transition process. The "Moving Your MobileMe Content" screen (shown in Figure 4-12) is displayed and the transfer process will commence. This could take 2 to 4 minutes.

**How to...**

## Manually Back up Outlook Data on Your Windows-Based PC

To create a backup of your Outlook 2007 or Outlook 2010 data (contacts, calendars, and so on) on your Windows-based PC, begin with the Contacts database. Use the Export Wizard that's built into the Outlook software.

To back up your calendar database, launch the Outlook software on your PC. Next, select the calendar you want to back up from the Calendar List. Be sure to uncheck all of the other calendars.

Choose File | Save As. When prompted, modify the save-related settings to include the entire Calendar, and then select a location to store the backup file that's about to be created. You will need to repeat this process for each separate Calendar being maintained by Outlook.

To back up your Safari Bookmarks on your Windows-based PC, launch the Safari web browser. Choose File | Export Bookmark. Select a storage location for the backup file, which will be called Safari Bookmarks.html.

If you're using Microsoft Internet Explorer on your PC, you'll need to back up that Bookmarks list as well while running that browser software. For information on how to do this, visit Microsoft's web site at http://windows.microsoft.com/en-US/windows-vista/Import-or-export-favorites-in-Internet-Explorer.

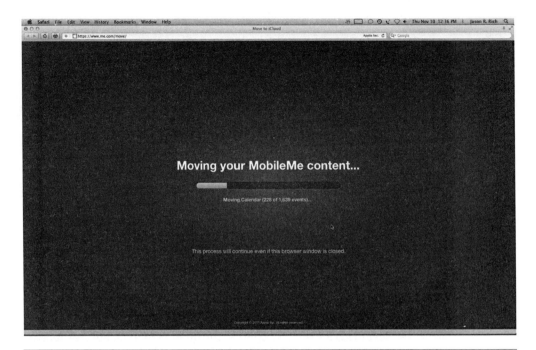

**FIGURE 4-12** The "Moving Your MobileMe Content" screen is displayed as your iCloud account is being created.

When the "Your iCloud Account Has Been Created" message appears, you're officially an iCloud user. Now you'll need to customize iCloud's functionality. A "Congratulations!" screen will be displayed. You'll then be prompted to sign into your new iCloud account (via www.iCloud.com). Notice that you're no longer using www.MobileMe.com to access this functionality. However, until June 2012, you can still use www.MobileMe.com to access your Galleries, iDisk (www.me.com/idisk), and iWeb data and content.

 How to turn on (or off) and customize each function of iCloud is the focus of Chapters 5–8, and 12–14. On your Mac, iCloud features are controlled primarily from the iCloud window within System Preferences. On a PC, the iCloud Control Panel is used.

When prompted, select your Language and Time Zone. You can also click the Add Photo option (shown in Figure 4-13) to associate your photo with your newly created iCloud account. Click the Done icon to continue. You'll be reminded to set up your devices to work with iCloud (shown in Figure 4-14). How to do this was explained within Chapter 3 and is reiterated in the various chapters that focus on specific iCloud-related features and functions.

**FIGURE 4-13**    When prompted, begin customizing your new iCloud account. Choose your Language and Time Zone.

The main iCloud.com menu screen is displayed (shown in Figure 4-15). At any time, you can return to this screen from any computer or mobile device that's connected to the Internet, by visiting www.iCloud.com and then signing in using your Apple ID and password.

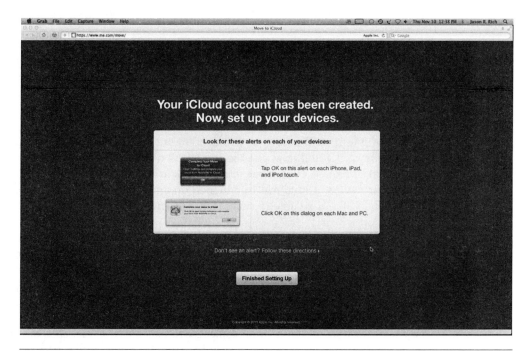

**FIGURE 4-14**    For iCloud to sync files and data between your computer(s) and iOS device(s), iCloud functionality must be turned on and set up on each iOS device separately.

**FIGURE 4-15** As soon as the transfer process is done, you'll be transferred to www.iCloud.com and the service's main menu will be displayed.

 Do not cancel your MobileMe account manually, especially before you make the transition to iCloud. When you manually cancel the account (as opposed to converting it to iCloud), all of your MobileMe-related data and files will be deleted and lost forever.

Whichever Apple ID and password you used to create your iCloud account is the Apple ID and password you'll now need to use on all of your Macs, Apple TV, and iOS mobile devices to link these computers and devices to the same iCloud account. On each computer or device, iCloud must be turned on and linked to the same iCloud account, or iCloud will not be able to share and synchronize data, files, documents, photos, and content.

 Although you can have multiple Apple ID accounts (which is possible, but not recommended), it is not possible to merge two or more Apple ID accounts into one. If you've made iTunes purchases using multiple Apple ID accounts, be sure to download all of your purchases to one computer or iOS device so they're saved in a single location before making the MobileMe-to-iCloud transition. Then, from within the iTunes software, authorize your computer to play content from each of your Apple IDs. (With iTunes software running on your Mac or PC, click the Store pull-down menu and select the Authorize This Computer command.)

## Deactivate the Backup Software on Your Mac

On your Mac, if in the past you used the free Backup software from Apple in conjunction with MobileMe to back up certain OS X-related data automatically, after you upgrade to iCloud, this software is no longer needed and will not function properly. You can manually deactivate it or simply delete the application from your Mac (it's stored within the Applications folder). This Backup application (which has a program icon that looks like an umbrella) was optional and was separate from Time Machine (which is still very much needed on your Mac).

## You Can Change the Name Used for Your Apple ID

You can change your Apple ID username without impacting the data related to the account or having to create a new account from scratch. Your Apple ID is used by iTunes, iChat, iCloud, FaceTime, iMessage, the App Store, iBookstore, and a variety of other Apple-related services. It's also used to request technical support from Apple.com or to make and track purchases from the Apple Online Store (www.Apple.com).

To change your Apple ID username, visit https://appleid.apple.com, and click the Manage Your Account option. When prompted, sign into your Apple ID account using your existing Apple ID and password.

When the My Apple ID screen appears, click the Edit option that's associated with any of the fields. To change your Apple ID, click the Edit field next to the Apple ID option. Remember that if your Apple ID ends with @mac.com or @me.com, it cannot be changed. Apple recommends that if you opt to change your Apple ID, you change it to your primary e-mail address.

Click the Save Changes option after you've made the desired changes to your Apple ID account.

# PART II

# Manage Your Music and Photos in the Cloud

# 5

# Manage Your Digital Music Library with iCloud

**HOW TO...**

- Set up an Apple ID to work with iTunes.
- Install and use iTunes on your Mac or PC to manage and acquire music.
- Link iTunes to iCloud and share your iTunes music purchases with other computers and iOS devices,

Apple has designed iCloud to handle many different tasks, mostly behind the scenes, to ensure that a wide range of files, data, and information are constantly available to you from your computers, Apple TV (for compatible content, such as music, TV shows, and movies), and/or all of your iOS mobile devices (including the iPhone, iPad, and iPod touch). Nowhere is this data syncing functionality more prevalent than with Apple's iTunes and the Music app on your iOS device. Thanks to iCloud, your iTunes music purchases are accessible when and where you want to listen to them.

iTunes is free and downloadable to your Mac or PC. This extremely versatile software was designed to help you manage your entire music library, sync data between your primary computer and iOS device, and serve as a portal for accessing the iTunes Store.

After you purchase content from the iTunes Store, App Store, iBookstore, or Newsstand, it's immediately downloaded to the computer or device from which it was purchased, but it's also saved to your iCloud account. Thus, it becomes immediately accessible on all of your computers and iOS devices that are linked to that account and that have access to the Internet. So, for example, if you purchase a song from iTunes, and you have a computer, iPhone, and iPad, you do not need to purchase the same song three times to enjoy listening to it on all three devices.

## Make Your Content Purchases from Apple's iTunes Store

You can shop for content from Apple through the iTunes Store, which is accessible via the iTunes software. You can download or purchase apps for your iPhone, iPad, or iPod touch; eBooks; TV shows; movies; or digital publications. When you shop for similar content on your iOS device, you can use the iTunes Store (via the iTunes app) to acquire TV shows and movies. You can also use the App Store (via the App Store app) to acquire apps for your iPhone, iPad, or iPod touch. The iBooks app is used to access iBookstore and to shop for eBooks. Use the Newsstand app (or the App Store app) to acquire digital editions of newspapers or magazines.

**Note**

To use iCloud with your Mac, you must first install OS X Lion v10.7.2 or later, and the latest version of iTunes (v10.5 or later), plus have an active Apple ID account. On a PC running Windows Vista Service Pack 2 or Windows 7, in addition to the latest version of the iTunes software, you'll need to download and install the free iCloud Control Panel (available from the Apple web site at www.apple.com/icloud/setup/pc.html). An active Apple ID is also required.

The following table shows from which Apple online-based service you can acquire various types of content and the costs of those services.

| Content Type | Service Used to Acquire Content | Cost | Rental Price |
|---|---|---|---|
| Music | iTunes Store | $.69 to $1.29 per song; $9.99 to $11.99 per album (prices vary) | N/A |
| Music videos | iTunes Store | $1.99 | N/A |
| Podcasts | iTunes Store | Free | N/A |
| TV show episodes | iTunes Store | $1.99 per episode (Standard Definition); $2.99 per episodes (High Definition); complete TV season prices by series | No longer available |
| Movies | iTunes Store | Varies | $3.99 (Standard Definition); $4.99 (High Definition) |
| Audiobooks | iTunes Store | $9.99 to $79.99 | N/A |

| Content Type | Service Used to Acquire Content | Cost | Rental Price |
|---|---|---|---|
| iTunes U educational programming | iTunes Store | Free | N/A |
| Ringtones (for the iPhone) | iTunes Store | $1.29 | N/A |
| eBooks | iBookstore (or select Books from the iTunes Store on your computer) | Varies; average bestseller price is $9.99 to $14.99 | N/A |
| Digital editions of newspapers and magazines | Newsstand (or the App Store) from your iOS device (or select App Store from the iTunes Store on your computer) | Single issue magazine $2.99 to $4.99; subscription prices vary | N/A |
| Apps for the iPhone, iPad, or iPod touch | App Store | Free or $.99 to $9.99 (or more) | N/A |

**Note**   If you're a Mac user, don't confuse the iOS App Store with the Mac App Store. The iOS App Store is where you get apps for your iPhone, iPad, and/or iPod touch. The Mac App Store is where you can acquire Mac software via the Web and is accessible by clicking the Mac App Store icon that's displayed on your Mac's Dock.

Using the iTunes software on your computer (or the iTunes app on your iOS device), you can browse through Apple's vast and ever-growing music selection comprising more than 20 million songs. As you're music shopping, you can preview music for free, and then, with a click of the mouse (on a computer) or the tap of a finger (on an iOS device), purchase individual songs or entire albums in digital format and enjoy them almost instantly.

**Did You Know?**

# Be Aware of the Limitations For iTunes Movie Rentals

Rented movies from the iTunes Store are stored on your computer, Apple TV, or iOS device for up to 30 days before being automatically deleted. However, after you begin playing a rented movie, you have 24 hours to watch it as often as you'd like before it is automatically deleted. Rented movies are downloaded to one computer or iOS device at a time and are not stored within your iCloud account.

# Shop for Music from the iTunes Store

The iTunes Store allows you to browse for music by genre, artist, song title, and a wide range of other options, so you can quickly find and purchase what you're looking for. Or you can utilize the iTunes Genius feature, which allows iTunes to recommend music to you, based on your past music purchases.

The iTunes Store is online-based, so to use it, your computer, Apple TV, or iOS mobile device requires access to the Web. After the music has been downloaded to your computer or device, a web connection is no longer needed to enjoy listening to it at any time, because it is stored on your computer, Apple TV, or iOS device.

Whether you're looking for the latest chart-topping hit from your favorite artist, a classic "oldies" song, or music from an unsigned or up-and-coming band or artist, chances are you'll find it for sale on iTunes.

After you select the Music option when visiting the iTunes Store, if you're looking for suggestions about what to purchase and download, check out the Featured, New, and What's Hot music sections. Or, if you know what you're looking for, enter the song title, album title, artist, or any other keyword related to that music into the iTunes Search field.

Each individual song or complete album offered by iTunes has its own listing within the iTunes Store. On a computer, when you click a song or album listing, this leads directly to an album page, which then displays all the information you need to know about the song and/or album on a single screen.

When viewing an iTunes listing for a song on an iOS device, the title of the song is displayed in boldface text. Just below the title is the recording artist, and below that is the song's release date. At the left of each listing is the album's cover art, and to the right is the song's Price icon. Near the bottom of each song listing is its average star-based rating, along with the total number of ratings the songs has received by fellow iTunes shoppers.

**How to...** **Discover Chart-Topping Music**

To discover the most popular music currently available from iTunes, access iTunes Top Charts. From your web browser, visit www.apple.com/itunes/ charts/songs to view a listing of the 100 current most popular songs on iTunes (based on purchased iTunes downloads). From the iTunes software on your computer, view several different Top Charts (for songs, albums, or music videos). These charts are displayed along the right margin of the main iTunes Store screen when you click the Music icon. From your iOS device, launch the iTunes app, and then select the Music option, followed by the Top Charts option, to see listings for popular music by genre or category.

**FIGURE 5-1**   Individual New & Noteworthy song listings display within the iTunes Store, accessed from a Mac, using the iTunes software.

Figure 5-1 shows sample song listings displayed on iTunes running on a Mac. You can click a listing to reveal more information or to purchase that music. Figure 5-2 shows similar information displayed within the iTunes app running on an iPad 2, and Figure 5-3 shows song listings displayed within the iTunes app running on an iPhone 4S.

**FIGURE 5-2**   When accessed using the iTunes app on the iPad 2, for example, music listings offer plenty of information about a song.

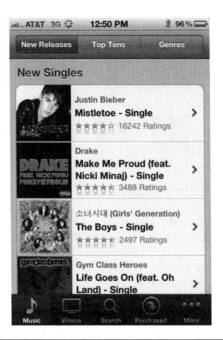

**FIGURE 5-3** Despite the smaller screen size, you can still efficiently shop for music from the iTunes Store using the iTunes app on your iPhone.

As you shop for complete albums on iTunes, the individual album listings include much of the same information as individual song listings. When you click the album title or cover artwork, the description screen includes a complete list of all songs on that album, which you can preview one at a time or purchase individually. Or you can purchase the entire album with just a few clicks of the mouse or taps on your iOS device's screen.

## Learn More About Music Before Purchasing It

Star-based ratings are a great way to clue you in as to a song's popularity. Songs can be rated from one to five stars, with five stars being the highest possible rating. So if a song has received thousands of ratings and has an average five-star rating, chances are it's a pretty good song.

By clicking or tapping an album cover or song title within a listing, you can view a detailed description page or window for that song or album (shown in Figure 5-4). Here, you can read full reviews written by fellow iTunes customers, plus see more details about how many one-, two-, three-, four-, and five-star ratings that song or album has received.

Before you make a purchase decision, you can also hear a preview of a song for free by tapping the song's title from within the description screen. If you like what you hear, tap the song's price icon to purchase and download that song from the iTunes Store.

**FIGURE 5-4**   When you click or tap a song's title or album cover artwork on an iPad, a detailed description window or screen is displayed.

That purchase will be downloaded directly to the computer or iOS device on which it was purchased; then it will become accessible to all of your computers and iOS devices via iCloud. The purchase price will be automatically charged to the credit or debit card that's linked to your Apple ID account, or it will be deducted from the iTunes Gift Card balance that's associated with your Apple ID account, if applicable.

To help you stay up to date on the latest music releases from popular artists, as well as new and up-and-coming artists, each week the iTunes Store offers a selection of free music you can download and enjoy. Once you download a free song, you own it (as if you purchased it), and it also becomes available to you via iCloud as part of your digital music library.

To find free music using iTunes on your computer, click the Music option (displayed near the top of the screen), and then look under the Music Quick Links heading (displayed near the top-left corner of the screen) for the Free Music option. Click Free Music to see what's being offered. To access free music on your iPad, launch the iTunes app and then tap the Music command icon. Scroll down to the bottom of the screen, and under the Quick Links heading, tap the Free Music option. On the iPhone, free music offerings are interspersed with regularly priced music listings.

# Browse the iTunes Store for Music by Genre

To browse the iTunes Store for music based on music genre, tap the Genres icon. More than 22 music genres, such as Alternative, Blues, Classical, Country, Hip Hop/Rap, Pop, R&B/Soul, and Rock, are available. On a computer, launch the iTunes software, select the iTunes Store, choose the Music option, and then, under the Music Quick Links heading, click the All Categories pull-down menu on the right side of the screen (shown in Figure 5-5). Then select a category or music genre.

On the iPhone, launch the iTunes app, tap the Music option, and then tap the Genres tab that's display near the top of the screen. On an iPad, launch the Music app, tap the Music command icon, and then tap the Genres icon that's displayed near the upper-left corner of the screen.

# Save Money Using iTunes' Complete My Album Feature

Once you purchase one or more songs from an album, if you decide that you want to purchase the entire album, iTunes offers the Complete My Album feature, which allows you to purchase the remaining songs on an album at a prorated (discounted) price. In other words, you don't have to repurchase music you already own. The discounted price will depend on how many songs from that particular album you've already purchased from the iTunes Store.

**FIGURE 5-5**   You can browse the music selection of the iTunes Store in several ways, such as sorting music listings by genre or category.

To use this feature on iTunes running on your computer, launch iTunes, and click the iTunes Store option (on the left side of the screen). Next, click the Music option (near the top-center of the screen). On the right side of the screen, under the Music Quick Links, click the Complete My Album feature. iTunes will analyze your past iTunes purchases and display which albums you can purchase at a discount; it will also display the regular price and discounted Buy For price (shown in Figure 5-6).

To use this feature on an iPhone, launch the iTunes app from the Home Screen. Tap the Music command icon that's displayed at the bottom of the screen, and then tap the New Releases tab that's displayed near the top of the screen. Using your finger, scroll down to the very bottom of the New Releases screen and tap the Complete My Album option.

On the iPad, to access the Complete My Album feature, from the Home Screen, launch the iTunes app. Tap the Music command icon that's displayed near the bottom-left corner of the screen, and then tap the Featured command tab that's displayed near the top-center of the screen. Using your finger, scroll down to the bottom of the Featured music screen. Under the Quick Links heading, tap the Complete My Album option. iTunes will analyze your past iTunes purchases and display what albums you can purchase at a discount. It will also display the regular price and discounted Buy For price (shown in Figure 5-7).

**FIGURE 5-6**    After purchasing one or more songs from a specific album, you can revisit the iTunes Store later and purchase the entire album at a prorated price, based on how many songs from an album you've already purchased separately.

**FIGURE 5-7** After selecting the Complete My Album feature, you'll see a listing of albums you're qualified to purchase at a discounted rate.

# Apple ID Required

When it comes to using your Mac, Apple TV, or iOS device with any of Apple's online-based services or iCloud, a single Apple ID is required. This Apple ID not only identifies who you are and provides you with a free e-mail account, it's also linked to a major credit card or debit card, which allows you to make online purchases from the iTunes Store, App Store, iBookstore, or Newsstand, for example, without having to re-enter your contact and credit card information with each purchase.

If you don't link a credit or debit card to your Apple ID account, you can purchase prepaid iTunes Gift Cards and then redeem them when making online purchases. iTunes Gift Cards are available from Apple Stores, convenience stores, supermarkets, pharmacies, gas stations, or wherever gift cards are sold. They're also available online from Apple's web site (www.apple.com/itunes/gifts). iTunes Gift Cards are available in $15.00, $25.00, and $50.00 denominations.

**How to...** ## Redeem an iTunes Gift Card and Make Purchases

To redeem an iTunes Gift Card and make purchases from the iTunes Store without using a credit card or debit card, select the Redeem option when visiting the iTunes Store. Once you enter the code displayed on the Gift Card, your iTunes account will have a credit balance, which you can then use to purchase music or other content.

On a computer running the iTunes Software, scroll down to the very bottom of the iTunes Store screen. The Redeem option is displayed under the Manage heading. On an iPhone, from the iTunes app, tap the Music icon, and then tap the New Releases icon. Scroll down to the very bottom of the New Releases screen and tap the Redeem option. On the iPad, from the iTunes app, tap the Music command icon; then scroll to the very bottom of the screen and tap the Redeem icon. iTunes Gift Cards are different from Apple Gift Cards. While an iTunes Gift Card can be used to purchase content online from the iTunes Store, App Store, iBookstore, or Newsstand, an Apple Gift Card is redeemable at Apple Stores (or Apple.com) for purchasing products, such as computers, iOS devices, or accessories.

If you already own a Mac, Apple TV, or iOS device, when you first set up that device, you are prompted to create an Apple ID. You're given this opportunity again any time you attempt to make an online purchase from the iTunes Store, App Store, iBookstore, or Newsstand, or when you first establish an iCloud account.

To establish a free Apple ID, visit https://appleid.apple.com and complete the online form. The process takes just a few minutes. You'll be required to supply your full name, address, and birthday, as well as create a security question and a unique password for the account. Your actual Apple ID will be your primary e-mail address, but it will have a separate Apple ID–specific password that you create. This password will potentially be different from the password you use to access your e-mail account. Once the Apple ID is established, you're given the option of linking a credit card or debit card to the account.

# Install and Set Up iTunes to Acquire and Manage Your Music Library

The iTunes software that runs on your Mac or PC can be used to manage your entire music library, including the following:

- Music purchased from the iTunes Store
- Music acquired from other online sources
- Digital music files you create from your audio CDs
- Music files transferred to your computer (via e-mail, for example)

# First, Get iTunes Running on Your Mac or PC

To be able to use iCloud to access your digital music library (or at least the music you purchase on iTunes), first install the latest version of iTunes on your primary computer, whether it's a Mac or PC. You can download this free software from www.apple.com/itunes.

## Installing and Using iTunes on a Mac

You'll then need to set up your free iCloud account, if you haven't already done so. Next, turn on iCloud functionality on your computer. On a Mac, access System Preferences (shown in Figure 5-8), and click the iCloud option. When prompted, enter your Apple ID and password that corresponds to your iCloud account. (If you're not automatically prompted to enter your Apple ID, click the Account Details option on the left side of the iCloud window shown in Figure 5-9.)

Next, launch iTunes (if it's not already running), and from the iTunes pull-down menu that's displayed at the top of the screen, select the Preferences option. The menus displayed within the pop-up window that appears on your computer screen allows you to customize operations relating specifically to iTunes, including how it functions with iCloud.

Click the Store option (displayed near the top-center of the Preferences window, shown in Figure 5-10). Near the top of this window, under the Automatic Downloads heading, you'll see a message that states, "iTunes can automatically download new purchases made on other devices using [insert your iCloud-related e-mail address]. To change to a different account, sign in to the iTunes Store." Just below this message will be three checkboxes: Music, Apps, and Books. Click each option to add a checkmark.

**FIGURE 5-8**   On your Mac, click the iCloud option from within System Preferences.

**FIGURE 5-9** Access this iCloud settings window within System Preferences, and then enter your Apple ID and password to activate iCloud on that computer.

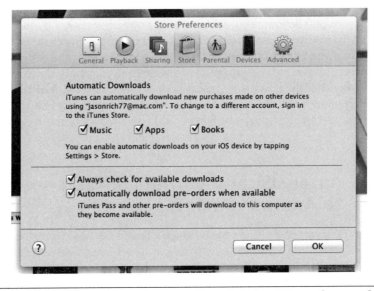

**FIGURE 5-10** Customize iCloud functionality related to iTunes from within the iTunes software on your computer.

Doing this allows your primary computer to download and store all new purchases you make via iTunes Store, the App Store, or iBookstore (including Newsstand) automatically. So, as you're using your iPhone or iPod touch, for example, when you download a new song or album, the next time you launch iTunes on your primary computer, that music will be downloaded from iCloud and automatically added to your iTunes music library on the computer as well.

**Note** If you do not add a checkmark to any or all of these checkboxes, the content that's purchased elsewhere will still be accessible from your primary computer via iCloud, but you'll need to select and download it manually.

Likewise, and by default, any time you make a purchase from the iTunes Store, App Store, or iBookstore using your primary computer, that content gets stored on your computer, but it is also saved to your iCloud account (so it becomes accessible from your other devices).

## Installing and Using iTunes on a PC

To get iTunes running on your Windows-based PC, so that it's able to access iCloud, first download the latest version of iTunes. Next, download and install the free iCloud Control Panel for Windows from Apple's web site (www.apple.com/icloud/setup/pc.html).

Once the software is installed, turn on your computer's iCloud functionality. To do this, from the Windows Start menu, select the Control Panel option. Then select the Network and Internet option followed by the iCloud option. When prompted, enter your Apple ID and password. Be sure it's the same Apple ID that you used to create your free iCloud account. Your computer is now set up to work with iCloud.

Next, launch the iTunes 10.5 (or later) software (if it's not already running). From the iTunes pull-down menu, select the Edit option, followed by the Preferences option, and then choose the Store option (displayed near the top-center of the window).

When the Store Preferences window appears, under the Automatic Downloads heading, you'll see the message, "iTunes can automatically download new purchases made on other devices using [insert your iCloud-related Email address]. To change to a different account, sign in to the iTunes Store." Just below this message will be three checkboxes: Music, Apps, and Books. Add checkmarks to these options.

**How to...** **Automatically Download Music to Another Device**

You can also set up your iPhone or iPad to download automatically from iCloud the music you purchase from iTunes using another computer or device. To do this, launch the Settings app. From the main Settings menu, scroll down to the Store option, and tap it. From the Store menu within Settings, turn on the virtual switches associated with Automatic Downloads of Music, Apps, and/or Books (shown in Figure 5-11 on an iPad 2).

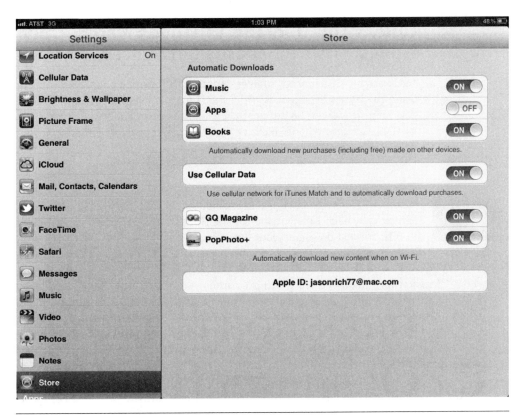

**FIGURE 5-11**   Turn on or off Automatic Downloads from within the Settings app to determine whether content will be downloaded automatically from iCloud to your iOS device as it's purchased in the future.

Just as on a Mac, this allows your primary computer to download and store automatically all new purchases you make via iTunes Store, the App Store, or iBookstore (including Newsstand). Then, as you're using your iPhone or iPod touch, when you download a new song or album, the next time you launch iTunes on your primary computer, that music will be downloaded from iCloud and automatically added to your iTunes music library on that computer.

# How Digital Music Becomes Accessible from iCloud

When you purchase music from the iTunes Store, it is automatically accessible when you run the iTunes software on your Mac or PC. When iTunes is running on your computer, click the Music option that's displayed under the Library heading on the left side of the screen to view your personal digital music library.

**Did You Know?**

# Unless You Upgrade to iTunes Match, Only iTunes Music Purchases Get Synced via iCloud

Music acquired from other sources can be transferred to your iOS device(s) using the iTunes Sync process from the iTunes software running on your computer. It will not be automatically transferred to iCloud and made available on your iPhone, iPad, or iPod touch, for example, unless you've upgraded to the iTunes Match service.

**Tip**

If you have iTunes on your primary computer set up to download new purchases automatically each time you launch the iTunes software, it will access iCloud via the Internet and download your latest music purchases, and then add them to your digital music library. (Your computer must have Internet access for this to work.)

Music that's acquired from other sources (not the iTunes Store) and saved on your computer's hard drive (or on another form of digital media) needs to be imported into your iTunes music library. When iTunes is running on your primary computer, choose File | Add To Library. You'll then need to locate the digital music file to import into iTunes by selecting the appropriate drive and/or directory, for example, where it is stored.

If you have one or more audio CDs that you want to transform into digital music files that can be stored and played using the iTunes software on your computer (and potentially transferred to your other devices), insert each audio CD into your computer's disc drive while iTunes is running on your computer. A pop-up window will appear on your screen (shown in Figure 5-12) that allows you to import each song from that audio CD to your iTunes music library so that it will be accessible and playable from iTunes.

The process of transferring music from audio CDs to your computer is called "ripping" the CDs. It takes several minutes to complete the process of converting and then transferring every song from an audio CD to your computer. This process needs to be done only once per song, however.

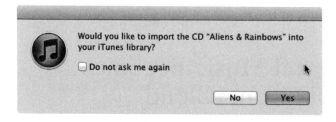

**FIGURE 5-12**   When you insert an audio CD into the disc drive of your computer, the iTunes software will invite you to "rip" that CD and import the music to your computer in the form of digital audio files.

Although your entire digital music library becomes accessible from iTunes running on your computer, by default, only the digital music you purchase from the iTunes Store automatically gets saved to your iCloud account and becomes accessible to all the computers and iOS devices that are linked to your iCloud account (including your Apple TV device). If you want access to your entire digital music library via iCloud, including music not purchased through iTunes, you'll need to subscribe to the iTunes Match premium service, which is described in Chapter 6.

## Access and Download Past iTunes Purchases from Your PC or Mac

If you've been using iTunes for a while and have purchased music using a variety of different devices, Apple has kept track of all of these past purchases and will make them available to all your devices that are linked to the same iCloud account. This includes music, music videos, ringtones, TV show episodes, entire TV show seasons, and purchased (but not rented) movies.

To access a past iTunes purchase that might not yet have been transferred to your primary computer, from the iTunes software on your computer, access your Purchase History. To do this, launch iTunes. On the left side of the iTunes screen, under the Store heading, click the Purchased icon.

The main area of the iTunes screen will display a detailed list of everything you've ever purchased from iTunes that's currently stored on your computer. If you have Automatic Downloads set up, this should be a comprehensive listing of all your recent iTunes purchases.

However, displayed near the bottom-right corner of the iTunes screen is a command option called Download Previous Purchases. Click this option to display a new screen within iTunes that offers a comprehensive listing of your music, TV show, movie, apps, and eBooks purchases, regardless of from which computer or iOS device that content was purchased, as long as it was purchased using the same Apple ID account that you just used to log into the iTunes Store.

You can also access the Purchased screen within iTunes by clicking the Purchased option that's displayed under the Music Quick Links menu (near the top-right of the iTunes Store screen).

Under the Purchased heading (shown in Figure 5-13) that's displayed near the top-left corner of the main iTunes screen are tabs for purchased Music, TV Shows, Movies, Apps, and Books, and possibly other types of content you've acquired in the past from iTunes. Tap one of these options to see a listing of content in that category that's currently stored within your iCloud account and that can be immediately downloaded to your primary computer without incurring additional charges.

When you tap the Music tab, for example, along the left side of the main iTunes screen will be a blank Search field. Below that, you'll see an option labeled All Songs. Using the Search field, enter a song title, artist's name, or any keyword or search phrase that will help you find the music you're looking for. Or tap on the All Songs option to

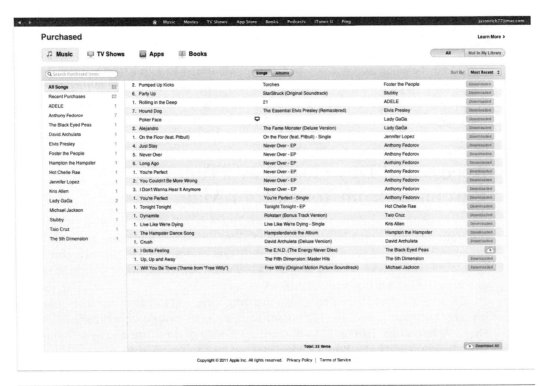

**FIGURE 5-13** From the iTunes software running on your Mac or PC, you can download past iTunes music purchases.

view a listing on the iTunes screen of all individual songs you've previously purchased from iTunes that are now stored within your iCloud account.

Below the All Songs option, a listing of recording artists whose music you own will be displayed. Click either the All Songs option or one artist's name to reveal a listing of songs you can download. Each listing will include the song's title, the album title, the artist, and either a Download or iCloud icon. Tap the Download or iCloud icon to download the song to your computer and automatically add it to your music library.

**Tip** Instead of downloading one song at a time, click the Download All icon that's displayed in the lower-right corner of the screen to acquire all of the listed music at once.

As you're looking at the All Songs display (or the listing of music you own from a particular artist), you can sort this listing in a variety of ways. For example, tap the All or Not In My Library icon to differentiate between songs already stored on the computer and songs available from iCloud that are not currently stored on your computer.

Or, next to the Sort By option that's displayed near the upper-right corner of the window, sort the listed iTunes content by Most Recent (based on purchase date) or alphabetically by Name. Above the album title column within the listing, click the Songs or Album tabs to sort the music by song title or group them together by the album from which they came.

Once you've transferred the previously purchased iTunes music from iCloud that you want stored on your computer, click the TV Shows, Movies, Apps, and/or Books tab to repeat this process. When you click the TV Shows tab, for example, you can view previously purchased TV show episodes as a comprehensive listing or sort them by series name, season, most recently purchased, or by episode title.

 When you transfer iTunes content to your primary computer, these files take up storage space on your computer's hard drive. You can potentially free up a lot of hard drive storage space by allowing your iTunes purchases to be stored on iCloud, and then download only the iTunes content you want to listen to or watch at any time.

# Access and Download Past iTunes Purchases from Your iPhone, iPad, or iPod touch

Just as you can easily access all of your past iTunes Store, App Store, and iBookstore (and Newsstand) purchases from iCloud using your computer, you can also do it from your iPhone, iPad, or iPod touch. However, the app you use to do this depends on the type of content you want to retrieve from iCloud.

## On the iPhone (or iPod touch)

To access and/or download your past music purchases, launch the iTunes app on your iOS device. Displayed at the bottom of the iTunes screen will be a handful of command icons: on the iPhone, these are Music, Videos, Search, Purchased, and More. Tap the Purchased command icon (shown in Figure 5-14).

When the Purchased screen appears on the iPhone, you'll be able to choose from several options, such as Music, TV shows, and/or Movies, depending on the type of content that's available. Tap the Music option.

Now the Purchased screen will display two command tabs, labeled All and Not On This iPhone (shown in Figure 5-15). Tap the Not On This iPhone option to display a listing of songs you've purchased that are available to you via iCloud but that are not currently stored on your iPhone.

 On a PC or Mac, the iTunes software is used to acquire, manage, and play your digital music. On an iOS device, such as an iPhone or iPad, the iTunes app is used to acquire music, but the Music app is used to play it.

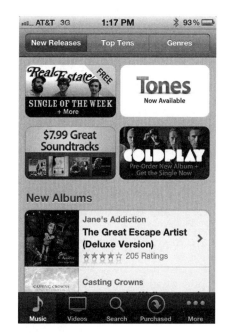

**FIGURE 5-14**  The main iTunes app screen running on an iPhone 4S looks the same on all iPhone models and on the iPod touch.

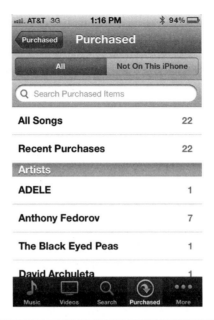

**FIGURE 5-15** From the Purchased screen, you can download past iTunes music purchases to your iPhone, where those music files will be saved and can then be played any time.

You can also find music listed within this screen using the blank search field, or by tapping the All Songs option to view a listing of songs. Under the artists heading, you can choose the music you want to transfer to your iPhone based on artist name.

If you tap All Songs, a listing of all previously purchased songs available on iCloud are displayed, which you can then sort by Most Recent, Song Name, or Artist Name, by tapping the appropriate command tab that's displayed at the top of the screen (shown in Figure 5-16).

When you find the song or songs you want to transfer (download) to your iPhone, tap the iCloud icon that corresponds to that music listing. The song will be downloaded and saved on your iPhone. To listen to it, launch the Music app.

## On the iPad

On the iPad, several command icons are displayed along the bottom of the screen within the iTunes app: Music, Movies, TV Shows, Ping, Podcasts, Audiobooks, iTunes U, Purchased, and Downloads (shown in Figure 5-17).

Tap the Purchased icon to view your past iTunes music purchases, and then tap the Not On This iPad tab to view music that's not currently stored on your tablet. Near the top-left corner of the screen, tap the View command icon and select Music (or choose to view your TV shows, movies, music videos, and so on, that are available from iCloud).

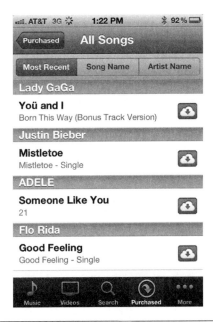

FIGURE 5-16  When you tap the All Songs option, you see a detailed listing of songs you've previously purchased and that are available to you via iCloud.

FIGURE 5-17  The iTunes app on the iPad allows you to shop for music from the iTunes Store after tapping the Music command icon at the bottom of the screen.

Then, along the left margin of the screen, tap the All Songs option to see a listing of songs you've purchased from iTunes that will then be displayed on the right side of the screen (shown in Figure 5-18).

Also near the top-center of the screen, tap the Songs or Albums tab to sort the listed music by song title or based on the album containing each song.

While you're viewing this All Songs screen on the iPad, click the iCloud or Download icon next to a song title to download it from iCloud to your tablet. Once it's downloaded and stored on your iPad, you can play the song using the Music app.

 Initially, it was rumored that iCloud would allow you to stream or download music. However, when the service actually launched, streaming capabilities were not activated. This, however, could change in the future. The benefit to streaming music from iCloud is that you don't need to store the music files on your computer or device.

**FIGURE 5-18** Display a listing of songs available from your iCloud account that are not already stored on your iPad.

# 6

# Use the Premium iTunes Match Service

## HOW TO...

- Share your entire digital music library with all of your computers and devices.
- Activate an iTunes Match subscription via iTunes on your primary computer.
- Discover how to use the iTunes Match feature of iTunes and iCloud.

You already know that one of the most popular features of iCloud is that it lets you share the music and content you acquire from iTunes on all of the computers and/ or mobile devices linked to your iCloud account. This feature is included with the basic iCloud service for free. It allows for as much online storage space as you need to store your online iTunes purchases, so they can be readily accessible from your primary computer, laptop computer, iPhone, iPad, iPod touch, and/or Apple TV, as long as those devices are connected to the Web.

But what about the portion of your digital music library that was not purchased from iTunes? You can purchase and/or download music from many other online-based music services, including Amazon MP3, which is described in Chapter 10. You can also download music for free (and legally) from some other web sites and online services, plus you can create your own MP3s by "ripping" your audio CDs and converting each song on your CDs into digital (MP3) files.

By default, the portion of your digital music library that was not acquired from iTunes is not compatible with iCloud. However, you can opt to upgrade your iCloud service, for $24.99 per year, to activate the optional iTunes Match service. This service allows you to store and access your entire digital music collection on iCloud and includes as much additional online storage space as is needed to store your entire music collection, regardless of where or how each song was acquired.

Once activated, iTunes Match examines the digital music collection that's stored on your computer's hard drive(s). It then compares it to the iTunes library of more than 20 million songs. When matches are found between your personal

## iTunes Match Offers the Highest-Quality Music Files

When iTunes Match determines that music from your personal digital music collection matches songs from the iTunes library, the iTunes Match service automatically gives you access to the highest quality recording of that song possible (iTunes Plus quality, which plays back at 256 Kbps), even if the version in your personal music library was saved in a lower quality. When you purchase music from iTunes, it's provided to you in an AAC format that's fully compatible with iTunes (and the Music app on your iOS device). To listen to that music with another digital audio player, it will need to be converted into .MP3 format, which can be done from within iTunes on your primary computer.

music collection and songs available from iTunes, those songs automatically become accessible to you on all of your computers and iOS devices via iCloud.

When matches between your music library and iTunes song collection can't be established, those unmatched songs within your music library are automatically uploaded to your iCloud account, and within a few minutes, they become fully accessible to you on all of your computers and mobile devices that are linked to that iCloud account.

# Signing up for iTunes Match

To activate an iTunes Match subscription, first download and install the latest version of iTunes on your primary computer. Next, launch iTunes on your computer, and then, on the left side of the screen, click the iTunes Match option under the Store heading (as shown in Figure 6-1).

 To ensure you have the latest version of iTunes installed on your computer, launch iTunes, and from the iTunes menu near the top-left corner of the screen, select the Check for Updates option. If a newer version of iTunes than the one installed on your computer is available, you'll be prompted to download and install the latest version.

You will be prompted to activate the iTunes Match feature, pay for the feature, and then enter your Apple ID password to confirm your purchase.

 As soon as you purchase an iTunes Match subscription, you will receive a confirmation e-mail from Apple that includes the date of purchase. Keep in mind that your subscription will automatically renew each year unless you turn off the auto-renew option.

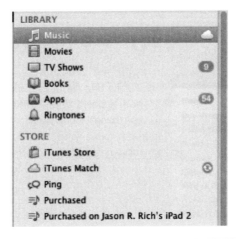

**FIGURE 6-1**   To activate iTunes Match, click the iTunes Match option displayed on the left side of the main iTunes screen.

Once activated, the iTunes Match feature will begin a three-step process of analyzing your personal digital music library, matching it with the song library offered on iTunes, and then uploading any songs from your library that could not already be found on iTunes. Depending on the size of your personal music library, this process will take from several minutes to several hours.

The three-step process occurs only once when you first activate the iTunes Match service. It begins with iTunes gathering information about your personal music library (as shown in Figure 6-2). The progress meter displayed near the center of the screen will keep you informed about how long this process will take based on the number of songs in your music collection.

As soon as this first step is completed, iTunes Match will immediately begin the second step, which is to match up as many songs in your personal music collection as possible with songs from the master iTunes library. As you can see in Figure 6-3,

**FIGURE 6-2**   When iTunes Match is activated, the service gathers information about your personal music library by analyzing the music stored on your computer.

FIGURE 6-3   Upon activating iTunes Match, Step Two of the activation procedure involves comparing your music library with the main iTunes music library.

a checkmark appears next to Step One, and a new progress bar shows how many songs from your collection have already been checked for a match (on the left side of the progress bar) versus how many songs from your personal library still need to be compared to iTunes library of songs. Once again, how long Step Two will take to complete will depend on how many songs are in your personal music library.

After the music library comparison is completed, you will discover that all of the songs that matched instantly become accessible to you on iCloud and can be enjoyed on any of your computers or mobile devices that are linked to your iCloud account. Step Three of the iTunes Match activation process will then commence, and all songs from your personal music library that didn't match up with songs found in the iTunes music library are uploaded, one at a time, from your primary computer to your online-based iCloud account.

Again, this process could take awhile if many songs didn't match up. For example, if you're a musician and record your own music or you have downloaded music that didn't include complete information about each song within its digital file, those songs will need to be uploaded to your iCloud account.

Near the center of the iTunes screen (as shown in Figure 6-4), yet another progress bar will be displayed. Below this progress bar is a message reminding you to turn on the iTunes Match feature on your iOS devices. How to do this will be explained shortly.

 iTunes Match devotes as much additional online storage space as required for all non-matching song uploads in the $24.99 annual fee.

As soon as Step Three of the iTunes Match activation process is complete, your entire music collection, including both iTunes purchases and music from your personal digital music collection acquired from other sources, will be available to you via iCloud.

**FIGURE 6-4**   All songs from your personal music library that didn't match up with the songs in iTunes' vast music library will be uploaded to your iCloud account.

Although you might be tempted to delete the music files on your computer's hard drive to free up space now that your entire digital music collection is stored on iCloud, you're better off transferring these files to an external hard drive and maintaining your own backup. This way, they'll always be available if your Internet connection fails and you can't access iCloud, or if another problem occurs.

When the message "Your iTunes library is now available in iCloud" is displayed near the top-center of the screen (Figure 6-5), the iTunes Match activation process is completed. At this point, you'll want to turn on the iTunes Match feature on your iOS mobile devices. In the meantime, click the Done icon that's displayed at the lower-right corner of the screen.

**FIGURE 6-5**   When you see this iTunes Match screen displayed, the iTunes Match activation process is complete.

# Cancel Your Auto-Renewing iTunes Match Subscription

Your iTunes Match subscription is auto-renewing, which means that every year you will automatically be charged $24.99 for the service until you cancel your subscription. To cancel your subscription from your primary computer, follow these steps:

1. Launch iTunes.
2. On the left side of the screen, under the Store heading, click iTunes Store.
3. At the upper-right corner of the screen, click the small, down-pointing arrow that appears to the right of your e-mail address or Apple ID account information displayed under the Search Store field. This small arrow icon will appear when you place your mouse over the correct location.
4. Choose the Account option from the pull-down menu that appears, as shown in the following illustration:

5. When prompted, enter your Apple ID password in the window that appears near the center of the iTunes screen (as shown next).

6. When the Account Information screen appears, scroll down until you see the iTunes in the Cloud heading that's displayed in blue (as shown next).

**iTunes in the Cloud**

| | |
|---|---|
| Manage Devices: | 3 devices are associated with this Apple ID and can download your purchases from iTunes in the Cloud beta. |
| iTunes Match: | Your subscription will automatically renew on Sep 11, 2012. |

Manage Devices >

Turn Off Auto-Renew

7. To the right of the iTunes Match option that's listed, click the Turn Off Auto-Renew option. Remember, to avoid being charged for an additional year, you must do this at least 24 hours before your existing subscription expires.

 As you're looking at the iTunes Account Information screen, under the iTunes in the Cloud heading will also be an option to view all computers and devices which are linked to your iCloud account. Click on the Manage Devices option to access this device listing and to remove one or more of the devices, if you so desire.

# Activate iTunes Match on Your iPhone or iPod touch

As soon as iTunes Match is activated, you'll also need to turn on this feature on each mobile device you'll be accessing your iCloud account from. Remember, iOS 5 must be running on your iPhone. The iTunes Match subscription fee allows you to access your music from multiple devices and/or computers. To activate iTunes Match on your iPhone (or iPod touch), follow these steps:

1. From your iPhone's Home Screen, launch the Settings app.
2. When the main Settings menu appears, scroll down to the Music app option, and tap it (as shown next).

3. At the top of the Music screen within Settings, tap the virtual switch next to iTunes Match (as shown next) to turn it on.

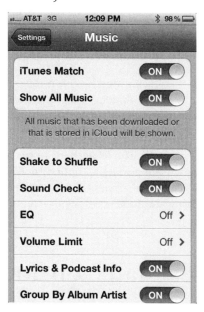

4. At the bottom of the screen, a pop-up window will appear that displays the message, "iTunes Match will replace the music library on this device." Two icons will also appear, labeled Enable and Cancel (as shown next). Tap the Enable icon.

5. Tap the Enable icon, and the music library currently stored on your iPhone will be erased. It will be replaced with access to your entire music library that's now available via iCloud.

You will be returned to the Music icon within the Settings app. Just below the iTunes Match option, however, a new Show All Music option will now be displayed along with a corresponding virtual on/off switch to the right. When the virtual switch is turned off, only music that has been downloaded from iCloud to the iPhone will be displayed within the Music app. If the virtual switch is turned on, all music that has been downloaded, as well as all music stored on iCloud, will be listed within the Music app.

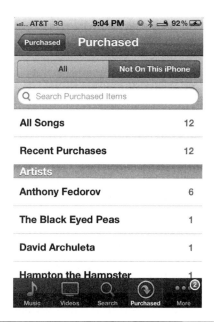

**FIGURE 6-6**    From the iTunes app on your iPhone, you can download music from your iCloud account and store it on your iOS mobile device; or you can stream music to your device from iCloud via the Internet.

6.  Tap the Home button on the iPhone to exit out of Settings and return to the Home Screen.
7.  From the Home Screen, launch the Music app to begin enjoying your music.

When you launch the Music app on your iPhone, all music stored on your iPhone will be displayed when you tap the Artists, Songs, or Albums icon displayed along the bottom of the screen. To download songs from your iCloud account (and store them on your iPhone), tap the Store icon within the Music app. When iTunes on your iPhone launches, tap the Purchased icon near the bottom of the screen.

From the Purchased screen within the iTunes app, tap the Not On This iPhone tab at the upper-right side of the screen (as shown in Figure 6-6). Next, tap on All Songs, Recent Purchases, or on one of the Artists listings to find the music you want to download to your iPhone from iCloud. Tap on the song listing(s) and when the cloud icon appears next to each listing, tap on it to download that song.

# Activate iTunes Match on Your iPad

As soon as iTunes Match is activated, you'll also need to turn on this feature on each mobile device you'll be accessing your iCloud account from. Remember, iOS 5 must be running on your iPad. To activate iTunes Match on your iPad, follow these steps:

1.  From your iPad's Home Screen, launch the Settings app.

2. From the Settings app, along the left side of the screen, you will see the main Settings menu. Scroll down to the Music option (as shown here).

3. On the right side of the screen, the Music menu will appear. The first option is iTunes Music. Tap the virtual switch next to the iTunes Match option to turn on this feature.

4. A pop-up window that says "iTunes Match will replace the music library on this device" will appear, along with an Enable and Cancel icons. Tap the Enable icon to continue.

5. Now, under the Music menu (on the right side of the screen), just below the iTunes Match option, a new Show All Music option is displayed. It is also associated with a virtual on/off switch (as shown next). When turned off, only music that has been downloaded to your iPad will be displayed within the Music app. When turned on, all music that has been downloaded to the iPad, or that is stored on iCloud, will be shown within the Music app. Turn this virtual switch to the on position by tapping it.

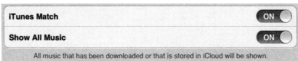

6. Tap the Home button on the iPad to exit Settings and return to the Home Screen.
7. From the Home Screen, launch the Music app to begin enjoying your music.

## How to... Download Music from iCloud

To download songs from your iCloud account (and store them on your iPad), tap the Songs, Artists, or Albums icon at the bottom of the screen. Choose which song(s) you want to download, and then tap the cloud icon that's associated with each song or album listing.

When you launch the Music app on your iPad, all music stored on your tablet or accessible from iCloud will be displayed when you tap the Playlists, Songs, Artists, or Albums icon along the bottom of the screen.

# Activate iTunes Match on Another Computer

You can set up your music library to be accessible from multiple PCs or Macs, including your desktop and laptop computer, for example, as long as they're linked to the same iCloud account. Once iTunes Match is set up on your primary computer, make sure that the latest version of iTunes is also installed on your other computers, and then activate the iTunes Match feature. To do this, follow these steps:

1. Launch iTunes on your secondary Mac or PC.
2. From the Store pull-down menu, select the Turn On iTunes Match option.
3. When the iTunes Match screen is displayed, click the Add This Computer option.
4. Within the Apple ID pop-up window that appears, enter the Apple ID and password that's associated with your iCloud account, and click the Add This Computer icon.
   iTunes Match will complete its three-step activation process on the secondary computer, just as it did on your primary computer. During this process, it will compare your personal music library that's stored on your secondary computer with the main iTunes music library. When necessary, it will then upload non-matching songs to the iCloud service and synchronize your entire personal music library listing. All of the music on your primary and secondary computers will be stored within your iCloud account as one personal music library, which will be accessible from any of your computers and/or mobile devices.
5. When the message "Your iTunes library is now available on iCloud" is displayed on your secondary computer, click Done.
6. From the main iTunes screen, click the Music icon at the upper-left corner.
   A comprehensive listing of your personal digital music library, including the music stored on iCloud, is displayed. You can access this music by clicking the Albums, Artists, Genres, or Composers tabs near the top-center of the screen.

 When you begin using your secondary computer with the iTunes Match service turned on, a pop-up window will appear once asking if you want to turn on automatic downloads for this computer. By clicking the Turn On Automatic Downloads icon, any time you make a new purchase on iTunes on any of your computers or devices, when you next use iTunes on this computer, those new purchases will automatically be downloaded (in addition to being available via iCloud).

When you're looking at a Listing View of your music, look under the Cloud column to see if a song is stored on your computer or is only on iCloud. If a cloud icon appears next to a song listing, it is available via iCloud but not yet stored on your computer's hard drive. To download a specific song, click the down-pointing arrow icon displayed under the iCloud column of your song listing that corresponds to the song you want to download (as shown in Figure 6-7).

As you're looking at a Listing View of your music, from iTunes' View pull-down menu, select the View Options option. A pop-up window will appear allowing you to choose which headings will be displayed as part of this listing. More than 40 options are available, including Album Title, Artist, Genre, Number of Plays, Rating, Release Date, File Size, and Time. Be sure the iCloud option is checked so you can easily differentiate between songs stored on your computer and those stored on iCloud.

**FIGURE 6-7**    As you access the Listing View of your music library within iTunes, you can easily determine whether a particular song is stored on your computer or whether it's accessible from iCloud.

As you add new music to your personal music library from other sources, you might need to have iTunes seek out and download album artwork to associate with your music selections. To do this, choose Advanced | Get Album Artwork.

# Keeping Your Music Library up to Date on iCloud

iTunes Match automatically keeps your entire personal music library available via iCloud, regardless of which computer or mobile device you use to acquire new music in the future. For example, if you access iTunes Store or another music service from your iPhone to purchase a few new songs, iTunes Match will sync those new additions to your personal music library stored in iCloud, ensuring that the new additions are accessible from all of your devices and computers.

 If the auto-update process isn't keeping up with new music added to your personal music library, access the Store pull-down menu and select the Update iTunes Match option from iTunes on your primary or secondary computer. This might be necessary if your laptop computer hasn't been connected to the Internet for a while, during which time new music was added to your iCloud account or stored on your laptop computer's hard drive after being ripped from a CD, for example.

As you'll discover in Chapter 10, using iTunes in conjunction with iTunes Match and iCloud is only one option when it comes to acquiring music, managing your personal music library, and making your music available via a cloud-based service to all of your computers and/or mobile devices. Each cloud-based service offers a different collection of features at a different price.

If you're a Mac user who wants to make your music library available with other Macs, in addition to your iPhone, iPad, iPod touch, and/or Apple TV, using iTunes in conjunction with iCloud and subscribing to iTunes Match probably makes the most sense in terms of functionality, pricing, and ease of use. Be sure to read Chapter 10, however, to learn about some other cloud-based options related to managing and enjoying music, including what's available from Amazon.com.

# 7

# Use iCloud to Store and Manage Your Digital Photos

**HOW TO...**

- Set up the Photo Stream feature of iCloud.
- Access Photo Stream from your iOS devices.
- Use Photo Stream with iPhoto '11 or Aperture 3 on your Mac.
- View images from Photo Stream on a PC.

Among the various types of data and content that iCloud allows you to share among your iOS mobile devices, your HD television set (via Apple TV), and your computer(s) are digital photos. You can do this by activating iCloud's Photo Stream feature.

Separate from the digital images stored on your primary computer or mobile devices, a Photo Stream is a collection of up to 1000 of the most recently shot or imported images that were taken using any of your mobile devices, imported into your mobile devices, or imported into your primary computer (from your digital camera, for example). These images are collected and shown in reverse chronological order, with the newest images displayed first.

Once your Photo Stream reaches 1000 images, or after 30 days have passed, the oldest images that are displayed within your Photo Stream are automatically removed to make room for new images. These images are then archived on your primary computer's hard drive or on an external hard drive that's connected to your primary computer (you select the destination). The former Photo Stream images will then remain there until you manually delete them.

The images that become part of your Photo Stream are stored online, on iCloud. Thus, they become available on all of your computers and/or mobile devices that are linked to your iCloud account. So if you activate this feature on your iPhone and iMac, for example, almost immediately after you snap a photo on your iPhone, it will automatically be uploaded to your Photo Stream and be accessible from your iMac (via iPhoto '11 or Aperture 3) and/or your iPad, without your having to copy, e-mail,

**How to...** Add Images to Photo Stream

You can import a photo into your iOS device so it can be included within your iCloud Photo Stream. You can snap a photo using the built-in camera on your iPhone, iPad, or iPod touch. Or you can use Apple's optional Camera Connection Kit ($29.00, http://store.apple.com/us/product/MC531ZM/A) to import images from your digital camera's memory card.

As you're surfing the Web, for example, you can also place and hold your finger on most images, and then tap the Save Image option to store that image or graphic within the Camera Roll Album of the Photos app, at which time it will also be added to your Photo Stream.

Once you save a new image to your iOS device, if the Photo Stream feature is turned on, that image will be uploaded to iCloud and almost immediately added to your Photo Stream.

On a Mac or PC, you can manually drag-and-drop or copy images stored elsewhere on your computer into the Photo Stream Album or directory.

or transfer the image, or use iTunes sync. For this feature to work, you'll need to be running the latest version of OS X Lion, iPhone '11, and/or Aperture 3 on your Mac. Older versions of the operating system and software don't have iCloud functionality or compatibility built in.

 For Photo Stream to work, each of your computers must have access to a high-speed Internet connection (such as Broadband or DSL), and your iOS devices need Internet access via a Wi-Fi connection. This feature does not work with a 3G Internet connection on your iPhone or iPad.

Once an image becomes part of your Photo Stream, you can manually save it to any of your computers or iOS mobile devices that are linked to your iCloud account, so they will remain on that computer or device indefinitely, until you manually delete them. Plus, you'll then be able to edit any saved image that has been copied from the Photo Stream Album or directory.

 When the Photo Stream feature was first introduced by Apple, the Photo Stream itself was not editable. In other words, you cannot pick and choose which images get uploaded and become accessible within your Photo Stream. With the release of iOS 5.1 in early-2012, this will likely change.

After you activate the Photo Stream feature, all new images added to your iOS mobile device(s) or computer(s) automatically become part of your Photo Stream until 30 days have passed or you reach the 1000-image capacity of your Photo Stream; at that point, the oldest images are replaced by any newer ones, and the older images are archived permanently on your primary computer's hard drive.

 Images stored within your Photo Stream on iCloud do not use the free 5GB of online storage space provided by Apple. So you can feel free to use Photo Stream with the highest resolution digital images possible, regardless of their individual file sizes.

# Turn on the Photo Stream Feature

Just as with all other iCloud-related features, you must manually turn on the Photo Stream feature on each of your computers and iOS devices separately, and make sure they're each set up to log into the same iCloud account. Note that even if this feature is turned on within your iPhone or iPad, it will not work unless a Wi-Fi Internet connection is present.

## Pros and Cons of Using Photo Stream

With Photo Stream, as soon as you shoot a photo on your iOS device or import a photo from your digital camera to your computer, it immediately becomes accessible, viewable, and potentially editable on your primary computer and/or other iOS devices, and/or viewable on your television screen. You do not have to transfer or copy your images manually among computers or devices that are linked to the same iCloud account.

By default, this feature also creates an online backup (on iCloud) of your newest images. The drawback of this feature, however, is that Photo Stream gathers and stores all of your new photos, or none of them, based on whether you turn on or off the Photo Stream feature.

When the Photo Stream feature is turned on, in addition to your favorite photos being added to your Photo Stream, all of the blurry, redundant, overexposed, or underexposed images also get uploaded to iCloud unless you delete them immediately after they're shot.

Because your Photo Stream is not editable, and you cannot pick and choose which images get added, as you're shooting photos on your iPhone or iPad, for example, anyone who uses your Mac will be able to view all of your images almost immediately as they're added to your Photo Stream. And although you can create an animated slide show of your Photo Stream using Apple TV, iPhoto '11 on your Mac, photo management/editing software on your PC, or the Photos app on your iOS device, your unwanted photos are displayed along with your favorite shots, all of which make up your Photo Stream.

**Note** To learn more about how to use Apple TV in conjunction with Photo Stream and other iCloud features, see Chapter 14.

For some purposes, Photo Stream is extremely practical. However, for people who want to sync or share only specific photos across multiple computers or devices, at least initially, Photo Stream is not the best solution.

## Download and Install the Latest Version of iPhoto '11 or Aperture 3

To make sure you're running the latest version of iPhoto '11 or Aperture 3, which offers iCloud functionality, launch either program on your Mac. Then, from the iPhoto or Aperture pull-down menu near the upper-left corner of the screen, select the Check For Updates option.

If you're already using iPhoto '11 but an updated version of the software is available, be sure to download and install it before attempting to use the iCloud feature to create and view an iCloud-based Photo Stream.

Your Mac should be running iPhoto '11 (version 9.2.1 or later), along with the most current version of OS X Lion (version 10.7.2 or later). If you're using Aperture 3, be sure to have version 3.2 (or later) installed on your Mac.

To learn more about Apple's optional Aperture 3 software ($79.99), visit www.apple.com/aperture. Sometime in 2012, Apple is expected to release Aperture 4, which will also be fully iCloud-compatible.

iPhoto '11 is part of Apple's iLife suite of software that comes bundled with all Macs. If you need to upgrade from an older edition of iPhoto (such as iPhoto '09), you can do this (for $14.99) by accessing Apple's Mac App Store or visiting www.apple.com/ilife/iphoto.

## Turn on Photo Stream on Your Mac

On a Mac, iCloud's Photo Stream feature is designed to work seamlessly with the latest version of iPhoto '11 or Aperture 3 (an optional and more advanced photo management and editing software package available from Apple). Before setting up this feature, however, you must create and activate a free iCloud account. It's then necessary to turn on iCloud's Photo Stream feature on the Mac itself, and then within whatever photo management/editing software you'll be using on your Mac. This process needs to be done only once.

To turn on the Photo Stream feature on your Mac, follow these steps:

1. Launch System Preferences on your Mac from the Dock or the Applications folder.
2. From the System Preferences window (shown in Figure 7-1), click the iCloud icon that's displayed below the Internet & Wireless heading.
3. When prompted, sign in to iCloud using your Apple ID and password when the iCloud window appears within System Preferences. If you're already signed into your iCloud account, this step is not necessary.
4. Once you're signed in, add a checkmark to the checkbox displayed next to the Photo Stream option (shown in Figure 7-2).

The Photo Stream option on your Mac is now turned on. However, you still need to turn on this functionality within the iPhoto '11 and/or the Aperture 3 software.

**FIGURE 7-1**   The System Preferences window on a Mac

**FIGURE 7-2**   The iCloud menu screen within System Preferences on a Mac looks almost identical to the iCloud Control Panel on a Windows PC.

To turn on the Photo Stream feature within iPhoto '11, follow these steps:

1. Launch the iPhoto '11 software on your Mac.
2. Along the left margin of the iPhoto '11 screen, click the Photo Stream option that's displayed within the Source List (shown in Figure 7-3).
3. In the main area of the iPhoto '11 screen, you'll be prompted to turn on the Photo Stream feature. Do this by clicking the large, blue-and-white Turn On Photo Stream icon near the center of the screen (also shown in Figure 7-3).

At this point, any new photos that have been added to your Photo Stream from other devices will be imported into the Photo Stream Album of iPhoto '11 and displayed. Depending on how many photos this is, the process could take several minutes.

From this point forward, any new photos you import into iPhoto '11 (from your digital camera's memory card, for example, or from other sources) will automatically be uploaded to iCloud and added to your Photo Stream.

When you configure iPhoto '11 on your Mac to work with Photo Stream, you can customize the photo importing settings from iPhoto's Preferences window (shown in Figure 7-4). From the iPhoto pull-down menu, choose the Preferences option, and then open the Photo Stream command tab.

After adding a checkmark to the Enable Photo Stream option, you can also add checkmarks to the Automatic Import and Automatic Upload options (shown in Figure 7-5). Automatic Import automatically adds photos into your iPhoto '11

**FIGURE 7-3** Be sure to turn on iCloud's Photo Stream option within iPhoto '11 or the Aperture 3 software on a Mac (shown here is iPhoto '11).

**FIGURE 7-4**   The Preferences window of iPhoto '11 on a Mac

Photo Library that have been added to your Photo Stream from other computers or devices that are also linked to your iCloud account. When Automatic Upload is activated by placing a checkmark next to this option, all new photos that are added to your iPhoto '11 Photo Library (from your digital camera or other sources) are automatically uploaded to iCloud and added to your Photo Stream.

For instructions on how to set up Aperture 3 (or later) on your Mac to work with iCloud's Photo Stream, visit the Support area of Apple's web site at www.apple.com/support/aperture.

**FIGURE 7-5**   Click the Enable Photo Stream option from the Photo Stream window.

# Turn on Photo Stream on Your PC

Once you turn on Photo Stream functionality to work with your PC, your Photo Stream images will be stored within a specific subfolder within your Pictures folder. You can then access, view, edit, print, and share those images using whatever photo management and editing software you typically use on your Windows-based computer.

To turn on Photo Stream functionality via iCloud on your PC, follow these steps:

1. Download and install the iCloud Control Panel software that's compatible with Windows Vista SP 2 and Windows 7. You can download this free software from Apple's web site at http://support.apple.com/kb/DL1455.
2. Once the iCloud Control Panel software is installed, from the Windows Start menu, choose Windows Control Panel.
3. From Control Panel, click the Network and Internet option.
4. Click the iCloud option, and log into your iCloud account when prompted by entering your Apple ID and password.
5. When the iCloud Control Panel window appears, add a checkmark next to the Photo Stream option. The iCloud Control Panel looks almost identical to the iCloud window within System Preferences on a Mac (refer to Figure 7-1).
6. Click the Options icon to the right of the Photo Stream option to customize your settings and activate (or deactivate) Photo Stream's Automatic Import and/or Automatic Upload features.

Unless you choose an alternative location, by default, your Photo Stream images will be stored on your PC at the following location: C:\Users\Apple\Pictures\Photo Stream\My Photo Stream.

 When your computer or iOS device accesses your Photo Stream from iCloud, it will download any and all new images that have already been added to the Photo Stream and store them temporarily within a Photo Stream Album on your computer or device. This Album will remain synchronized with Photo Stream and update automatically as new photos are added.

# Turn on Photo Stream on Your iPhone, iPad, or iPod touch

If you have multiple iOS devices, you'll need to turn on iCloud's Photo Stream feature on each device separately. To turn on Photo Stream functionality on any of your iOS devices after upgrading to iOS 5, follow these steps:

1. Create your iCloud account (if you have not already done so).
2. Launch the Settings app from the Home Screen.
3. From the main Settings menu, select the iCloud option by tapping it.

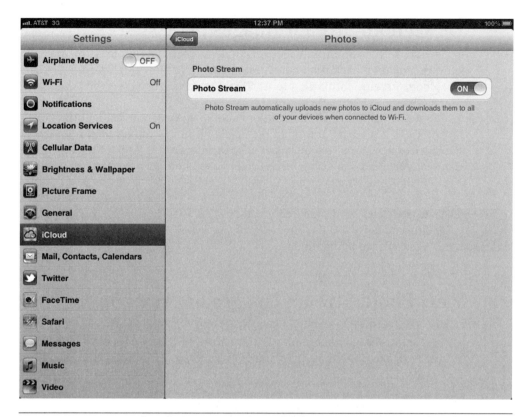

**FIGURE 7-6**   From the Photos menu screen within Settings, turn on the Photo Stream option, as shown here on the iPad 2.

4. When the iCloud menu screen appears within Settings, log into your iCloud account (if prompted to do so) using your Apple ID and password.
5. Tap the Photo Stream option on the iCloud menu within Settings.
6. From the Photos menu screen (shown in Figure 7-6), tap the virtual on/off switch next to the Photo Stream option to turn it on.

From this point forward, Photo Stream will automatically upload to iCloud all new photos added to your iPhone, iPad, or iPod touch and download them to all of your devices that are linked to the same iCloud account and that have the Photo Stream feature turned on.

# How to View Your Photo Stream Images

Images stored within your Photo Stream can be viewed on a Mac, PC, on your HD television or monitor (via Apple TV), or on an iPhone, iPad, or iPod touch (using the Photos app that comes preinstalled with iOS 5).

## View Photo Stream Images on a Mac

To view your Photo Stream images on a Mac, launch the iPhoto '11 or Aperture 3 software, and then click the Photo Stream Album to view the images stored within your Photo Stream. Within iPhoto '11, Photo Stream is listed on the left side of the screen (shown in Figure 7-7).

iPhoto '11 displays a thumbnail for each image that's stored within your Photo Stream. Click any image thumbnail to display it in full-screen mode. To use any of iPhoto '11 or Aperture 3's features to edit, print, or share a Photo Stream image, for example, you'll need to copy the image to your Photo Library first, and then store it within a different Album (not the Photo Stream Album).

 When iCloud was introduced in fall 2011, it was not possible to view your Photo Stream from a web browser by accessing www.iCloud.com. This, however, will most likely change in the future.

## View Photo Stream Images on Any iOS Device

To view images from your Photo Stream on your iOS device(s), launch the Photos app and select the Photo Stream Album (shown in Figure 7-8 on an iPad 2). As you're looking at image thumbnails, tap one of them to view it in full-screen mode.

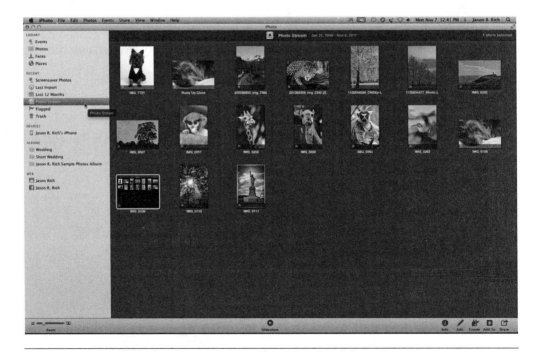

**FIGURE 7-7** Select Photo Stream from the left side of the iPhoto '11 screen to view your Photo Stream images on a Mac.

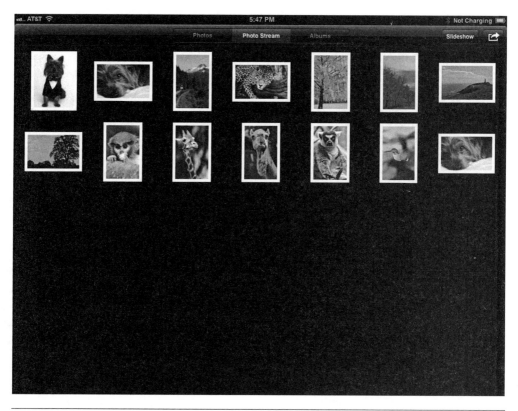

**FIGURE 7-8**    Photo Stream images can be viewed on an iPad 2 that's connected to a Wi-Fi Internet connection.

As you're looking at the Photo Stream Album on your iOS device (with the image thumbnails displayed on the screen), you can tap the Share command icon, select one or more image thumbnails by tapping them, and then tap the Save icon to transfer and save one or more images at a time to the Camera Roll Album. Once saved within the Camera Roll Album, the images will remain there until they're manually deleted.

**How to...    Save an Image in the Camera Roll Album**

When you're viewing an image from your Photo Stream on your iOS device, you can save it to another Album within the Photos app, where it can be stored indefinitely and/or edited. First view that image in full-screen mode. Then tap the Share icon, and select the Save To Camera Roll option from the Share menu (shown in Figure 7-9). Or tap the Edit icon, and use any of the photo editing tools on the image that are available within the Photos app (including Rotate, Enhance, Red-Eye, or Crop). When you click the Save command, the image will be saved to your Camera Roll Album, not the Photo Stream Album.

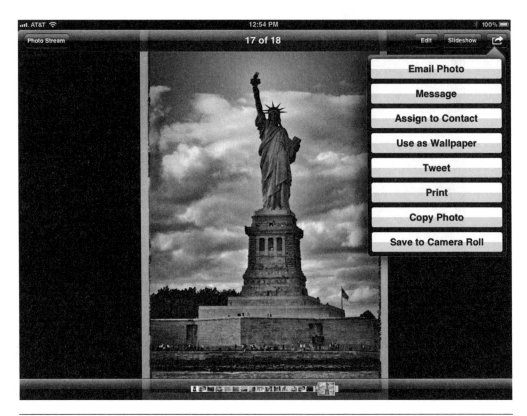

**FIGURE 7-9**   While viewing a Photo Stream image in full-screen mode on your iOS device, tap on the Share icon and select the Save To Camera Roll option.

Plus, they can be viewed, edited, enhanced, shared, or printed from within the Camera Roll Album.

Or, as you're viewing the Photo Stream Album on your iOS device (with the thumbnails for the images displayed on the screen), after tapping the Share command, you can select one or more image thumbnails, and then tap the Share or Copy command icon. Share allows you to send the selected image(s) via e-mail or text message to someone else, or you can print the images using iOS 5's AirPrint feature. The Copy command allows you to create a duplicate of the image.

# View Photo Stream Images on Your PC

On a PC, access the subdirectory where your Photo Stream images are stored, and use your photo management/editing software to view them.

**How to...**   ## View Photo Stream Images as an Animated Slide Show

To view your Photo Stream images as an animated slide show on your iOS device, select the Photo Stream Album after launching the Photos app, and then tap the Slide Show command icon. From the Slideshow Options window, select your favorite slide transition animation and/or background music, and then tap the Start Slideshow icon to view the animated slideshow in full-screen mode. It will showcase all of your Photo Stream images and continue running until you tap anywhere on the device's screen.

# View Photo Stream Images on Your HD Television

To view your Photo Stream images on an Apple TV, the optional $99.00 Apple TV device must be connected to your HD television set or monitor and also connected to a high-speed Wi-Fi or Ethernet Internet connection.

From Apple TV's main menu, after signing in to your iCloud account, select the Photo Stream option. It's listed under the Internet heading within the main menu. Thumbnails representing images from your Photo Stream will be displayed on your television screen. Use Apple TV's remote control to select the Slideshow option or to highlight and select one image at a time to view it in full-screen mode.

While viewing Photo Stream images on your television via Apple TV, select the Settings option to add music to the slide show and to choose a slide show theme.

Keep in mind that Photo Stream is used to share and synchronize digital images, not video clips shot using your iOS device. The Photo Stream feature supports digital images stored in the JPEG, TIFF, PNG, and many RAW photo formats only.

**Did You Know?**   ## Image Resolution Is Maintained on a Computer, But Not on an iOS Device

When uploaded to iCloud, your digital images are always kept in their existing resolution, and they're kept at that resolution when they are downloaded to your Mac or PC for viewing. However, when you view Photo Stream images on your Apple TV, iPhone, iPad, or iPod touch, when the images are downloaded from iCloud, they are automatically optimized for those devices. In most cases, an "optimized" photo will have a 2048×1536 resolution when it's downloaded from iCloud to your Apple TV or iOS device.

# Manually Add Images to Your Photo Stream from Your Computer

Once you've activated Photo Stream on one or more of your computers and/or iOS devices that are linked to the same iCloud account, you can begin adding digital photos to the Photo Stream.

By default, whenever you import any new photos to your Mac or PC, they'll automatically be uploaded to iCloud and added to your Photo Stream. Likewise, when you snap photos using your iPhone, iPad, or iPod touch, and/or import photos into your iOS device, those images will also automatically be uploaded to iCloud and included within your Photo Stream.

However, on your Mac, for example, if other images are stored on your computer (within iPhoto '11 or Aperture 3) that you want to add to your Photo Stream, you can drag the thumbnails representing those images from their current Albums or Events to the Photo Stream Album (listed within the Source list on the left side of the iPhoto '11 screen).

On a PC, you can drag-and-drop or copy images you want to add manually to your Photo Stream into the Photo Stream subdirectory on your computer. By default (unless you change it), this subdirectory can be found at C:\Users\Apple\Pictures\Photo Stream\My Photo Stream.

 If images are stored on your iPhone, iPad, or iPod touch that you want to add to your Photo Stream, you'll need to edit those images manually first using the Photos app. Your iOS device considers the edited images as new images that will be automatically added to your Photo Stream.

# Edit Photos in Your Photo Stream

Once an image becomes part of your Photo Stream, you can transfer it out of the Photo Stream Album to edit it on a Mac, PC, or an iOS device. However, before you can edit an image from Photo Stream, you must transfer it to another folder or album.

On a Mac that's running iPhoto '11, a photo must be copied or transferred from the Photo Stream Album to any other Album or Event folder.

To edit an image from your Photo Stream on your iOS device, follow these steps:

1. Launch the Photos app from the Home Screen.
2. Open the Album in which those images are stored on your iOS device.
3. As you're viewing the image thumbnails, tap one image at a time to view it in full-screen mode.

4. Tap the Edit icon to edit the image using the Rotate, Enhance, Red-Eye, and/or Crop tool of the Photos app.
5. Tap the Save icon, followed by the Save to Camera Roll option (shown in Figure 7-10).
6. As soon as the newly edited image is saved to the Camera Roll Album, your iOS device will perceive it as a new image, automatically upload it to iCloud, and add it to your Photo Stream.

By default, every image that's added to your Photo Stream automatically gets stored within the Photo Library on your primary computer's hard drive. This includes images shot using your digital camera and imported to your computer, or images shot using your iOS device's built-in camera, for example. All images will remain within the Photo Library on your primary computer indefinitely, until they are manually deleted (even if they're automatically removed and archived from your Photo Stream after 30 days or the 1000-image limit of Photo Stream is reached).

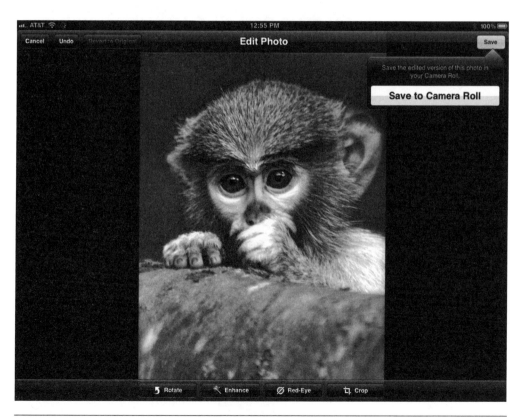

**FIGURE 7-10**   After editing a Photo Stream image on your iOS device within the Photos app, tap the Save icon and select the Save To Camera Roll option.

# Delete Your Entire Photo Stream

Although you cannot edit your Photo Stream, delete individual photos from it, or pick and choose which photos become part of it, you can manually delete your entire Photo Stream from the Web and start it again from scratch.

To do this from a Mac, PC, or any mobile device, you'll need to use your web browser and visit the iCloud web site (www.iCloud.com). Follow these steps:

1. When you access the main screen of iCloud.com, you'll see your account name displayed in the upper-right corner (as shown next). Click or tap it to reveal the Account pop-up window.

2. As you're viewing the Account window (shown next), click or tap the Advanced option. It's displayed just below the Time Zone field.

3. When the Advanced menu window appears, tap the Reset Photo Stream option. A message will appear (shown next) stating that all of the photos that were previously included within your Photo Stream have been removed. They are no longer being stored on iCloud.

4. If the images have already been sent to your computer or iOS mobile device, they'll need to be deleted from those Photo Stream folders or Albums as well.

# Remove Photo Stream Images from Your iOS Device

After you have reset your Photo Stream while visiting www.iCloud.com, you will still need to remove the Photo Stream images manually from your iPhone, iPad, or iPod touch. However, if you want to save any individual photos from your Photo Stream to your iOS device, you should do so before proceeding.

   To remove your entire Photo Stream (and all photos within it) from your iOS device, follow these steps:

1. Launch the Settings app from the Home Screen, and select the iCloud option.
2. From the main Settings menu, tap the Photo Stream option.
3. When the Photos menu screen appears within Settings, tap the virtual on/off switch that's associated with the Photo Stream option, and turn it off.
4. A pop-up message screen will appear that states, "Turning off Photo Stream will delete all Photo Stream photos from your iPad/iPhone." Tap the Delete Photos icon (shown next). All images within the Photo Stream Album within the Photos app will be deleted.

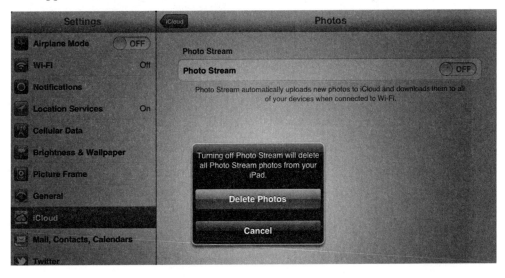

# Remove Photo Stream Images from iPhoto '11 on Your Mac

After you have reset you Photo Stream while visiting www.iCloud.com, you will still need to remove the Photo Stream images manually from the Photo Stream Album within iPhoto '11 or Aperture 3 on your Mac. However, if you want to save any individual photos from your Photo Stream, be sure to transfer or copy those individual images to another Album prior to proceeding.

To remove images in your Photo Stream Album that are stored within iPhoto '11 or Aperture 3 on your Mac, follow these steps:

1. Launch the iPhoto '11 or Aperture 3 software on your Mac.
2. From the iPhoto or Aperture pull-down menu near the top-left corner of the screen, select the Preferences option. (See Figure 7-4.)
3. When the Preferences window is displayed, click the Photo Stream command tab near the top-center of the window. (See Figure 7-5.)
4. The Photo Stream window will replace the Preferences window and will display three options, each with an associated checkbox. Using the mouse, remove the checkmark from the Enable Photo Stream option.
5. A pop-up message (shown next) appears that states, "Turning off Photo Stream will remove photos from the Photo Stream view. Previously imported photos will remain in your library." Click Turn Off to continue.

6. The images in your Photo Stream Album within iPhoto will be deleted. When the image deletion process is complete, click the checkbox next to the Enable Photo Stream option to turn this feature back on.

# Remove Photo Stream Images from Your PC

After you have reset your Photo Stream while visiting www.iCloud.com, you will still need to remove the Photo Stream images manually from the My Photo Stream folder. However, if you want to save any individual photos from your Photo Stream, be sure to transfer or copy those individual images to another subfolder within your Pictures folder, for example, prior to proceeding.

To remove images in your Photo Stream Album that are stored within the My Photo Stream directory on your PC, access the directory located at C:\Users\Apple\ Pictures\Photo Stream\My Photo Stream (by default), and delete its contents.

# Turn off Photo Stream Without Deleting Photos on Your Mac

On your Mac, you can turn off the Photo Stream feature without deleting any images stored on your computer (or from the Photo Stream itself). However, when you turn off the Photo Stream feature within iPhoto '11 or Aperture 3, for example, the Photo Stream Album will no longer be accessible.

Meanwhile, any new photos you take on other devices or computers, and that are added to your Photo Stream, will not be sent (downloaded) on the Mac(s) on which the Photo Stream feature has been turned off. And any images you add to your Mac on which the Photo Stream feature is turned off will not automatically be uploaded to iCloud and added to your Photo Stream.

 Remember that images stored within your Photo Stream remain there for up to 30 days, after which time they're automatically deleted from all devices connected to your iCloud account, but archived on your primary computer. However, once your Photo Stream includes 1000 images, as new images are added, the oldest ones are automatically removed for your Photo Stream (even if it's before the 30-day period ends).

To turn off the Photo Stream option within iPhoto '11 on your Mac, from the iPhoto pull-down menu, select the Preferences option, and then click Photo Stream. Remove the checkmark from the Enable Photo Stream option and click Turn Off.

 If you turn off Photo Stream functionality on your Mac (from within System Preferences) or on any of your iOS devices, the Photo Stream folder or Album that's storing Photo Stream images on that computer or device will be deleted.

# Share Images Among Computers and Devices

Although all of the different steps described in this chapter are required if you want to activate the iCloud Photo Stream feature and then use it with a Mac, PC, Apple TV, and/or iOS devices, once you set up Photo Stream and turn it on, all the Photo Stream images automatically remain synchronized on each of your computers or iOS devices. In other words, you don't have to take any additional steps to view your latest images on any computer or iOS device that's linked to your iCloud account.

If, however, on your Mac, you begin importing new images from your digital camera, but they're not showing up within your Photo Stream, this is probably because you don't have the Automatic Upload feature activated. To activate the feature, select the Preferences option from within iPhoto '11 or Aperture 3, and then select the Photo Stream option. Place a checkmark next to the Automatic Upload feature.

On your iOS device, if you don't see your Photo Stream at all or it's not being updated with images added to your Photo Stream from other devices, this is probably because your iPhone, iPad, or iPod touch is not currently connected to the Internet via a Wi-Fi connection. As soon as you connect to a Wi-Fi hotspot (or your home wireless network) and launch the Photos app, your Photo Stream images will synchronize with your iOS device.

When using Apple TV, if you have trouble accessing your Photo Stream from iCloud, make sure your Apple TV is connected to the Internet and that you're signed in using the same Apple ID and password you used to create your iCloud account. Plus, make sure you have the most recent version of the Apple TV operating system installed, which as of this writing is version 4.4.4 or later.

 If your Apple TV operating system needs to be updated to work with iCloud, follow the directions provided on the Apple web site at http://support.apple .com/kb/HT1600.

# PART III

## Share Documents, Music, Data, and More via iCloud and Other Services

# 8

## Share Documents and Files with iCloud

**HOW TO...**

- Use iWork.com in conjunction with iCloud.
- Transfer Microsoft Word, PowerPoint, and Excel, or Apple iWork documents and files between your computers using iWork.com and iCloud.
- Transfer Microsoft Word, PowerPoint, and Excel, or Apple iWork documents and files between a computer and your iPhone, iPad, or iPad touch using iCloud.
- Set up your iPhone, iPad, and/or iPod touch to sync documents using iCloud.

Whether you need to synchronize files and documents between computers linked to the same iCloud account, between your computer and iOS device(s), or among multiple iOS devices, one of the most useful features of iCloud is its ability to transfer and synchronize documents and files related to a growing number of software programs and apps, including Microsoft Word, Excel, and PowerPoint, and Apple Pages, Numbers, and Keynote (also known as Apple iWork applications). Once these files are transferred to iWork.com and/or iCloud, they become readily accessible on other computers and/or iOS devices that are linked to the same account.

What gets a little bit confusing, however, are the different methods required to get Microsoft Office or Apple iWork files transferred to your iOS devices and then synchronized among various computers and/or devices using Apple's cloud-based services. This chapter outlines the different procedures.

## Set up a Free iWork.com Account

Before you can transfer Microsoft Office or iWork for Mac files to iWork.com (which links to iCloud), you must first set up a free iWork.com account in addition to an iCloud account. iWork.com is a free service used exclusively to share iWork

(Pages, Numbers, and Keynote) documents and files among multiple users, various computers, or with iOS devices via the Web.

Every iWork.com account comes with 1 gigabyte of free online storage space.

    iWork.com is a cloud-based file sharing service developed by Apple and designed specifically for sharing iWork-related documents and files created or edited using Pages, Numbers, and Keynote. However, if you first import a Microsoft Word document into Pages, an Excel spreadsheet into Numbers, or a PowerPoint presentation into Keynote, you can then transfer and share those files via iWork.com as well.

    To set up an iWork.com account, visit iWork.com using any computer or iOS device, and sign in to the service using your existing Apple ID and password that are linked to your iCloud account. The process takes less than 30 seconds. After the iWork.com account is established, you can transfer documents from the iWork for Mac apps to iWork.com. You can also send files and documents from your iOS devices (including your iPhone and iPad) to iWork.com (or vice versa).

    After setting up an iWork account, when you visit www.iCloud.com, you'll discover an iWork icon is added to the web page for managing iWork.com files via iCloud (shown in Figure 8-1). Files stored on iWork.com can be accessed directly from iCloud by visiting www.iCloud.com/iWork or by pointing your web browser to www.iWork.com.

**FIGURE 8-1** When you create an iWork.com account, it becomes accessible online from the iCloud web site (www.iCloud.com).

## Documents Created with iWork Can Be Used with Microsoft Office on Your Computer

Documents created using the iWork for iOS apps (Pages, Numbers, and Keynote) on your iPhone or iPad can be uploaded to iWork.com in Word, Excel, or PowerPoint format and then accessed using a computer that's running Microsoft Office applications (Word, Excel, or PowerPoint).

# Transfer Office and iWork Documents to iWork.com

Although it is easy to transfer a Pages for Mac, Numbers for Mac, or Keynote for Mac document or file from your computer to iWork.com, and then make it available to your computers and iOS devices, there is not yet a quick and direct process for transferring Microsoft Office files created on a computer to iWork.com or iCloud.

To do this, you first need to import a Word document into Pages, for example, and then use Pages' Share Via iWork.com command (available from the Share pull-down menu) to upload that Word (now Pages) file to iWork.com (shown in Figure 8-2).

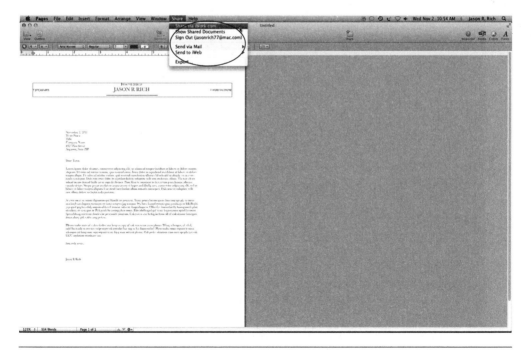

**FIGURE 8-2** The Mac version of Pages, Numbers, and Keynote each have a Share pull-down menu, where you can export a file or document to be shared with other people, computers, or iOS devices via iWork.com.

## Microsoft Office Is a Suite of Popular Applications

Microsoft Office includes Mac and PC software applications, including Microsoft Word (for word processing), PowerPoint (for digital slide presentations), and Excel (for spreadsheet management). Apple offers its iWork software, which includes Pages (a word processor), Numbers (for spreadsheet management), and Keynote (for digital slide presentations).

## Download iWork Software from the Mac App Store

To learn more about the Mac versions of Pages, Numbers and Keynote, which can be purchased for $29.99 each, and downloaded from the Mac App Store, visit http://www.apple.com/iwork, or click on the Mac App Store icon on your Mac's Dock.

(It can be converted back into a Word formatted document later.) The same process would be used for Excel documents (which first need to be imported into Numbers), or PowerPoint files (which first need to be imported into Keynote).

If you want to use your iPhone, iPad, or iPod touch to access Microsoft Office documents or files created using your computer, you can transfer those files and documents and ultimately make them available on iCloud in several ways.

For example, when you transfer a document or file to iWork.com, you can make it private, so only you can access it. Or you can make it available to select people by password-protecting it. You can also make the document or file public, which means anyone who looks for it can access it.

## Use a Mac to Password-Protect a File Being Uploaded to iWork.Com

From your Mac, to add a password to a document and limit who can view it via iWork .com, first open the Pages, Numbers, or Keynote document you want to share. From the Share pull-down menu, choose the Share Via iWork.com option. Then sign in to iWork. com when prompted using your Apple ID and password. Next, click the Share With Viewers option (as opposed to the Publish On The Web or Upload For Private Use option).

Within the Viewers field, type the e-mail address for each person who will have access to the document or file (shown in Figure 8-3). Type in the Subject field and, if you want, add a message.

When the window expands, decide if people invited to access your documents will be able to leave comments related to the documents or download them, by placing checkmarks next to the Allow Viewers To options. Then, add checkmarks,

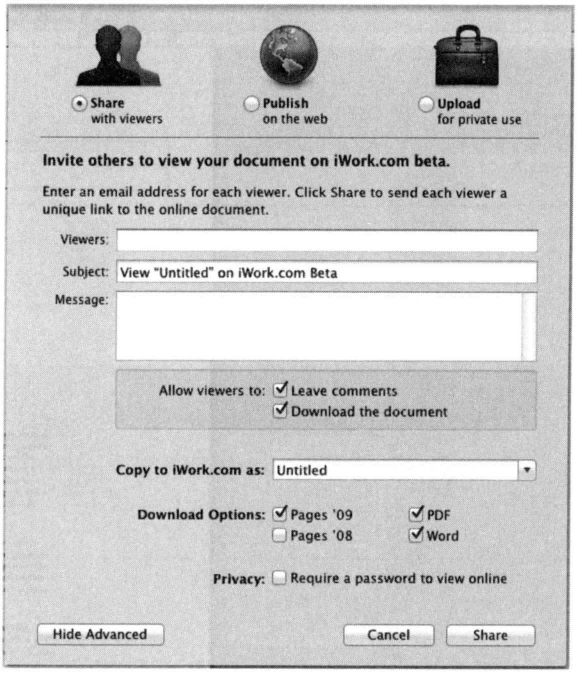

**FIGURE 8-3**    From your Mac, add an optional password to an iWork file or document you're about to upload to iWork.com.

as appropriate, to the Download Options, in order to select the file formats in which you want to make the document or file accessible. These options differ slightly if you're using Pages, Numbers, or Keynote.

Next to the Privacy option, add a checkmark next to the Require A Password To View Online option. When the Set A Password For This Document On iWork.com window appears, enter and then re-enter the password that you want to associate with the document or file. Click the Set Password icon to continue. To upload the document or file (with the password option activated) from your Mac to iWork.com, click the Share icon.

# Use an iOS Device to Password-Protect a File Being Uploaded to iWork.Com

The process for uploading a password-protected document or file from an iWork for iOS app using an iPhone or iPad, for example, is similar. Follow these steps:

1. From the Document Manager screen within Pages, Numbers, or Keynote on your iPhone or iPad, tap the Edit icon in the upper-right corner of the screen (shown in Figure 8-4).
2. When the document or file thumbnails start to shake, tap the file or document thumbnail that represents the file you want to upload to iWork.com.

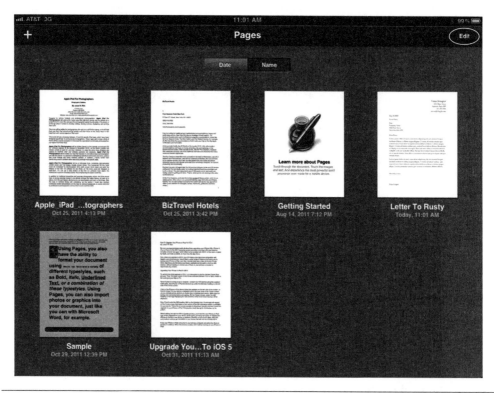

**FIGURE 8-4**   Tap the Edit icon within the Document Manager screen of Pages, Numbers, or Keynote, to prepare the document or file to be exported to iWork.com.

3. Once the document or file is selected and highlighted, tap the Share icon, and then choose the Share Via iWork.com option.

4. When promoted, log into your iWork.com account using your Apple ID and password.

5. When the Share Via iWork.com screen (shown in Figure 8-5) appears, enter the e-mail addresses for the people with whom you want to share the document or file. If these recipients have contact entries stored within the Contacts app of your iOS device, you can enter their names in the To field. You can then edit the Subject field, plus add a Message to the document being exported.

6. To add a password to the document or file prior to exporting it, tap the Sharing Options command on the right side of the Share Via iWork.com window (across from the Message heading).

7. From the Sharing Options window that appears (shown in Figure 8-6), tap the Password option and enter the password you want to assign to that document. Also from this Sharing Options window, you can adjust other settings related to the document you're about to export, such as what file format download options you want to make available to others.

8. Tap the Share icon in the upper-right corner of the Share Via iWork.com window (on the iPad) or screen (on the iPhone) to upload the now password-protected document or file to iWork.com.

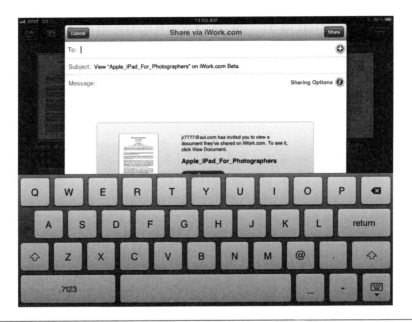

**FIGURE 8-5** Fill in the fields within the Share Via iWork.com window or screen (depending on which iOS device you're using) to prepare the document or file for uploading to iWork.com.

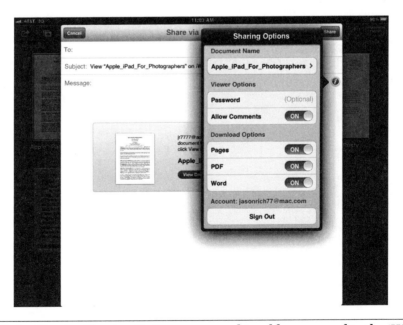

**FIGURE 8-6** Tap the Sharing Options command to add a password to the iWork document or file, plus customize additional settings before uploading a file or document to iWork.com.

# E-mail Yourself Office Documents or Files from Your Computer

You can transfer a Microsoft Word, PowerPoint, or Excel document or file from your computer to your iOS device (without first importing it into Pages, Numbers, or Keynote on your Mac) by e-mailing that document or file as an attachment to yourself. Then open the e-mail using the Mail app within your iOS device. This process works for PC users as well.

On your iOS device, you will need to install an app that's capable of opening, viewing, editing, printing, and sharing Microsoft Office files and documents. The three iWork for iOS apps are designed for this purpose, but others are also available from the App Store.

From your computer, after you've attached the Microsoft Office document or file to an e-mail, send it to yourself. Then, from your iOS device, launch the Mail app and access the appropriate e-mail account. You will see the incoming e-mail listed in your Inbox.

Tap the message listing to open the e-mail and view it. Within the body of the e-mail, you will see an icon representing the file attachment (shown in Figure 8-7). Place and hold your finger on that attachment icon until the Quick Look and Open In command tabs appear.

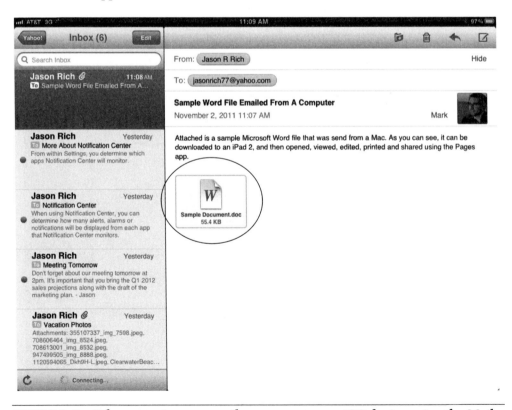

**FIGURE 8-7**   When you view an e-mail message on your iOS device using the Mail app (shown here on the iPad 2) with an attached document or file, you'll see an icon for it embedded within the body of the e-mail.

If the attachment is a Word document, and Pages is installed on your iOS device, the Open In command tab will say Open In Pages. Likewise, if it's an Excel or PowerPoint file, the Open In command tab will say Open In Numbers or Open In Keynote, respectively, assuming you have Numbers and/or Keynote installed on your iOS device.

The appropriate iWork for iOS app will then launch automatically, and the Word, Excel, or PowerPoint file will be imported and opened within the applicable app. As soon as you do this, if you have that iWork for iOS app set up to sync with iCloud automatically, the file will be uploaded to iCloud. It then becomes available on any computer or iOS device that's linked to your iCloud account.

Once a file is imported into Pages, Numbers, or Keynote on your iOS device, you can export it directly to iWork.com, where it becomes accessible from any computer (including computers or devices not linked to your iCloud account). Thus, you'll be able to access the document or file from any computer using any web browser by logging into your free iWork.com account (www.iWork.com), or using your iCloud account by visiting www.iCloud.com/iWork.

You're now free to edit or modify the newly imported document or file on your iOS device. As you make changes, they will automatically become available to all of your computers and devices via iCloud.com, or the files can be manually exported to iWork.com. How to export files from Pages, Numbers, and Keynote running on your iPhone or iPad to iWork.com will be explained shortly.

# Transfer iWork for Mac Files to iWork.com and iCloud

Any of the iWork for Mac software applications allow you to upload files directly to iWork.com from within the app and then access those files from iCloud or iWork.com from your iOS device. You can also e-mail documents or files from within the iWork programs to access them from your other computer(s) and iOS devices or to share them with specific other people.

When you're ready to transfer an iWork for Mac document or file from your Mac-based computer to iWork.com, click the Share pull-down menu from the Pages, Numbers, or Keynote program, and select the Share via iWork.com option. You'll be prompted to provide your Apple ID and password. Enter this information, and click the Sign In icon.

Any time you opt to share a document through an iWork software application on your Mac, the Share window will appear, where you can choose between sharing the document or file with viewers, publishing the file on the Web, or uploading the file to iWork.com for private use. Click your selection, and then click the Upload icon.

 Depending on the files size and the speed of your Internet connection, the file will be transferred from your Mac (running iWork software) to iWork.com in less than one minute.

You can now log into iWork.com and download that file or document from any computer or using Safari on your iOS device. If it started as a Pages document, for example, you can download it from iWork.com as a Pages, PDF, or Word document.

From Safari on your iOS device, after you access iWork.com and open a Page document, Numbers spreadsheet file, or Keynote presentation, you can tap that document or filename and an Open In command tab will appear. Again, if it's a Pages document, the tab will say Open In Pages. If it's a Numbers or Keynote file, the command tab will say Open In Numbers or Open In Keynote, respectively. The appropriate app must be installed on your iOS device for this to work.

Once the file is transferred from iWork.com to your iOS device, if that iWork for iOS app is set up to work with iCloud, the file will automatically be uploaded to your iCloud account and also stored on your iPhone, iPad, or iPod touch. After it's available on iCloud, the document becomes automatically accessible from any computer or iOS device that's linked to that account.

# Share iWork for iOS Files on Your iPhone or iPad with Other Computers/Devices

Whether you're using Pages, Numbers, or Keynote on your iPhone, iPad, or iPod touch, you can set up your iOS device to sync files with your iCloud account automatically. Doing this, however, is a two-step process. First, turn on iCloud functionality on your iOS device. Then, one at a time, activate the iCloud feature for each specific iWork for iOS app.

 A growing number of third-party iPhone and iPad apps also offer the ability to sync app-specific data and files automatically via iCloud.

## Turn on iCloud Functionality for iWork Apps on an iOS Device

Follow these steps to set up your iWork for iOS apps to work automatically with iCloud (after you have created an iCloud account). Keep in mind that your iOS device will need access to the Internet to link with iCloud.

1. Launch the Settings app from the Home Screen of your iOS device.
2. From the main Settings menu, select the iCloud option.
3. When the iCloud menu screen appears, make sure the e-mail address you have associated with your iCloud account is displayed within the Account field near the top of the iCloud menu screen (shown in Figure 8-8 on the iPhone and Figure 8-9 on the iPad). If no e-mail address is listed here, or you need to change it, tap the Account field.

**FIGURE 8-8** The iCloud menu within Settings on the iPhone

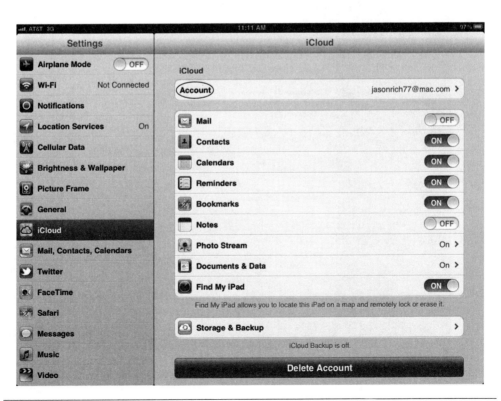

**FIGURE 8-9** The iCloud menu within Settings on the iPad

The Account screen within Settings will be displayed (shown in Figure 8-10). Using your iOS device's virtual keyboard, enter the Apple ID and Password associated with your iCloud account, and then tap the Done icon.

4. From the iCloud menu screen within Settings, scroll down to the Documents & Data option, and make sure the virtual switch associated with this feature is turned on. This turns on iCloud functionality on your iOS device.

5. Next, you'll need to choose which specific iCloud features you want to activate. Tap the left-pointing arrow-shaped Settings icon in the upper-left corner of the screen to return to the main Settings menu.

6. Once you're viewing the main Settings menu again, scroll down to the Pages menu option and tap it.

7. At the top of the Pages menu screen within Settings, tap the virtual switch to the right of the Use iCloud option for Pages to turn it on. This option is near the top of the screen (shown in Figure 8-11). This step turns on iCloud functionality in conjunction with the Pages app.

Now, when you launch the Pages app on your iOS device, it will automatically access your iCloud account and retrieve any Pages documents created on other

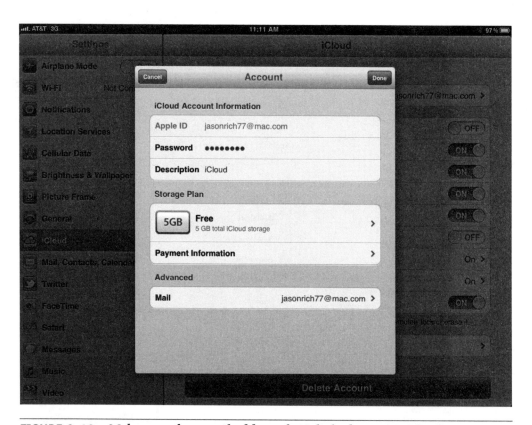

**FIGURE 8-10** Make sure the e-mail address that's linked to your iCloud account is displayed on the Account screen within Settings, shown here on the iPad. The available options are identical on the iPhone.

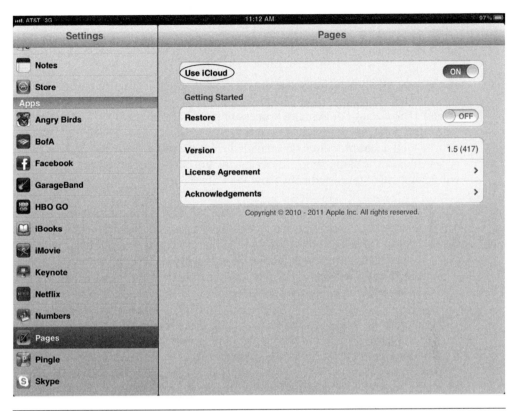

**FIGURE 8-11**   The Pages screen within Settings shown on the iPad. It's virtually the same on the iPhone.

computers or devices. They'll be displayed within the Document Manager screen of Pages.

At the same time, if you have created or modified a document within Pages on your iOS device, it will now automatically sync with iCloud, so the most recent version of that document is always available on the computer or device from which you access it.

8. Tap the left-pointing arrow-shaped Settings icon to return to the main Settings menu.

9. Repeat steps 6 through 8 for the Numbers and Keynote apps as well, if these apps are also installed on your iOS device.

10. On each of your iOS devices you'll be using, including your iPhone, iPad, and iPod touch, repeat steps 1 through 9.

# Use iWork for iOS Apps with iCloud

After iCloud functionality is turned on for iWork apps, the process of syncing documents and files between your iOS device and iCloud happens automatically.

The process for using Pages, Numbers, and Keynote in conjunction with iCloud is identical for all three apps. Explained here is how to use Pages on your iOS device with iCloud, but a similar process applies to Numbers and Keynote as well.

When you launch the Pages app on your iPhone, for example, the "Updating Documents" message will appear near the top-center of the Pages Document Manager screen. The document syncing process happens automatically. During this process, assuming your iOS device has access to the Web, any new Pages files added to your iCloud account will be downloaded from iCloud to your iOS device and made accessible. At the same time, any Pages documents you created on your iOS device will be uploaded (automatically) to your iCloud account.

 If a document or file is created on your iOS device using Pages, Numbers, or Keynote, but the iOS device doesn't have access to the Internet to sync that file, a small arrow icon will appear on the file's thumbnail on the Document Manager screen. Later, when your iOS device does get access to the Internet, as long as the Pages, Numbers, or Keynote app gets launched (or is open), the file will automatically be uploaded to iCloud.

When this updating process is completed, from the Pages Document Manager screen (shown in Figure 8-12 on the iPhone, and in Figure 8-13 on the iPad), tap the thumbnail for any document you want to open, view, edit, or print using your iOS device. From the Document Manager screen, you can also tap the Edit icon, and then select and highlight a document thumbnail so you can share, copy, rename, or delete it.

**FIGURE 8-12** This is the Document Manager screen of Pages on the iPhone. Numbers and Keynote have similar Document Manager screens.

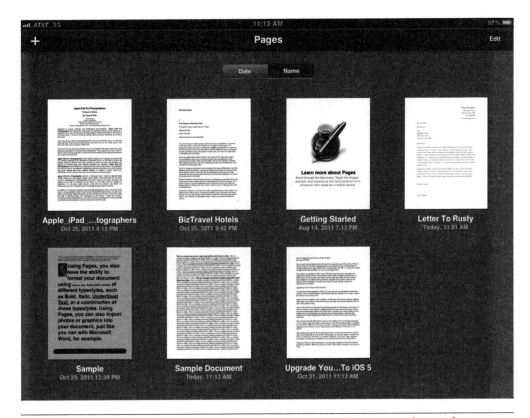

**FIGURE 8-13**   This is the Document Manager screen of Pages on the iPad.

iWork for iOS documents and files that are synced via iCloud are accessible from other iOS devices. From a computer, you'll need to access the document or file from iWork.com by visiting www.iWork.com or www.iCloud.com/iWork after the file is manually exported from your iOS device to iWork.com.

# Manually Export a Document from an iWork App on an iOS Device

When using the Pages, Numbers, or Keynote app on your iPhone, iPad, or iPod touch, you can work from the Document Manager screen to import or export documents and files, as well as create new documents or files, rename documents or files, copy documents or files, or delete documents or files.

To create a new document or import a document from iTunes, iDisk, or WebDAV, tap the plus-sign icon in the upper-left corner of the Document Manager screen of Pages, Numbers, or Keynote. To rename a document or file, tap the filename under its thumbnail, and then use the virtual keyboard to enter a new filename (shown in Figure 8-14 on the iPhone).

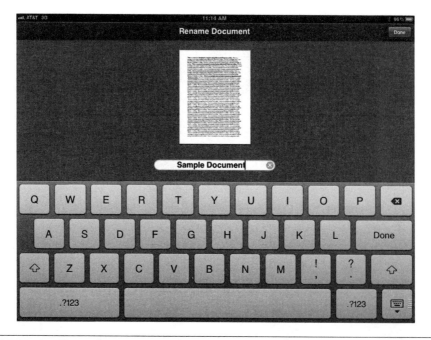

FIGURE 8-14 From the Document Manager screen of Pages, Numbers, or Keynote, tap the filename displayed under a document or file thumbnail to rename it.

If you want to export a document or file manually from an iWork for iOS app, tap the Edit icon near the upper-right corner of the Document Manager screen of the app you're using. The document or file thumbnails will start to shake.

Tap the document or file thumbnail you want to export. Once a document is selected and highlighted within the Document Manager screen of Pages, Numbers, or Keynote, it will be framed within a yellow box. Simultaneously, the Share, Copy, and Trash command icons on the screen become active.

 You can select one thumbnail at a time to be manually exported. However, you can select and highlight multiple thumbnails to use the Document Copy or Delete options as you're using Edit mode from the Document Manager screen of Pages, Numbers, or Keynote.

## Share iWork Documents via E-mail on Your iOS Device

From within an iWork for iOS app, tap the Share icon, and then, to send the document to one or more people via e-mail, tap the Share via Email icon (shown in Figure 8-15). When you do this, the Email Document screen (shown in Figure 8-16) will appear, allowing you to select in which format you want to export the document. When using Pages, for example, your options include Pages, PDF, or Word. Tap your selection.

Next, the New Message screen will be displayed. Using the virtual keyboard, fill in the To field of the outgoing e-mail with one or more recipients' e-mail addresses.

**FIGURE 8-15** To e-mail a document from within an iWork for iOS app, tap the Share icon from the Document Manager screen after selecting and highlighting a document or file thumbnail.

You can then tap the Subject heading to edit the subject, and tap anywhere within the body of the outgoing e-mail message to add text to that message.

The iWork for iOS document or file (which is now in Pages/Numbers/Keynote, PDF, or Word/Excel/PowerPoint format) is automatically attached to the e-mail (as shown in Figure 8-17). Tap the Send icon to send the e-mail to the recipients.

When you manually export a Pages document from the Document Manager screen (or from the Tools menu), you can convert the document being exported into Pages, PDF, or Word format. Likewise, if you're using Numbers, the file can be exported in Numbers, PDF, or Excel format (shown in Figure 8-18). Or, if you're using Keynote, the file can be exported in Keynote for Mac, PDF, or PowerPoint format (shown in Figure 8-19).

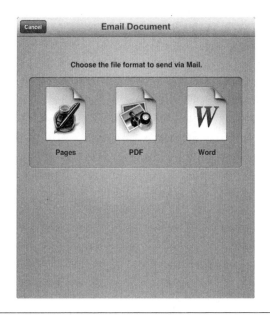

**FIGURE 8-16** Once you opt to export a document or file via e-mail, you can choose the file format.

**FIGURE 8-17** As you prepare the e-mail to be sent, notice that the iWork for iOS document or file is automatically embedded within the outgoing e-mail message.

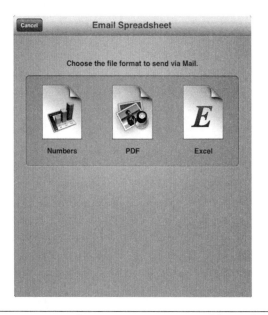

**FIGURE 8-18** When using Numbers, you can export a file in the Numbers, PDF, or Excel file format.

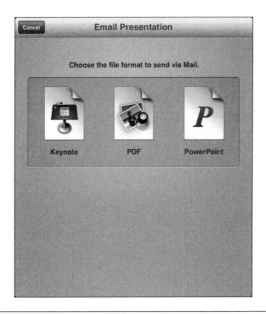

**FIGURE 8-19** When using Keynote, you can export a presentation file in the Keynote, PDF, or PowerPoint format.

However, with iCloud functionality turned on, the Pages, Numbers, or Keynote file that is automatically uploaded and synced with iCloud will remain in its native format.

## Export Files to iWork.com from iWork Apps on Your iOS Device

Instead of exporting the file and sending it via e-mail, after selecting a document from the Document Manager screen and tapping the Share icon, you can tap the Share via iWork.com icon to upload that file to your iWork.com account.

You'll have the option of exporting the Pages document, for example, in Pages, PDF, or Word format. Once uploaded to iWork.com, the document can be accessed by anyone (on an iOS device or on a Mac) to whom you've granted access permission, as well as by your other computers or iOS devices.

## The Pages Word Processor Can Automatically Sync Files via iCloud

When iCloud functionality is turned on for Pages on your iOS device, your documents automatically sync with iCloud. You don't have to do anything to make this happen. However, you can manually export one Pages document at a time from your iOS device to your iWork.com account, which allows you to share it with other people (as opposed to computers or devices that are linked to your iCloud account).

**Use the Tools Menu Within Pages to Share and Print Documents**

While you're editing a document using Pages (or working with a Numbers spreadsheet or a Keynote presentation), by tapping the wrench-shaped icon, you can access the app's Tools menu. From this menu, you can quickly share the document or file you're working with by tapping the Share And Print option. When the Share And Print menu screen appears (shown here), tap the Email Document, Share via iWork.com, Copy to iTunes, Copy to iDisk, or Copy to WebDAV menu option.

| Share and Print |
|---|
| ✉ Email Document |
| 🖨 Print > |
| Share via iWork.com |
| 🎵 Send to iTunes |
| Copy to iDisk |
| Copy to WebDAV |

## Export Files to iTunes, iDisk, or WebDAV from an iWork App on an iOS Device

By tapping the Share icon, you can also sync the iWork for iOS document or file to your primary computer via the iTunes Sync process. To do this, tap the Copy To iTunes option. Or you can upload the document to iDisk or WebDAV.

 If you delete a file from the Document Manager screen on your iOS device, it will delete that file from your device as well as your iCloud account.

# Other Third-Party Apps with iCloud Compatibility

If you begin using other apps (along with iWork for iOS apps) that offer iCloud compatibility, you'll need to make sure that iCloud functionality is set up on your iOS device to work with those apps. From within the Settings app, tap the iCloud option from the main Settings menu, and make sure the Documents & Data option is turned on. Then return to the main Settings menu and select the specific app that offers iCloud compatibility. Make sure the virtual on/off switch associated with iCloud functionality for that app is turned on as well.

One iCloud-compatible program and app is called SingleText for the Mac, iPhone, and iPad ($ .99, http://itunes.apple.com/us/app/singletext/id471095690?mt=12). It's a basic text-editing tool that allows you to transfer the documents you create between your Mac and iOS devices via iCloud.

**Did You Know?**

## Many Third-Party Apps Now Offer iCloud Compatibility

You'll find other iCloud compatible apps for your iOS device by browsing the App Store from iTunes on your computer or using the App Store app on your iPhone, iPad, or iPod touch. To find iCloud-compatible Mac software, visit the online-based Mac App Store by clicking the Mac App Store icon on your Mac's Dock.

Other applications include Bento (www.filemaker.com/products/bento), a database management application for the Mac, iPhone, and iPad, and Awesome Idea + iCloud, which is used for brainstorming and list management (http://itunes.apple.com/us/app/awesome-idea-icloud/id462788426?mt = 8). Both applications are also iCloud compatible.

# 9

## Cloud-Based File/Document Sharing Alternatives to iCloud

**HOW TO...**

- Use Dropbox as a cloud-based file sharing service.
- Tap the capabilities of WebDAV instead of, or in addition to, iCloud.

Many cloud-based file sharing services are basically online file and document storage options that allow you to maintain a remote and secure backup of your important documents and files and share those files or documents with others without having to use e-mail. These services can also simplify how you collaborate with others on projects via the Internet, when you and your collaborators are working from different locations.

For a while, file sharing and storage were the primary uses of cloud-based file sharing services, and they continue to be used today for these purposes among PC, Mac, and mobile device users. The focus on this chapter is to introduce you to two other cloud-based file sharing options beyond Apple's iCloud that can be used to share documents and files with other people and make it easier to collaborate on projects via the Web.

You may be thinking, "I already have iCloud, and it's free, so why would I need to use another cloud-based file sharing service?" It's true that iCloud offers a vast collection of features and functionality that's never before been available in a cloud-based file sharing service (including full integration with the OS X Lion operating system on the Mac and the iOS 5 operating system for the iPhone and iPad). iCloud also lets you create backups and access your files, data, photos, documents, and iTunes content from any of your own computers or devices that are linked to your personal iCloud account.

What iCloud doesn't yet offer (at least when the service was launched) is an easy way to share documents, data, files, and photos with other people who are using computers and/or mobile devices that are not linked to your secure iCloud account.

Thus, iCloud is not yet the ideal service to use for collaborations or sharing specific files and documents with others. Hence, in addition to using Apple's iCloud, if you want to share data, documents, files, and photos, for example, as well as collaborate with others, you'll probably want to use another cloud-based file sharing service, such as Dropbox, or a cloud-based service that's compatible with WebDAV.

**Note** Although the focus of this chapter is on cloud-based file and document sharing services that are alternatives to iCloud, Chapter 10 offers information about cloud-based services for managing your digital music library, including offerings from Amazon.com and Google Music. Unless you upgrade to Apple's premium iTunes Match service for $24.99 per year (refer to Chapter 6), iCloud can be used to manage and share only the music and content you've purchased from the iTunes Store, as opposed to your entire digital music library. However, if you want to acquire music and content legally from other services, and then make that content available to all of your computers and mobile devices, you'll probably want to use another cloud-based file sharing service in addition to the basic iCloud service.

iCloud is also designed primarily for use by home computer users, not by businesses. Many companies with their own IT infrastructures have already begun to use secure, multiuser cloud-based file sharing services, which employees can tap into from their desk at work, from home, or while on the go using a mobile device.

In addition, many software developers are starting to make their applications online-based. So instead of installing an application on your computer's hard drive, and then running it from your computer, the online-based software as well as files or documents created using that software are accessible from any web browser. Companies such as Microsoft (with its Office 365 suite) and Google have been pioneers in offering online-based apps and file sharing, for such tasks as word processing, spreadsheet management, database management, scheduling, and contact management. You'll learn more about these options, and how cloud-based computing is being used for these purposes, in Chapter 11.

**Did You Know?**

# Cloud-Based Services Can Also Be Used to Back Up Important Files and Data

Mac, iPhone, and/or iPad users can use iCloud for sharing content, documents, and files among your own devices, and for maintaining a remote backup of important information. Services such as Dropbox can also be used for creating and maintaining secure online backups of important information (which is also offered by iCloud), but these services are also ideal for sharing files with others and collaborating with other people on projects that involve using the same files and data.

To use any cloud-based file sharing service, all devices from which you plan to upload or download content must have access to the Internet. When using a cloud-based document sharing service such as Dropbox, you can easily do the following:

- Back up important files from a computer or mobile device to a remote (cloud-based) server, where it will be stored securely.
- Share content on your primary computer with another PC or Mac, or retrieve a file from another PC or Mac.
- Share content from your primary computer with your mobile device(s), such as an iPhone and/or iPad.
- Create files, documents, or data on your mobile device, and share that content with your computer(s) or other mobile devices that have access to the same cloud-based account.
- Share content and collaborate on creating, editing, or reviewing files or data with other people using equipment with access to the Web.

# Introduction to Dropbox

Since September 2008, Dropbox has been offering cloud-based file and document sharing services to consumers and small business operators. The service now has more than 25 million registered users from more than 175 countries and continues to grow in popularity because it's easy to use and inexpensive; in fact, to get started using Dropbox takes less than five minutes—and it's free to sign up for 2GB of storage space.

When you register to use Dropbox, you'll be required to set up a free account. (The process for doing this will be explained in the next section.) You'll then need to download free Dropbox software (and/or an app) that's compatible with your computer or mobile device. The Dropbox account you set up automatically comes with 2GB of online storage space. However, by upgrading to a paid subscription, you can increase your online storage space to 50GB ($9.99 per month) or 100GB ($19.99 per month).

Once you've set up a Dropbox account, it's password protected and secure. Just as when you organize your files on a computer's hard drive with a hierarchy of folders and subfolders, you can set up and use as many separate folders within your Dropbox

**Did You Know?**

## Access Files Stored on Dropbox from Almost Any Internet-Connected Device

One appealing feature of Dropbox is that it allows you to access your files, data, and documents from almost any device that's capable of connecting to the Internet. The service works with Windows, Mac OS, and Linux-based computers. Plus, apps are available for the Apple iPhone and iPad, as well as Android, Windows Mobile, and Blackberry mobile devices.

account as you need, and each can be shared with specific people, if you so choose. Thus, you can invite others to access only specific folders within your Dropbox account, allowing you to share files or content, without giving other people full access to your Dropbox account.

 Dropbox also allows you to create and share photo galleries, which are viewable by anyone you choose.

As you begin to use Dropbox as a remote storage option for your important documents, files, and data, any changes you make on your primary computer (or mobile device) to individual files are backed up in your Dropbox account. However, to save time, only the changed portion of those files are uploaded. The end result is that the most current versions of the documents, data, photos, videos, or files that you manually select can always be available to you (on all of your computers and/or mobile devices), as well as to your collaborators, via your online-based Dropbox account.

 When you store information on Dropbox, the latest encryption technology is used to ensure security. The service also automatically keeps a one-month history of your work, and during that period, it allows you to undelete files you accidently delete from your Dropbox account.

Yet another useful feature of Dropbox is that you can access your files, data, documents, and photos from any Internet-connected computer or mobile device, directly from the Dropbox.com web site.

# Get Started Using Dropbox

To begin using Dropbox for free, simply access the Dropbox.com web site from your computer's web browser, and from Dropbox's main web page, click the large blue Download Dropbox icon (as shown in Figure 9-1). The web site will determine what operating system your computer is using and allow you to download the appropriate version of the required software automatically.

If you want to use a mobile device to access Dropbox, download the free Dropbox app. For example, if you use an iPhone or iPad, visit Apple's App Store. From the Search field within the App Store, enter the keyword **Dropbox**, and then download and install the free hybrid iPhone/iPad app.

On your computer or mobile device, after the Dropbox software downloads (which takes less than a minute using a high-speed Internet connection), run the Dropbox installer. When the Dropbox software (or app) is launched for the first time, you'll be asked to enter your e-mail address and password, or click or tap the Create Account button to establish a new account.

To create a new account on your computer or mobile device, when prompted, enter your first name, last name, e-mail address, and password. The e-mail address you supply must be active, unique to you, and not previously registered with the

**FIGURE 9-1**   To get started, click the Download Dropbox icon on the Dropbox .com website.

Dropbox service. Next, if you're working from a mobile device, tap the Create Account icon (shown in Figure 9-2 on the iPad 2). Before you can complete your account registration, you will need to agree to the Terms of Service by clicking (computer) or tapping (mobile device) the I Agree icon in the Dropbox Terms of Service window.

After you've set up your new Dropbox account, a brief on-screen tutorial will appear to show you what the service offers and how to use it. You'll learn that when you access your newly created, online-based Dropbox account (which is accessible using the Dropbox software on your computer, from a Dropbox app on your mobile device, or from the Dropbox.com web site), it has already created two folders: Photos and Public.

 Also saved within your newly created Dropbox account will be a PDF file, called Getting Started. This is a quick start guide to using Dropbox, which you can open, read, and then delete from your account.

On your primary computer, you'll discover that a new Dropbox folder appears when you access a list of available hard drives or storage media connected to your computer. The same folder names that appear when you access your Dropbox account will be displayed here. On a Mac, for example, click the Finder icon on the Dock at the bottom of the screen. Along the left side of the screen (within the Sidebar), under the Favorites heading, is a Dropbox listing (as shown in Figure 9-3). Click it to view your Dropbox folders.

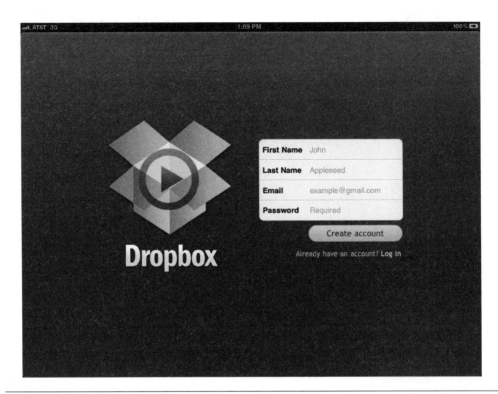

**FIGURE 9-2** Creating a new Dropbox account takes just minutes and can be done from a computer or mobile device.

**FIGURE 9-3** You can move files to Dropbox from your primary computer.

You'll next want to install the Dropbox software or app on your other computer(s) and/or mobile devices. This time, however, instead of setting up a new account, you'll log in by entering the same e-mail address and password you initially used to set up the account. Each time you do this on a separate computer or device, it will link that computer or device to your Dropbox account, allowing you to transfer and/or synchronize documents, data, files, photos, or videos quickly and easily.

After the Dropbox software is installed on your primary computer, you can treat your Dropbox folder just as you would an external hard drive or USB thumb drive and copy any files you want to share or save within your Dropbox online account to your Dropbox Public or Photos folder, or you can create any additional folders (or subfolders) within your Dropbox account to store and organize files.

 You can create folders and subfolders for your Dropbox account from a Mac OS, from a PC running Windows, or from a mobile device.

## Create Dropbox Folders Using Your Mac

To create an unlimited number of folders within your Dropbox account, click the Finder icon on your Mac's main screen and follow these steps:

1. From the Favorites area on the left side of the Mac's screen, click the Dropbox option.
2. At this point, you can create a new folder or add a subfolder to any existing folder. To create a subfolder, double-click an existing folder displayed within Finder's Dropbox window. When the contents of that folder are displayed, follow the next steps to create a subfolder within the primary folder you selected. Or skip this step to create a new top-level folder that will appear alongside the main Public and Photos folders.
3. When the Dropbox window opens within Finder, click the gear-shaped icon displayed at the top of the screen, and select the New Folder option from the pull-down menu (as shown in Figure 9-4).
4. When the new main folder is created, it will appear next to the Photos and Public folder; by default, it will be named Untitled Folder. It's also possible, however, to create subfolders. If it's a subfolder it won't appear next to the Photos and Public folder, however.
5. Click the folder icon once to highlight it, and then click the gear-shaped icon again. This time, choose the Get Info icon related to that folder.
6. When the Untitled Folder Info window opens, click the Name & Extension field and type a custom name for the newly created but untitled folder.
7. You can now drag-and-drop, or use the Select, Copy and Paste, or the Save As... command, to add files, documents, and/or data to this folder. As soon as you do this, those files will be uploaded to the Dropbox service, and will be accessible online from your other computers and mobile devices, as well as by the people you opt to share them with.

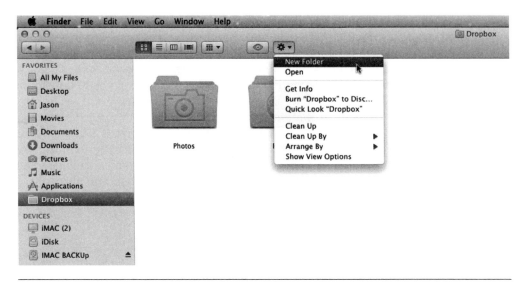

**FIGURE 9-4** Click the gear-shaped icon within Finder to create a new folder.

On your primary computer, you must manually pick which files will be uploaded to Dropbox, and then decide in which online-based folder that content will be stored. It's not an automated process as it is with iCloud. Using Dropbox, you can then opt to make a folder's content available to other specific users by using the Share Folder command.

# Use Dropbox with Your iPhone or iPad

When using Dropbox in conjunction with your iPhone or iPad, the Dropbox app allows you to import documents and files with ease from the Web to your iOS device. However, to access those files or documents, you'll need to have a compatible app already installed on your iPhone or iPad. For example, to import a Word or Pages document, the Pages app (or another compatible app) is needed. To download and access an Excel or Numbers spreadsheet, the Numbers app (or another compatible app) is required.

Using the QuickLook feature built into iOS 5, you can view a PDF file on the screen, but to do anything with that file, you'll need an optional PDF reader app installed on your iOS device. (In addition to allowing you to view eBooks, the iBooks app can also be used as a PDF file reader on your iPhone or iPad.)

When you download a photo or video clip from Dropbox to your iPhone or iPad, the Photos app (which comes preinstalled on your iOS device) is used to view this content. Or you can use another app that can access your device's Photos folders.

To export files, documents, or data from your iPhone or iPad to your Dropbox account, you'll need to use a third-party app that offers Dropbox functionality and export the file or data directly from within that app. You'll discover that hundreds of third-party apps offer both iCloud and Dropbox compatibility.

**Many Third-Party Apps Now Support Dropbox**

More than 230 third-party iPhone and iPad apps, as well as apps for other mobile devices, are currently compatible with the Dropbox service, including GoodReader, Documents To Go, and Quickoffice. These apps allow you to import and export files or documents from that app running on your iPhone or iPad and share them with other computers, devices, or users.

While you can import iWork for iOS files and documents (including Word, Excel, and PowerPoint files) from Dropbox to your Apple mobile device, you can export them only via iCloud, as the Pages, Numbers, and Keynote apps do not have Dropbox compatibility built in. They do, however, support iCloud and WebDAV.

## Transfer a Word Document to Your iPad via Dropbox

Once your primary computer and iPad are both linked to your Dropbox account, from your computer, you can use the Save As command within Microsoft Word, for example, to save the Word document within your Dropbox Public folder, just as you'd save a file to your hard drive or a USB thumb drive (as shown in Figure 9-5).

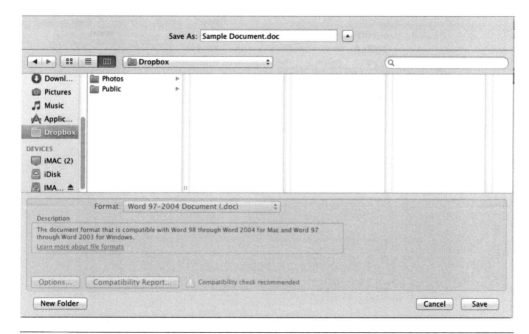

**FIGURE 9-5**   Use the Save As command (or equivalent) to save a file to a Dropbox folder.

The following steps apply to Microsoft Word documents, Excel spreadsheets, PowerPoint presentation files, and other documents or files that are compatible with apps on your iPad or iPhone. After the file from your computer, for example, is saved to your Dropbox account, follow these steps to import it into your iPad (or iPhone):

1. Launch the Dropbox app on your iPad (or iPhone).
2. Displayed at the bottom-left corner of the iPad screen when the Dropbox app is running are four command icons: Dropbox, Favorites, Uploads, and Settings. Tap the Dropbox icon (shown in Figure 9-6).
3. Tap the Public folder. Within the Public Folder, you'll see the Word document you just saved on your primary computer.
4. Tap the document name (as shown in Figure 9-7), and the file will be displayed on the right side of the iPad's screen.
5. To open the file within Pages, so you can edit, print, and share it, tap the Share icon displayed in the upper-right corner of the iPad's screen, and then tap the Open In...Pages command. (If you have another app that's capable of accessing and reading Word or Pages documents, it will be listed here.)

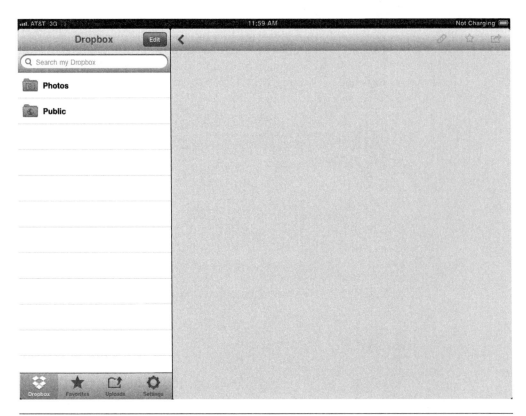

**FIGURE 9-6** Choose Dropbox's Public folder, or another folder, that holds the file you want to copy.

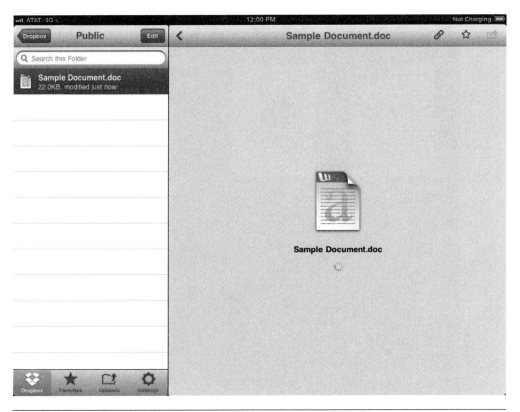

**FIGURE 9-7** Tap the filename on the left side of the iPad's screen to view it on the right.

6. Pages will then launch on your iPad, and the Word document (created on your primary computer that you just imported from Dropbox) will be listed on the Document Menu screen within Pages (as shown in Figure 9-8). Tap the thumbnail image of the document, and it will open within the Pages app. It will automatically be imported as a Pages-formatted document, even though it was created using Word. (Later, when you're exporting the file, you can change it back into a Word-formatted document.)

7. You can now read, edit, print, and share the Pages document using your iPad. If the app you're using to read the document is also compatible with Dropbox (such as Quickoffice Pro HD), you'll be able to tap the Share command within that app to send the revised document back to Dropbox, exported as a Word document or PDF file, for example.

This process for transferring a document to your iPad from Dropbox also works with other types of files that were created using the Mac version of Numbers or

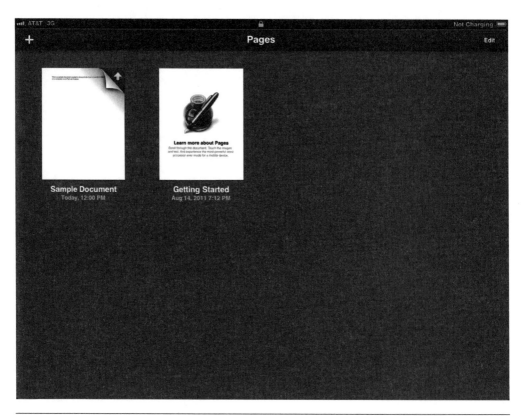

**FIGURE 9-8** The file imported from Dropbox will be displayed within the Document Menu screen of Pages on the iPad.

Microsoft Excel (on a PC or Mac) and/or the Mac version of Keynote or Microsoft PowerPoint (on a PC or Mac), for example. Plus, the same process can be used for transferring files from Dropbox to an iPhone.

**How to...** | **Use Dropbox to Store and Share Photos and Videos**

The Dropbox app for the iPhone or iPad allows you to upload picture and video files (not including copyrighted iTunes content) stored within the Photos app and share them via the Photos folder in Dropbox. To do this, launch the Dropbox app, tap the Uploads icon (displayed at the bottom of the screen), and then tap the plus sign icon displayed near the top-left area of the screen. Choose the photo(s) or video clip(s) you want to share via Dropbox by selecting them from your Photo Albums, and then at the bottom of the Photo Albums window, select the Dropbox folder.

# Manage Files Directly from Dropbox.com

From the Dropbox.com web site on any computer or mobile device, you can sign in and gain full access to your files, documents, and data. You can also create, move, or delete folders. Plus, you can create a Shared folder (or transform a regular folder into a Shared folder.)

You can use a Shared folder within Dropbox to share specific files or documents from your Dropbox account with other people.

When someone is granted access to one of your Shared folders, that folder name will appear within the person's Dropbox account as well, and the files within that folder will automatically sync to the person's computer or device, as well as to yours. Thus, when changes are made to files or documents stored within a Shared folder, those changes will be updated on all applicable computers and devices automatically, and almost instantaneously. All parties require their own Dropbox account.

When you transform a folder into a Shared folder, the people you invite to access that folder will gain access to all of that folder's contents. Keep in mind, however, you cannot share a subfolder within your Public folder. While anyone with access to the Shared folder can add, delete, or modify files within it, only the person who initially created the Shared folder can grant or retract other people's access to it.

In addition to accessing your Dropbox files from your primary computer using the Dropbox software, or from your mobile device using the Dropbox app, you can just as easily manage your files and folders from the main Dropbox web page. Here's how:

1. Launch your favorite web browser (such as Safari or Internet Explorer).
2. Using your web browser, enter the URL for Dropbox (**http://www.Dropbox.com**).
3. In the upper-right corner of the screen, click the Sign In option.
4. Sign in to your Dropbox account using your e-mail address and password.
5. To manage folders and files stored within your Dropbox account, click the Files tab displayed near the top-center of the screen (as shown in Figure 9-9).

From the main Dropbox.com web page, after you sign in, you will have access to each of your private and Shared folders that contain the files, documents, or data you have uploaded to the service. After clicking the Files tab displayed near the top-center of the screen, you can upload additional content to specific folders, create new folders, share a folder, show recently deleted files, download the contents of a folder to whatever computer you're currently using, or view a gallery of digital images stored within your Dropbox account.

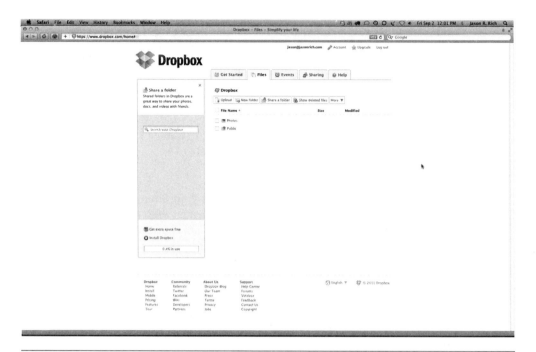

**FIGURE 9-9** You can manage your Dropbox account and access files from it directly from the Dropbox.com web site.

# Dropbox vs. iCloud: Similarities and Differences

In terms of features and functionality, here's a brief summary of what Dropbox and iCloud have in common, including redundancies in what they offer:

- Creating and using a Dropbox account is free of charge; however, for a fee, you can acquire more online storage space as needed.
- Dropbox allows you to create a reliable, secure, and password-protected backup of your important files, documents, data, and photos. The backup files are stored on a cloud-based server (in a remote location), rather than on your computer's hard drive or an external hard drive connected to your computer.
- Once files, documents, data, or photos, for example, are uploaded to your Dropbox account, you can access them from any other computer or mobile device that's also linked to that Dropbox account (using the same e-mail address and password).
- Dropbox compatibility is built into a growing number of third-party apps for the iPhone and iPad, allowing you to upload and download content directly from within those apps.

 If you want to collaborate on projects and share files, documents, photos, or data with people in other locations, and easily synchronize and/or transfer content between users, Dropbox makes this easy using the service's Share A Folder feature.

Although Dropbox and iCloud are both cloud-based file sharing services, both of which are feature-packed and extremely useful, they each offer some different features. Here's a brief summary of how Dropbox differs from iCloud, and why you might want to use one service as opposed to the other:

- Many of the data backup and synchronization features of iCloud are designed to work automatically, behind the scenes, after an iCloud account is set up. However, in most cases, content needs to be manually copied to a Dropbox folder before it gets synchronized to a Dropbox account (and other computers or devices linked to that account).
- Dropbox allows specific content stored within your Dropbox account to be shared easily with others, while iCloud allows you to share your iCloud-stored content only with computers or mobile devices linked to your specific iCloud account. The benefit to Dropbox is that you can have hundreds or thousands of files stored within your Dropbox account, but you can pick and choose one or more specific files or folders that you want to share with specific people, while keeping everything else private and secure.
- Dropbox is not compatible with Apple's iWork for iOS apps (Pages, Numbers, and Keynote), but it is compatible with a growing number of other third-party apps designed for the iPhone and iPad.
- iCloud can be used to manage your music and iTunes content library. Dropbox does not have this functionality.
- iCloud can automatically create a backup of your mobile device and save the files on iCloud. Dropbox does not offer this feature.
- iCloud can be used to sync specific data automatically from apps, such as Contacts and Calendar on your iOS mobile device, with your primary computer. Dropbox doesn't offer this feature.

 To access a current listing of Dropbox-compatible third-party software for Macs and PCs, as well as apps for the Apple iPhone, iPad, Windows Mobile, Blackberry, and Android mobile devices (including phones and tablets), visit https://www.dropbox.com/apps.

# Introduction to WebDAV

Another popular example of cloud-based file sharing functionality that can be used for sharing documents, data, files, and photos is WebDAV (also referred to as DAV). This functionality is also readily accessible by any PC or Mac that's connected to the Internet, as well as virtually any other mobile device, including the iPhone and iPad.

WebDAV stands for Web-based Distributed Authoring and Versioning. It allows you to access, edit, and manage files that are stored on a remote server (as opposed to on the hard drive within your primary computer, for example). Like Dropbox, WebDAV can be used for file sharing and collaboration between two or more people. In the process of collaboration, WebDAV prevents older versions of files from being overwritten and makes the most current revisions or versions of a document or file readily available to everyone collaborating on its creation or modification. Unlike iCloud or Dropbox, WebDAV is open-source, meaning that it's not owned or operated by any one company and is available for free. Software developers are free to include WebDAV compatibility into their software or apps for free, and without limitation.

In addition to iCloud, Apple's iWork for iOS apps (Pages, Numbers, and Keynote for the iPhone and iPad) are fully compatible with WebDAV. Thus, WebDAV can be used for easily synchronizing and transferring files among computers and devices that are linked to the same WebDAV account and server.

 Because WebDAV is open source, it is not owned or hosted by any particular company. Thus, to use it, you'll need access to a remote server that supports WebDAV. Many companies that have their own cloud-based file sharing functionality are WebDAV-compatible. Apple's now defunct MobileMe service offered iDisk, which was WebDAV-compatible. However, MobileMe has been replaced by iCloud, and the MobileMe service will be discontinued altogether in June 2012. iCloud is also WebDAV-compatible.

The features and functionality you can access when using WebDAV as a remote backup, file sharing, or file collaboration tool will depend entirely on the software (or app) you're using to access your WebDAV account and server.

You can sign up for a free WebDAV-compatible hosting service using OffSiteBox .com (https://offsitebox.com), which supplies the off-site server and online storage space needed to use WebDAV. OffSiteBox.com is just one example of a service that's available on the Web that offers WebDAV compatibility to individuals and small businesses. A basic OffSiteBox.com account includes 1GB of free online storage space that can be upgraded for a monthly fee. For example, 10GB of online storage through OffSiteBox.com is priced at $4.95 per month, or 100GB of online storage is priced at $34.95 per month. Many website hosting services, for example, also offer WebDAV hosting for a monthly fee.

 Using WebDAV in conjunction with a fee-based WebDAV hosting service is ideal for file sharing or collaboration with multiple users if your own network doesn't offer this functionality.

# Copy a File or Document from Your Primary Computer to Your iPhone or iPad

Using your iPhone or iPad, launch the third-party app that's WebDAV-compatible and into which you want to upload a file or document. For example, the iWork for iOS apps allow you to access a WebDAV account to import files or documents into Pages, Numbers, and/or Keynote.

To import a Word or Pages document into your iPhone or iPad, for example, do the following:

1. Launch Pages on your iOS mobile device.
2. From the main Document Menu screen that appears when you launch the Pages app, tap the plus sign icon in the upper-left corner of the screen.
3. Next, tap the Copy From WebDAV icon in the little window that appears (as shown in Figure 9-10).
4. You'll need to sign into your WebDAV account. To do this, enter the appropriate WebDAV server address, as well as your user name and password.
5. The Pages app (or any of the iWork for iOS apps) will then display all compatible documents or files that can be imported directly into your iPhone or iPad from your WebDAV account. Tap a file thumbnail to import and load it, in this case, into Pages.

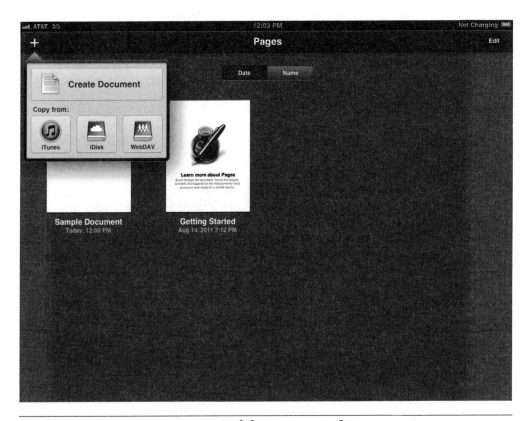

**FIGURE 9-10**   You can import a Word document sent from your primary computer via a WebDAV-compatible cloud-based file sharing service.

## Transfer and Share a File or Document from Your iPhone or iPad to WebDAV

You can also transfer and share files or documents from your iPhone or iPad to WebDAV as you're working with an iPhone or iPad app that's compatible with WebDAV, such as Pages, Numbers, or Keynote.

1. From the main Document Menu of one of these apps, tap the Edit icon in the upper-right corner of the screen.
2. When the thumbnails that represent your individual files or documents start to shake, tap the file(s) that you want to export from your iPhone or iPad to your WebDAV account. A yellow box will appear around the file's thumbnail.
3. Tap the Share icon in the upper-left corner of the screen, and choose the Copy To WebDAV option.
4. If you haven't already done so, you'll need to sign in to your WebDAV account by entering the server address, user name and password that's associated with your account. You will then be prompted to choose an export file format, such as Pages, Numbers, or Keynote (for Mac); Microsoft Word, Excel or PowerPoint; or PDF. The file you selected will be uploaded from your iPhone or iPad to your WebDAV account, where it can then be accessed by other computers or mobile devices.

**How to...** ## Choose a File Sharing Service

You might find it advantageous to use iCloud for many of its features and functions, but also use a service such as Dropbox, for example, when you want to share or collaborate with others (as opposed to syncing files or data on multiple computers and/or devices linked to your iCloud account).

Keeping in mind that iCloud is free and is fully integrated into iOS X Lion as well as iOS 5 (for iPhone and iPad), if you opt to use another cloud-based file sharing service for the purpose of backing up, synchronizing or sharing documents and files, choose a service that offers the functionality you need and that's offered for free or at a competitive price.

# 10

# Cloud-Based Music Service Alternatives to iCloud

**HOW TO...**

- Manage your digital music library using cloud-based options other than iCloud.
- Use Amazon Cloud Drive, Amazon MP3, and Amazon Cloud Player.
- Use Google Music.
- Differentiate between iCloud and other cloud-based music management options, including Spotify and Sony's Music Unlimited.

As you learned back in Chapter 1, Apple's iCloud isn't the only cloud-based file sharing service in the virtual sky. In fact, depending on what you're trying to accomplish using cloud-based computing technology, you'll find a wide range of options. Many of the available cloud-based file sharing services are designed to handle specific tasks, such as serving as a remote online backup and storage solution for your important data and files, or allowing you to share documents, files, and data among multiple computers, devices, and/or users.

Cloud-based computing has also proven itself to be invaluable when it comes to managing a digital music collection, especially if you want to access your favorite tunes on your primary computer, laptop computer, mobile phone, tablet, and/or home theater system.

 **Note** When it comes to managing your music library, Apple's iCloud works in conjunction with all of your iTunes purchases. If you want the service to manage all of your digital music, including songs not acquired from iTunes, you'll need to pay for Apple's premium iTunes Match service ($24.99 per year). Details about iTunes Match can be found in Chapter 6.

## Did You Know?

## Using iCloud Has Its Benefits

For Mac OS and iOS users, the biggest benefit to using iCloud instead of another cloud-based file sharing service is that it is fully integrated with Mac OS X Lion and the iOS for the iPhone, iPad, and iPod Touch. So in addition to iCloud's wide range of functions, many of its features work automatically and entirely in the background. Thus, the latest versions or revisions of your files, data, documents, photos, and music, for example, are always accessible when you want or need them, regardless of what Apple equipment you're using.

iCloud also works seamlessly with iTunes and the iTunes Store, so all of your purchased content (including music, television show episodes, movies, music videos, podcasts, and so on) are automatically downloaded to the computer or device on which they're purchased. They're also saved to your iCloud account, so that content becomes accessible from any other computer or iOS device that's linked to your account.

This allows you to purchase a song on your iPhone, for example, but enjoy listening to it on your Mac or on your home theater system via Apple TV, without having to repurchase that song multiple times or manually copy and transfer it to each of your computers and devices.

As an Apple user, however, you have options for purchasing, using, and storing digital music other than the iTunes Store, the iTunes software (and/or app), and iCloud. In fact, a growing number of options are offered by some of Apple's biggest and most powerful competitors, including Amazon.com and Google. Using these alternative services, you can purchase music, manage your personal digital music library, stream music from the Web, and make your music collection available on all of your Internet-connected computers and mobile devices, without using Apple's iTunes or iCloud.

Remember, however, that not only does Apple's iCloud allow you to manage your digital music library, but it also has a wide range of other uses designed primarily for Apple Mac and iOS device users. This functionality is not built into the services offered by iCloud's competitors, especially those that were designed exclusively for digital music management.

The iCloud alternatives featured in this chapter, as well as the many others offered on the Internet, are ideal for people who have an already established and vast digital music collection from a variety of sources (including several different online music stores and by "ripping" their own audio CDs and transforming their content into digital audio files).

# The Benefits of Keeping Your Music in the Cloud

Without using a cloud-based service to manage your music, every song you maintain in your personal music library as a digital file takes up space on your computer's hard drive or within the storage medium built into your mobile device. A single song file saved in the popular MP3 format is between 3MB and 5MB in size. If only a few songs are stored on your computer, you really don't need to worry about filling up your available storage with music files.

However, if your music library consists of 5000, 10,000 or 20,000 songs, now you're talking about needing a significant amount of storage space for that digital music library (which probably won't even fit on your mobile phone or MP3 player). For example, an Apple iPod Touch (with 8GB of memory) will hold approximately 1750 songs assuming no other content is stored within it (such as apps or data).

By storing your digital music library on a cloud-based service, as long as your computer or mobile device is connected to the Web, you'll have immediate access to an unlimited number of songs that you own or acquire the rights to listen to, without using up any storage space on your computer or mobile device. Some of the cloud-based services used for music management will stream the songs you want to hear but won't permanently store those music files on your computer or mobile device, unless you set up this option for offline listening (when no Internet connection is available). When it first launched in October 2011, music streaming was not yet possible using iCloud.

 Whether you opt to use iCloud or another cloud-based service to manage your digital music library, choose only one service. Otherwise, you could wind up with music spread out over multiple and incompatible services, and you might not be able to find or access particular songs when and where you want them. Determine which computers or devices you want to use to access your music. Also, determine what's involved in converting your audio CD library into digital form, so those songs can become accessible via the cloud-based service you opt to use.

# Amazon.com Cloud-Based Services

Many people know Amazon.com as the massive online retailer. Amazon started off as an online-based bookstore, but it has expanded its service by offering a wide range of other products. Since its launch in July 1995, Amazon.com has become the world's most successful online retailer, which now sells everything from books, movies, music, and games, to electronics, computers, toys, jewelry, and sporting goods.

With its line of Kindle eBook readers and tablets, Amazon.com has also been a pioneer in distributing and selling eBooks and allowing those digital books to be read on state-of-the-art, but highly affordable eBook readers (as well as many other devices).

 If you're already a Kindle eBook reader user, you can use the free Kindle app to read Kindle-formatted eBooks on your iPhone, iPad, or iPod touch.

Recently, Amazon.com has launched three cloud-based services that work seamlessly together. When combined, these services offer much of the same features and functionality offered by iCloud, but they are available to PC and Mac users, as well as users of many different mobile devices.

- **Amazon Cloud Drive**   This cloud-based file sharing service can be used by PC and Mac users as well as mobile device users to back up and share all types of data, documents, files, photos, videos, and music. It works much like Dropbox (described in Chapter 9) and offers many of the same file-sharing and syncing features offered by iCloud.
- **Amazon Cloud Player for the Web**   When it comes to experiencing your music on a wide range of computers and devices, Amazon Cloud Player for the Web allows you to use your web browser to access any of the music content that's stored within your Amazon Cloud Drive account, and then play it on whatever device or computer you happen to be using. This is a browser-based digital music player. Specialized software and apps are also available for PCs, Macs, and many mobile devices for accessing and managing your digital music library that's stored online using the Amazon Cloud Drive service.
- **Amazon MP3**   Designed to compete with Apple's iTunes Store, the Amazon MP3 store sells digital music from most of the major record labels, recording artists, and music groups (including unsigned and independent artists, and those represented by small, independent record labels). Like the iTunes Store, Amazon MP3 offers an ever-growing collection of music for sale in the form of individual songs or complete albums, often at highly competitive prices. The music you purchase from Amazon MP3 will work on any MP3 digital music player, including computers, mobile phones, iPods, tablets, and other devices.

# What Amazon.com's Cloud Drive Offers

When you set up a free Amazon Cloud Drive account, it includes 5GB of online storage space that you can use to store your files, data, documents, photos, videos, and music. All files that are saved to Amazon's Cloud Drive are stored on Amazon .com's secure servers. If you opt to shop for your digital music using Amazon MP3, all of those purchases will automatically be stored within your Amazon Cloud Drive account, and the additional online storage space required for those purchases is provided for free.

For storing your personal files, data, documents, photos, videos, and personal music library, if you require more than the free 5GB of online storage space, additional (and secure) online storage space can be purchased for an annual fee. As you can see from the following chart, Amazon.com's pricing for online storage space related to its cloud-based file sharing service is extremely competitive.

| Additional Storage Space | Amazon.com Price* | Apple iCloud Price** |
| --- | --- | --- |
| 5GB | Free | Free |
| 20GB | $20 per year | $40 per year |
| 50GB | $50 per year | $100 per year |
| 100GB | $100 per year | N/A |
| 200GB | $200 per year | N/A |
| 500GB | $500 per year | N/A |
| 1000GB | $1000 per year | N/A |

*Prices are subject to change, but all include unlimited additional online storage space for music purchased from the Amazon MP3 store.
**Prices are subject to change, but all include unlimited additional online storage space for all iTunes Store, iBookstore, Newsstand, Mac App Store, and iOS App Store purchases.

A single Amazon Cloud Drive account can be used by up to eight different computers and/or compatible mobile devices that are linked to the same account. For managing your digital music library, Amazon Cloud Drive works seamlessly with Amazon Cloud Player for the Web, as well as with other Amazon Cloud Player software applications and apps. However, the service can also be used for backing up, sharing, or syncing photos, videos, documents, and other data.

To set up a free Amazon Cloud Drive account, visit www.amazon.com/clouddrive from any computer or device that's connected to the Internet. If you already have an Amazon.com account (used for shopping), that same account allows you to create a free Amazon Cloud Drive account using the same e-mail address and password.

## Set Up a Free Amazon Cloud Drive Account

If you don't yet have an Amazon.com account set up, from the sign-in screen (at www.amazon.com/clouddrive), enter the e-mail address you want to associate with the account, and then select the No, I Am A New Consumer option when prompted for your password (as shown in Figure 10-1).

Next, click the Sign In Using Our Secure Server icon. From the new account Registration screen (shown in Figure 10-2), you'll be prompted to enter your full name, e-mail address (twice), and your mobile phone number (optional). You'll then be asked to create a custom password for the new account and enter it twice. Click the Create Account icon to continue.

**FIGURE 10-1** You can set up a free Amazon Cloud Drive Account in just minutes.

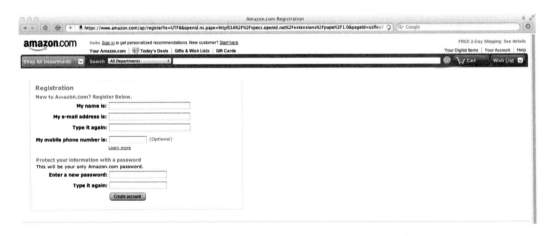

**FIGURE 10-2** Supply the information requested on the Registration screen to set up your Amazon Cloud Drive account.

The main Amazon Cloud Drive screen (shown in Figure 10-3) appears next, where you can begin uploading your files.

## Managing Your Amazon Cloud Drive Account

Unless you're using specialized software or an app to access your Amazon Cloud Drive account, the main way to upload and then access the files, documents, data, photos, videos, and music stored on this service is via your web browser (by visiting www.amazon.com/clouddrive). The main Amazon Cloud Drive screen allows you to view all files currently stored on the cloud-based service. Or you can opt to view just the files you've manually uploaded yourself, or just the music files purchased from

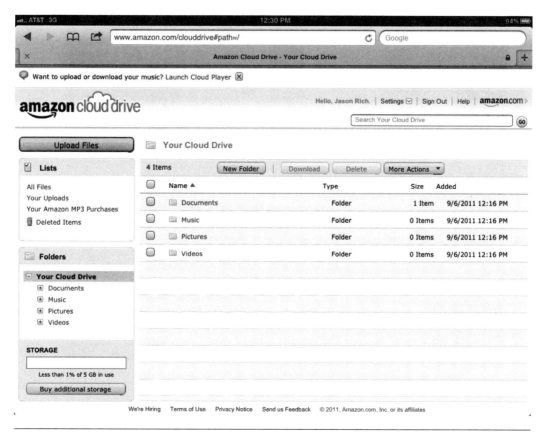

**FIGURE 10-3**    The Amazon Cloud Drive screen can be accessed from any device using a web browser (shown here on an iPad 2, but it looks identical on a Mac or PC, for example).

Amazon MP3. As you're viewing files stored on the service, you can manually transfer any of them to the device you're currently using or delete them from your Amazon Cloud Drive account.

To make it easier to organize your files, your Amazon Cloud Drive account provides four main default folders: Documents, Music, Pictures, and Videos. Within each of these main folders, you can create an unlimited number of subfolders and/or store an unlimited number of files (based on the storage capacity limit for your account).

**How to...    Access Your Amazon Cloud Drive Account**

To see a listing of the files you have stored on your Amazon Cloud Drive account, access the options displayed on the left side of the main Amazon Cloud Drive screen when you visit www.amazon.com/clouddrive and have signed into your account (Figure 10-3).

To view the various folders within your Amazon Cloud Drive account (and see their contents), use the Folders options displayed on the left side of the main Amazon Cloud Drive screen when you visit www.amazon.com/clouddrive and sign into your account.

 Displayed in the lower-left corner of the main Amazon Cloud Drive screen is a Storage meter that graphically depicts how much of your available online storage space is currently being utilized. When you first open your account, below this graphic meter will be a message that says, "0% of 5GB in use." As you upload files to store on Amazon Cloud Drive, you will use some of your available storage space.

When you're ready to begin manually uploading files to Amazon Cloud Drive, simply click the Upload Files icon that's displayed in several places on the main screen. Uploading files is a two-step process, which the service will walk you through using easy-to-understand pop-up windows and prompts. First, choose which Amazon Cloud Drive folder to which you want to upload the files, and then select the specific files from your computer or mobile device that you want to upload. Keep in mind that the maximum file size for an individual file is 2GB.

 Although you can download certain types of files from Amazon Cloud Drive to your iOS device (such as your iPhone or iPad), it is not currently possible to upload files from your iOS device to Amazon Cloud Drive. This could change if third-party app developers incorporate Amazon Cloud Drive functionality into their apps.

After a file has been uploaded to a specific main folder or subfolder that you create, it will be accessible from any computer or device from which you access your Amazon Cloud Drive account. As you view various files online, you'll see Action Buttons associated with them. These Action Buttons allow you to perform specific tasks with a single click, such as create a new folder, download the file, delete the file, rename the file, or copy the file. You can also click the file to view it if it's a document, PDF file, or photo, for example.

 To listen to your digital music stored within your Amazon Cloud Drive account, whether you've uploaded the MP3 file or purchased it from Amazon MP3, you'll use the Amazon Cloud Player, which is accessible from Amazon.com's website (www.amazon.com/mp3). For your Android-compatible mobile device, be sure to download the free Amazon Cloud Player for Android app. There's also a free Amazon Cloud Player app available for Blackberry mobile devices and for the Kindle Fire tablet.

**How to...** **Purchase Additional Online Storage Space As Needed**

To purchase additional online storage on the Amazon Cloud Drive service, click the Buy Additional Storage icon that's displayed in the lower-left corner of the main Amazon Cloud Drive screen.

### You Can Listen to Amazon MP3 Music Purchases on Your iOS Device

Your Amazon MP3 purchases, as well as any music stored within your Amazon Cloud Drive account, are accessible from your Apple iPad or iPhone. Use Safari on your iOS mobile device to access the Amazon MP3 store, Amazon Cloud Player, and/or Amazon Cloud Drive service. No special app is required, but your iOS device must be connected to the Internet using a 3G or Wi-Fi connection.

In terms of your digital music files, you can stream them from your Amazon Cloud Drive account (so no storage space is used on your computer or mobile device to store the music files), or you can opt to download songs to your computer or compatible mobile device, and store them there, so the song(s) will be accessible even when you don't have access to the Internet.

## Using Amazon Cloud Player

Once you have added music to your digital music library that's stored within your Amazon Cloud Player account, use the Amazon Cloud Player to listen to your music and create customized playlists. From the Amazon Cloud Player (shown in Figure 10-4), you can also download music files that you own to your PC, Mac, or Android mobile device. It is not currently possible to download music files from Amazon Cloud Player (or Amazon MP3 Store) directly to your iPhone, iPad, or iPod touch.

To access the Amazon Cloud Player, point your web browser to www.amazon .com/gp/dmusic/mp3/player, or from the main Amazon Cloud Drive screen, click the Launch Cloud Player option that's displayed in the upper-left corner.

From the main Amazon Cloud Player screen, you can upload your own digital music (MP3 files) to your Amazon Cloud Drive account or access the Amazon MP3 store (shown in Figure 10-5) to purchase music. On the left side of the screen, you can view your Cloud Drive music categorized by songs, albums, artists, or genres. You can also view your latest purchases or latest uploads, and then create a new playlist by clicking on the Create New Playlist option and manually selecting which of your songs you want to add to that playlist.

After highlighting Playlists, Albums, or individual songs from the main area of the screen, use the music controls (displayed in the lower-left corner) to play, rewind, or fast-forward your music. You can also adjust the volume, put songs in auto repeat mode, and/or shuffle your song list or playlist using on-screen icons.

Because Amazon Cloud Player pulls music from your Amazon Cloud Drive account (on the Internet), the songs and playlists you create on one computer or device will always be accessible on any computer or device from which you later access Amazon Cloud Player.

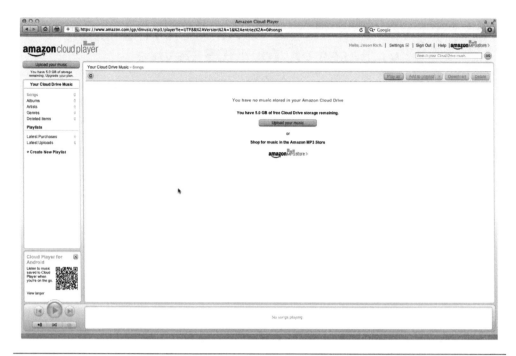

**FIGURE 10-4** Amazon Cloud Player is a web-based digital music player that you access using your web browser.

**FIGURE 10-5** The main screen of the Amazon MP3 store, from which you can find and purchase music.

# Acquiring Music from the Amazon MP3 Store

Designed to offer an alternative to purchasing and downloading music from Apple's iTunes Store, the Amazon MP3 store offers an ever-growing library of music (comprising more than 18 million individual songs). As with iTunes, songs can be purchased individually, or you can purchase an entire album with a single click of the mouse. Your purchases will be downloaded to the PC, Mac, or Android mobile device on which they were purchased, and they'll be stored within your Amazon Cloud Drive account.

When you access the main Amazon MP3 store using your web browser from any computer or device, you'll first need to sign into your account. You'll then be able to search for and purchase new music.

One reason to purchase music from Amazon MP3 as opposed to iTunes is lower prices. A best-selling single typically sells for between $.69 and $1.29 on Amazon MP3, while on iTunes, that same song will be priced between $.99 and $1.29. Some full albums are priced as low as $5.00 on Amazon MP3.

As you begin exploring the offerings of Amazon MP3, you'll discover the service offers some exclusive music (not found on iTunes). However, iTunes also offers exclusive music not accessible from Amazon MP3 or other services. On both services, you'll be able to preview and purchase music from many of the most popular record labels and recording artists from the past and present. The music that's available spans across many music genres.

# Amazon's Cloud-Based Offerings vs. iCloud Offerings

When you begin exploring the features and functions offered by Amazon's cloud-based services, you'll discover many similarities between these services and those from Apple's iCloud. There are, however, some major differences.

Apple's iCloud service is designed to work with your Mac or PC, in conjunction with your iOS mobile devices, and when it comes to managing music, iCloud requires that you use the iTunes software (or app) as well as the iTunes Store to make music purchases. To manage all of your music, including purchases from sources other than iTunes, you'll need to upgrade to the iTunes Match premium service for $24.99 per year.

Music purchased from Amazon MP3 cannot be directly saved on an Apple iOS device or downloaded from your Amazon Cloud Drive account. To transfer music to your iOS device, you'll still need to use iTunes to import MP3 files not purchased through iTunes (and/or use the iTunes Match service). Music can, however, be streamed on your iOS device from Amazon Cloud Player.

## Amazon.com's Online-Based Music Services and Cloud Services Are Nicely Integrated

You can begin using Amazon MP3 and Amazon Cloud Player in conjunction with your free Amazon Cloud Drive account without having to purchase any new music by taking advantage of the free "Artists on the Rise" and "Free Songs & Special Deals" music downloads available from Amazon MP3. The free offerings change weekly and can introduce you to up-and-coming artists. To find these free music downloads, from the main Amazon MP3 store screen, click the Free Music From Rising Artists or Free Songs & Special Deals option. Both are displayed along the left side of the screen, under the Popular Features and Categories headings, respectively. The Artists on the Rise screen is shown in the following illustration.

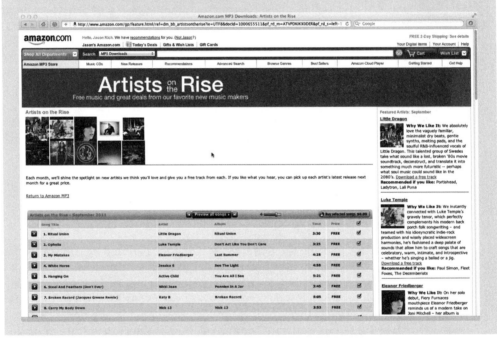

The file sharing and data synchronization features offered by iCloud happen automatically, in the background, among Macs and iOS devices. All file transfers using Amazon's cloud-based services occur manually. However, if you own or use a combination of PCs, Macs, iOS devices, and/or other mobile devices (such as Android or Blackberry devices), you might find it easier to manage files and music using Amazon's cloud-based offerings as opposed to iCloud. Whether you should use Apple's iCloud or Amazon's cloud-based services is a personal decision, based on what features and functionality you need and will find useful, as well as what computer systems and mobile devices you'll be sharing music and other information with.

**Did You Know?**

## In the Cloud, Sharing Files Between Users Isn't Always Easy

At the time of launch, neither iCloud nor Amazon Cloud Drive allowed for easy file sharing or collaboration among several users, without giving other users full access to your entire iCloud or Amazon Cloud Drive account. For online-based collaborations and file sharing with other people, the Dropbox file sharing service (or a similar service) will be most useful. iCloud and Amazon Cloud Drive are ideal for wirelessly sharing your own files and data between several of your own computers and/or mobile devices via the web.

# Google Music Cloud-Based Music Management

If you look at the actions of Apple, Microsoft, Amazon.com, Google, and many other media companies, it's clear that the future of computing lies in cloud-based file sharing services when it comes to managing, transferring, and synchronizing data, documents, files, photos, and music. In keeping up with this fast-evolving and growing trend, Google has also launched a cloud-based music service that is compatible with PCs, Macs, and a wide range of Android-compatible mobile devices.

As of late 2011, the Google Music service (also referred to as Music by Google) was still in its beta-testing stage and wasn't yet available to the general public. However, based on product announcements and online demos, the Google Music service could become a major player in the battle for domination within the cloud-based music management genre of personal computing.

At least initially, the Google Music service is available for free. This includes an account with enough online storage space to hold 20,000 songs. Since Google Music does not sell music, you're free to shop for music using any service, or you can rip your own music CDs and then upload the MP3 files to enjoy listening to them via the Google Music service.

**Note**   To access the Google Music service and set up a free account, visit http://music .google.com using a web browser from any computer or mobile device. To view a free YouTube video that explains more about Google Music, visit www.youtube .com/watch?v=ZrNhKcxBbZo.

Via the free Google Music Manager software for PC or Mac (shown in Figure 10-6), the Google Music service allows you to create an online-based personal music library comprising up to 20,000 songs that you acquire from any source, including your existing iTunes library. These music files are stored on the Goggle Music cloud-based service (for free) and become accessible on any computer, tablet, or mobile phone that's connected to the Internet.

**FIGURE 10-6** Use the Google Music Manager software on your PC or Mac (or the Android app) to build your online music library, which you can then enjoy from the browser-based Music Player.

The service also allows you to create personalized playlists and access those playlists from any device or computer. You can enjoy your favorite music pretty much anytime and anywhere, without first having to copy or transfer each song to a particular computer or device.

 The benefit of storing your music online with a cloud-based music service such as Google Music is that you need to purchase a song or album only once, but it is available to you on any computer or mobile device you own or use, without your having to repurchase the same content multiple times or manually transfer that content to each computer or device. You can also purchase your music from any source on the Web. You're not limited to one online music store, such as Amazon MP3 or the iTunes Store.

You can access your Google Music account and listen to your music using the browser-based Google Music Player (shown in Figure 10-7), which can be accessed from any device that's connected to the Internet, and stream your music from the cloud-based service to your computer or mobile device. For Android-compatible mobile devices, a free app is available from the Android Market.

When your computer or device is not connected to the Internet, you can pre-download specific songs, albums, and/or playlists to your computer or mobile device for offline listening. If you need help creating a playlist, the service will access details about your existing music library and then automatically create a 25-song customized

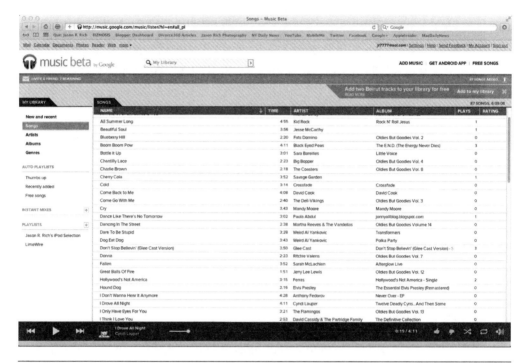

**FIGURE 10-7**    Use the browser-based Google Music Player to listen to your music stored on the cloud-based Google Music service.

playlist it deems appropriate. To do this, use the Instant Mixes feature that's built into the Google Music Player.

If you're already managing your digital music library with iTunes, you can easily upload your entire iTunes library to Google Music (including your playlists), and then access that music library from any device or computer without needing iTunes.

As you're using the Google Music Player, you can sort your song library by song title, artist, album title, or music genre. You can also assign a "thumbs up" or "thumbs down" to songs and manage your playlists from the command options available on the left side of the screen.

 Using Google's Magnifier feature, which is part of the Google Music service, you can access new music for free, plus watch exclusive artist interviews and live performances.

One of the fun features of Google Music is the Free Music option. Click it to access an ever-changing selection of free music from well-known artists that you can add to your Google Music account with a click of the mouse. After choosing a music genre, your web browser will display a current listing of free music from which you can choose. Just click the Add Free Music icon, and that free music will be added to your personal music library that's accessible from the Google Music Player.

As Google Music gets introduced to the general public in 2012, it will no doubt become popular among computer enthusiasts who already rely heavily on Google's other online services, as well as people who use Android-based mobile devices (as opposed to iOS devices, such as the iPhone, iPad, or iPod Touch). The Google Music service, like similar services, will also evolve over time.

# Other Music-Oriented Cloud Services

Keeping your digital music library stored on a cloud-based service makes a lot of sense, especially if you want to access that music from several different computers and/or devices, or you don't want to take up space on your computer or mobile device to store your music library. If you have only a few dozen songs or several hundred songs to store on your iPhone, iPod touch, or iPad, for example, it is easy to do and doesn't take up much space. However, if your personal music library consists of thousands of songs, you're now talking about a lot of required storage space if you want immediate access to your entire music library without using a cloud-based service.

## Spotify Music Streaming Option

Spotify is yet another cloud-based music service which recently launched in the United States after achieving immense popularity in Europe (with more than 10 million users). This service offers on-demand access to more than 15 million songs that you can listen to online (by streaming it from Spotify's cloud-based servers or by downloading individual songs that you own to your digital music player). The service, like so many others, allows you to create and manage personal playlists, plus you can share playlists with others using Spotify (by accessing websites such as www.ShareMyPlaylists.com and www.SpotiSeek.com). To set up a Spotify account and begin using this service, visit www.Spotify.com.

One nice feature of Spotify is that the service nicely integrates with Twitter, Facebook, Short Message Service (SMS), and e-mail, so you can recommend music to others and easily share links to your favorite tunes.

When it launched in the United States in mid-2011, Spotify offered three tiers of service. Spotify Free is an advertiser-supported service that allows you to stream music you already own from the Spotify cloud-based service and listen to that music on your computers and/or mobile devices. Using this service and setting up an account is free, but you need to agree to view ads on your computer or mobile device's screen in conjunction with using the service, plus you need to share details about Spotify with your friends via Facebook.

With a few limitations, the Spotify Free service allows you to listen to the service's entire music collection, but you'll be subjected to ads. You can upgrade to a paid service to avoid the ads. Paid subscribers can use the Spotify mobile app to download, store, and play favorite songs and playlists even when no Internet connection is available.

Spotify Unlimited ($4.99 per month) offers ad-free access to the service's library of 15 million songs, which you can stream and listen to from the cloud-based service. The Spotify Premium Service ($9.99 per month) allows you to stream music or download music to your computer or mobile device on an unlimited basis.

Once you set up a Spotify account, your music preferences and playlists are all stored online, so when you access the account from any computer or device, your customizations and personal music selections and playlists are always at your fingertips. In addition to having a powerful search feature for finding new music (or music that's new to you), the Artist Radio feature offers a dedicated radio stream that will introduce you to new music. There's also a Related Artists feature that examines your musical preferences and then suggests additional music you might like (which is a feature similar to iTunes' Genius).

Unlike many of the other cloud-based music services featured within this book, Spotify does not require you to purchase music before you can stream it from the Web and listen to it. The monthly fee associated with your Spotify account includes unlimited access to the service's entire music library for streaming purposes from any of your computers or mobile services.

 To help you enjoy Spotify on your iPhone, iPad, or iPod touch, be sure to download the free Spotify app for iPhone (which also works with other iOS devices). It's available from the App Store. You'll need to download the free Spotify software on a Mac or PC to use this service with your computer.

## Music Unlimited Cloud-Based Music Service

Yet another cloud-based solution for managing your music is Music Unlimited from Sony Entertainment Network (www.sonyentertainmentnetwork.com/music-unlimited). This service offers a library of more than 10 million songs that you can access and stream from your cloud-based Music Unlimited account to a compatible computer or device, including a Sony PS3 video game system, an Android-compatible mobile device, a Sony Bravia television, or any computer with access to the Web.

Music Unlimited has two plans. The Basic plan ($3.99 per month) allows you to stream music to multiple computers and devices, sync music, and access the service's basic music channels. A Premium plan ($9.99 per month) offers access to premium music channels, and the ability to create and edit playlists and maintain a personalized music library.

 Although Music Unlimited is compatible with Macs, it does not currently work with iOS mobile devices, such as an iPhone or iPod touch.

# More Options

If you explore the Web, you'll find other cloud-based music services similar to those described here, offered by many different companies. Even though this aspect of cloud-based computing is still in its infancy, several major corporate players, including Walmart, for example, have already entered and then quickly exited the online music sales and distribution business. In the months and years to come, cloud-based music services will continue to evolve.

As the music industry (including the major and independent record labels) plays catch-up and adapts its music sales model from selling physical CDs in retail stores to selling digital content via the Web in this digital era, we'll no doubt see new and exciting ways to acquire, experience, and share digital music via the Web in conjunction with a wide range of devices, computers, home theater systems, mobile phones, tablets, video game consoles, and car audio systems. Many, if not all of these music distribution methods, will likely be cloud-based in the foreseeable future.

# 11

# The Microsoft 365 and Google Docs Alternatives to iCloud

**HOW TO...**

- Collaborate with others on work-related documents and presentations via the Web.
- Access all of your documents and files via the Web on any computer or device.
- Utilize online-based software to get your work done from any device linked to the Web.

One of the more useful features of iCloud is its ability to back up and sync automatically all of your iWork for Mac and iWork for iOS files, granting you immediate access to any related document or file, from any compatible device, at any time.

Although iCloud makes your iWork and Microsoft Office files available to all of your computers and mobile devices via the Web, it's not currently ideal for collaborating with other people or for sharing specific files with devices not already linked to your iCloud account. Utilizing cloud-based computing technologies, both Microsoft and Google offer browser-based applications, as well as document and file management, which is

 **iCloud Offers Its "Documents in the Cloud" Feature**

The document management capabilities of iCloud also allow you to share and sync Microsoft Office documents and files, including Word documents, PowerPoint presentations, and Excel spreadsheet files, if you first upload them to iWork.com or import them into one of the iWork for Mac or iWork for iOS applications. How to do this is explained in Chapter 8. Apple refers to this feature as "Documents in the Cloud."

## There's No Need to Install Specialized Software

Instead of your having to install software on your computer, a browser-based app is accessed from your computer or mobile device using its web browser and operates within the browser when you are connected to the Internet. The benefit to using browser-based apps and storing files and documents on a cloud-based system is that there are, theoretically, far fewer compatibility issues between PCs, Macs, and mobile devices. The potential drawback is that a web connection is always needed to use the online-based app to access your files and data.

designed around the concept of online collaboration with other people, while also giving you access to specific applications and related data from any device that's connected to the Internet.

**Note** Web-based or browser-based apps sometimes run slower than traditional software and offer fewer features than their traditional software counterparts.

Both Microsoft and Google have been pioneers in combining cloud-computing technology with browser-based applications that offer word processing, spreadsheet management, digital slide show presentation capabilities, and other applications in an online environment that can be used by one person on multiple devices or by multiple users on multiple devices. Currently, iCloud does not utilize browser-based applications, but its iWork software for Mac and iWork for iOS apps are fully compatible with iCloud in terms of backing up and syncing documents, data, and files. (Using iWork with iCloud is covered in Chapter 8.) Many third-party software and iOS app developers have also begun including iCloud compatibility into their software and apps.

As a reminder, Apple's suite of iWork apps comprises Pages (a word processor compatible with Word), Numbers (a spreadsheet management program compatible with Excel) and Keynote (for creating and presenting digital slide shows, compatible with PowerPoint). All three applications are available for both the Mac and iOS devices (iPhone, iPad, and iPod touch).

# Microsoft Takes to the Cloud with Office 365

In mid-2011, Microsoft released Microsoft Office 365, a cloud-based version of its popular Office suite of applications. Office 365 is designed to allow groups to communicate and collaborate easily online using already familiar Microsoft applications. In addition to offering browser-based applications, including Word, PowerPoint, Excel, OneNote, and Outlook, Office 365 has integrated instant messaging, e-mail, and scheduling.

You can also use it to host virtual meetings, so people at different locations can connect, communicate, share information, and collaborate using a PC, Mac, or almost any mobile device that connects to the web.

Microsoft Office 365 is an example of cloud computing in which the software and all related files, data, and documents are stored on web-based servers. No software, except for a web browser, is needed to access, create, or edit Microsoft Office–compatible documents or files while you're online. However, to work offline, you will still need to have Microsoft Office (or compatible) software running on your computer or mobile device, and you must remember to download the needed files or documents from Office 365 to your computer or mobile device.

To make Office 365 affordable and accessible to entrepreneurs, small business operators, and major corporations alike, a variety of service plans are available, ranging in price from $2 to $27 per user, per month. For the average small business operator or entrepreneur, a comprehensive Office 365 subscription plan is available for $6 per month, per user.

 A free, 30-day trial of Microsoft Office 365 is available by accessing www.office365 .com. You can also register online and begin using Office 365 within minutes from this web site.

The biggest benefit to Office 365 is that all of the browser-based applications can be used from any device that connects to the Web. So you can begin creating a document on your Windows-based desktop computer, continue working on it from a MacBook, and then review or modify your work from an iPhone, iPad, Windows Mobile phone, Blackberry, Android-compatible phone, or any other mobile phone or tablet that has a web browser and an Internet connection. This cross-platform compatibility also applies to e-mail, scheduling, and calendars, as well as contact management databases.

 If you already use Microsoft Office on your desktop or laptop computer, those software applications will work seamlessly with Office 365, whether or not your computer is connected to the Web.

Another benefit to using Office 365 if you're an established Microsoft Office user is that there's no learning curve when it comes to using the online-based Microsoft Office web apps. These web apps are online companions to Word, Excel, PowerPoint, OneNote, and Outlook, for example, that offer a similar design and user interface, except you can access, view, and edit documents and files directly from your web browser.

With its focus on multiperson collaborations, Office 365 automatically tracks edits and modifications made by each user of every document and file, regardless of what type of computer or device they're using, and makes sure that every user has immediate access to the latest version of that document or file. Using the Microsoft Office web apps, everyone has access to the same set of editing features and formatting tools.

Once a user has access to Office 365, a click of the mouse or a tap on a tablet's screen, for example, launches the online-based Office web app of their choice. This app selection is made after signing in to the Office 365 web site and providing a Microsoft Online Services ID and password.

Figure 11-1 shows the app selection screen when Office 365 is accessed from the Safari web browser on an iMac. The screen looks almost identical if accessed from any other web browser on a PC or Mac, from a tablet, or from a smartphone. Figure 11-2 shows the same screen on an iPad 2, running the Safari web browser app.

Figure 11-3 shows what the main screen of the Word app looks like. Many of the formatting and editing commands and tools will look extremely familiar if you're already a Microsoft Word user. The documents created using this app are automatically stored online and securely linked directly to your Office 365 account.

When you click the File tab (displayed near the upper-left corner of the screen), you can save your file online or save it on your computer to work on it using the traditional version of Word, without having to be connected to the Web, or you can open the file in Word (as shown in Figure 11-4).

As you'd expect from Word, when using the cloud-based version, you have access to many different fonts and type styles that can be incorporated into your documents. Click the Insert tab to create and add tables, clip art, digital photos, and/or web links to your document.

**FIGURE 11-1** Microsoft Office 365 gives you quick access to Office web apps and other features of Office 365.

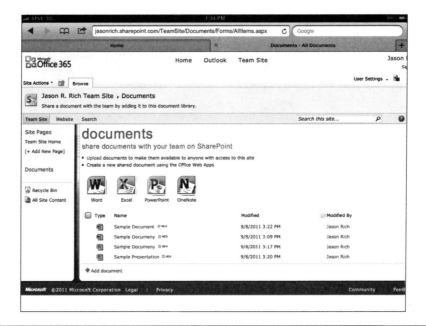

**FIGURE 11-2**   Whether you run Office 365 on a computer or an iPad 2 (as shown here), the screen and functionality of the service is identical.

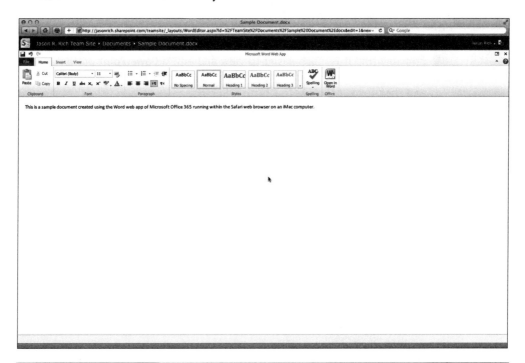

**FIGURE 11-3**   The Word web app offered as part of Office 365 allows one or more people to collaborate on Word documents via the Web.

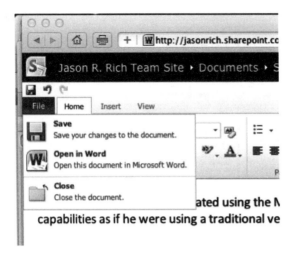

**FIGURE 11-4** When you're working on a document, you can opt to save your document online within your cloud-based account.

From the main Office 365 screen, you can just as easily launch the web app edition of Microsoft PowerPoint (shown in Figure 11-5) or Microsoft Excel (shown in Figure 11-6) to create or collaborate on the creation of a PowerPoint slide presentation or a Microsoft Excel spreadsheet.

**Tip** Instead of creating a PowerPoint presentation from scratch using Office 365, you'll probably find it is much easier to view and edit a PowerPoint presentation that you previously created using the traditional PowerPoint software on your computer, and then upload the file to Office 365, since the web app is less feature-packed and robust than the actual software, especially when it comes to formatting slides, utilizing themes, adding transitions and incorporating animated effects.

From any web app's main screen, you can also load a file or document created and saved on your computer or load a document (created by you or someone else on your team) that is saved as part of your cloud-based account. Depending on the Microsoft Office 365 plan to which you subscribe, from one to several hundred users can share files, documents, and data securely via the Web.

**How to...** # Share Files with Your Collaborators

Documents or files you plan to share or collaborate on with others are stored online within a SharePoint Online folder, as opposed to an individual user's online-based folder. When a document is stored within a SharePoint folder, it can be accessed simultaneously by multiple people who are authorized to access that folder.

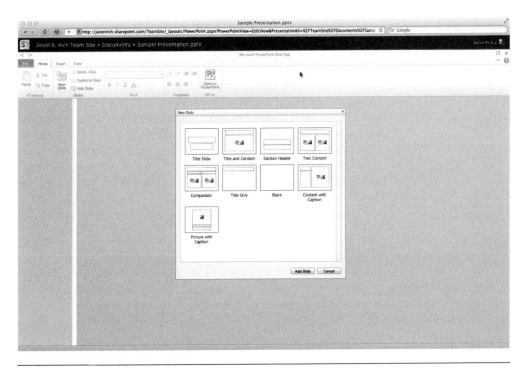

**FIGURE 11-5**   A sample of the Microsoft PowerPoint web app

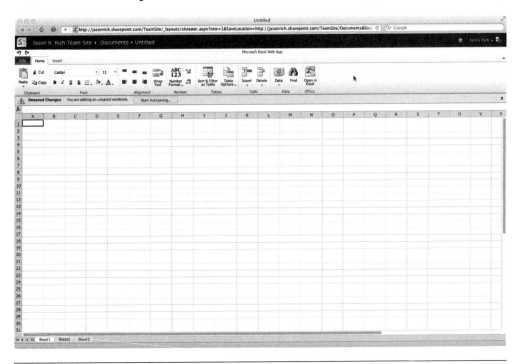

**FIGURE 11-6**   A sample of the Microsoft Excel web app

## Documents Created on Your iPad Can Be Shared via Office 365

Using Office 365, you can create a document or file on your iPad (that's connected to the Web), for example, without using Pages, Numbers, or Keynote. Instead, you'd access Office 365 from the Safari browser. When you create a document, spreadsheet, or presentation using Office 365, you know it will be 100-percent compatible with the Microsoft Office software running on your primary computer, regardless of whether it's on a Mac or PC. Plus you'll be able to share that file or document instantly with others who are also linked to your Office 365 account.

Each user of Microsoft Office 365 also receives an e-mail account with 25GB of online storage space. This account connects to Microsoft Outlook for managing contacts and scheduling, whether you're working online or offline. Meanwhile, everything you do within the Office 365 environment is kept secure and virus-free on Microsoft's cloud-based servers.

**Caution** The concept of fully utilizing cloud-based computing to host web-based applications and data is still relatively new, and is not 100-percent reliable. During the period this chapter was being written, Microsoft experienced a technical problem with its online services, which kept Office 365 users from accessing their accounts and data for several hours. Furthermore, while the web-based applications help to insure cross-platform compatibility, they are not anywhere near as robust as their traditional software counterparts in terms of features and functionality. Many users might find it more feasible to continue to utilize their existing applications that are stored on their computers and/or mobile devices, but use a cloud-based service, such as iCloud or Office 365, to back up, sync, collaborate, and transfer documents and files between computers, devices and/or users.

# Google Docs: Another Cloud-Based Application Option

Using a suite of browser-based applications developed by Google, this cloud-based service allows you to perform basic word processing, spreadsheet management, or online presentation management from virtually any device that connects to the Web. When it comes to creating a document using the Google Docs word processor, for example, you can create text, add bulleted lists, insert columns and tables, incorporate images, and adjust fonts, typestyles, and formatting.

However, Google Docs also allows you to load your existing files and documents created using traditional software applications, such as Word, Excel, PowerPoint, Pages, Numbers, and Keynote, for example, and use those files in Google's cloud-based environment. The service allows you to import .doc, .xls, .odt, .ods, .rtf, .csv, and .ppt files. Once they are loaded into the browser-based apps, you can use an intuitive user interface to work with those documents or files in an online environment.

Like virtually all of Google's online-based services, using Google Docs is free of charge. You simply need to set up a Google account, which can be the same account you already use to access other Google services, such as Google+, Gmail, or YouTube.

Google Docs can be used to create, view, and edit documents and files online, as well as to maintain a remote backup of your files and transfer files between your own computers and mobile devices. Using an e-mail–based invitation system, you can also share specific files or documents with others, and then use Google Docs online collaboration tools to modify those files together or separately, and share the results instantly.

The service can also be used as an online-based presentation tool. You'll discover an on-screen chat window that allows you to communicate with your collaborators online as you're showing off or working together on a document, presentation, or spreadsheet, for example.

As you'd expect from a cloud-based service, all of your files, documents, and data are saved automatically on Google's servers and become accessible from any computer or device that's connected to the Web and has a web browser, such as Microsoft Internet Explorer (on a PC) or Safari (on a Mac). From your mobile device, you can also use its built-in web browser or a specially designed app available from the app store associated with your device.

In addition to storing your files on Google's cloud-based servers, files can also be copied to your computer or mobile device easily, so you can work with them offline using traditional software or an app. When storing your files online, you can create an unlimited number of folders and subfolders to keep them organized and secure. It's also possible to publish a file or document as a standard web page with one click, and then control exactly who has access to that web page.

If you already use other online-based Google services, such as Blogger.com to create and manage a blog or Picasa to manage and edit your online photos, you'll discover that Google Docs works seamlessly with these other services.

**Did You Know?**

## Using a Third-Party App Makes Using Google Docs More Efficient

For the Apple iPhone and iPad, you can purchase and download any of several different third-party apps from the App Store that make accessing the Google Docs service faster, easier, and more efficient. For example, you'll find GoDocs for Google Docs, gogoDocs Google Docs, PowerDocs HD, and Google Apps Browser, which range in price from $.99 to $4.99.

The big difference between Microsoft Office 365 and Google Docs is the price. Google Docs is free of charge. All you need is a free Google account to begin using it. To set up a free Google account or use Google Docs, visit https://docs .google.com.

# Do Browser-Based Apps Make Sense for You?

To recap, using a cloud-based service that offers web-based apps in addition to storing your files, documents, and data online offers both advantages and potential disadvantages. These types of services are a good choice if you know you'll have access to the Internet just about any time you want to create, view, and/or manage your files and documents. Otherwise, you'll need to plan in advance, and remember to download manually all of the files and documents you'll want or need to access, so they'll be available to you offline when no Internet connection is available.

In theory, web-based apps solve the cross-platform compatibility issues you might otherwise run into when you transfer a document from a PC to a Mac, or from your desktop computer to a mobile device, for example. However, if you use traditional word processing, spreadsheet management, and/or slide show presentation software, you'll discover that these software applications offer a Save As command that allows you to export a document or file into a format that will be compatible with whatever computer or device to which you'll be sending it.

Plus, if the software is saved on your computer and/or mobile device, it's always accessible, whether or not an Internet connection is present. You can easily keep copies of your important files and documents both on your computer or mobile device and stored on a cloud-based service.

When you use iCloud, for example, transferring files, documents, and data among your Mac and mobile devices (or between Macs) is an extremely easy process, and depending on the Mac software or iOS app you're using, it might also be set up to transfer files to your iCloud account automatically.

Refer to Chapter 8 for more information on using iCloud to manage and share documents and files.

# PART IV

# Use iCloud with Your iPhone and iPad Running iOS 5

# 12

## Manage Apps, App-Related Data, and eBooks with iCloud

**HOW TO...**

- Synchronize Contacts, Calendar, and your iCloud e-mail data.
- Set up iCloud to synchronize apps, eBooks, and web browser bookmarks.
- Keep all of your devices and computers up to date with the latest information.

Setting up your free iCloud account is your first step toward being able to use the features of Apple's cloud-based service from your computers and iOS devices. However, each device you'll be using with iCloud needs to be set up separately so that the specific iCloud-related features you want to use will ultimately work automatically and behind the scenes.

This chapter explains how to set up the Mail, Contacts, Calendars, Reminders, and Safari apps on your iPhone or iPad so they synchronize data with iCloud (and ultimately with your other computers and iOS devices that are linked to the same iCloud account). When you're using your iPhone, for example, if you add or update a contact entry using the Contacts app, add or change an appointment using the Calendar, create or change a to-do list item within the Reminders app, or add or modify a bookmark you save when surfing the Web using Safari, those additions or changes will almost instantly and automatically be uploaded to iCloud, and then shared with your primary computer and/or other iOS devices.

Thus, after you make those additions or changes on your iPhone, you should be able to access your primary computer or iPad, for example, and see up-to-date information. Likewise, any additions or changes made on your computer or iPad will be reflected almost instantly on your iPhone.

 For iCloud to synchronize data between your computer(s) and iOS devices automatically, each must be connected to the Internet. Your iPhone or iPad will be able to use either a 3G or Wi-Fi connection for this purpose. If no Internet connection is available, the additions or changes will not immediately upload to iCloud or will not be downloaded by your other computers or devices from iCloud.

The necessary uploads or downloads, however, will automatically occur when an Internet connection is reestablished.

Remember that the iCloud functionality for the Mail, Contacts, Calendars, Reminders, and Safari apps need to be activated and set up by you once, on each of your iOS devices and computers, in order for them to synchronize app-related data. Once set up, the data synchronization happens in almost real-time in the background. You don't have to take any further actions to ensure that all of your most up-to-date data for the relevant apps is stored on iCloud, and thus made available to your other computer(s) and/or iOS devices that are linked to the same iCloud account.

On each computer or iOS device, make sure that when you activate iCloud, you enter the same account-related e-mail address that was used to create the iCloud account. This is essential if you want all of your computers or iOS devices to be able to share and synchronize data.

## Download the Free iCloud Control Panel Software

If you're a Windows PC user, multiple references are made to the iCloud Control Panel throughout this chapter. This is a free software download available from Apple. You can download it by pointing your web browser to http://support.apple.com/kb/DL1455 (as shown next).

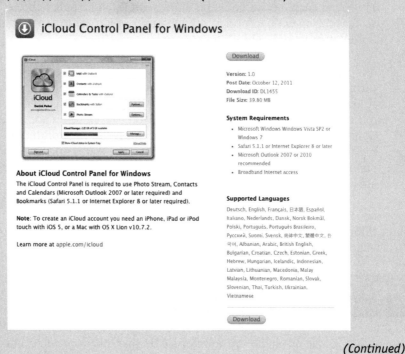

*(Continued)*

This software is compatible with Windows Vista SP2 and Windows 7, Safari 5.1.1, Microsoft Explorer (version 8 or later), and Microsoft Outlook 2007 or 2010. In some cases, it must also be used in conjunction with the iTunes (version 10.5 or later) software.

# Set up Your iCloud-Specific E-mail Account

When you first established an iCloud account, it came with a free e-mail address. Or if you already had a MobileMe account, when you transferred that account to iCloud, the MobileMe-related e-mail account automatically became your iCloud e-mail account. This e-mail address uses a [*username*]@me.com or [*username*]@mac.com format.

**How to...** ## Access Your iCloud-Related E-mail Account

To access your iCloud-related e-mail account (shown next) from any computer or wireless device that's connected to the Internet, point your web browser to www.iCloud.com/mail.

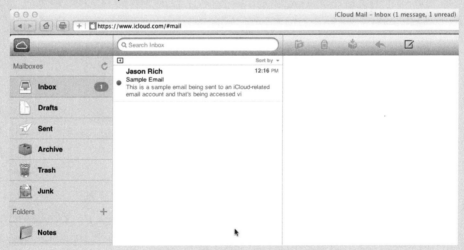

You'll be able to sign into the iCloud service using your Apple ID username and password, and you can then manage your e-mail account. Any updates or changes made to the account (to your Inbox, for example) will be reflected on all of your computers or iOS devices. From the iCloud Mail web site, you can read incoming e-mails, compose and send outgoing e-mails, or organize e-mail messages into various folders, just as you can using the Mail software on your Mac or the Mail app on your iOS device.

See Chapter 4 for detailed instructions on how to convert a MobileMe account into an iCloud account (before June 2012).

Once your iCloud account is active, your iCloud-related e-mail address will automatically remain synchronized on all of your computers and iOS devices if you turn on iCloud's Mail feature on each computer or device. This feature works only with your iCloud-related e-mail address, not with the other e-mail accounts you manage from your computer(s) or iOS devices.

To turn on the iCloud e-mail sync feature on your iOS device, follow these steps:

1. Launch the Settings app from the Home Screen.
2. From the main Settings menu, tap the iCloud option.
3. Make sure the e-mail address that is displayed within the Account field of the iCloud menu screen within Settings has the appropriate iCloud-related e-mail account listed.
4. Tap the virtual on/off switch associated with the Mail option on the iCloud menu screen, and turn it on (shown in Figure 12-1).
5. Repeat this process on each of your iOS devices.

**FIGURE 12-1**  Turn on the Mail setting from the iCloud menu screen within Settings on your iOS device. It's shown here on an iPad 2.

On your Mac, you'll also need to turn on the Mail synchronization feature for your iCloud-related e-mail account. To do this, follow these steps:

1. Click the System Preferences icon on your Mac's Dock, or launch it from the Applications folder to open the System Preferences window (shown in Figure 12-2).
2. Under the Internet & Wireless heading, click the iCloud option.
3. Using the mouse, add a checkmark to the checkbox displayed next to the Mail & Notes option (shown in Figure 12-3).

On your Mac, if you have not yet added the e-mail address that's associated with your iCloud account, here's how to do this so that it becomes listed on the left side of the Mail, Contacts & Calendars window:

1. Click the System Preferences icon on the Mac's Dock, or launch it from the Applications folder.
2. Under the Internet and Wireless heading, click the Mail, Contacts & Calendars option.
3. Near the lower-left corner of the Mail, Contacts & Calendars window (shown in Figure 12-4), click the plus sign icon to add an e-mail account to your Mac, or click the Add Account option displayed under the list of already added e-mail accounts (if applicable) on the left side of the window.

**FIGURE 12-2**   The System Preferences window on a Mac

**FIGURE 12-3** The iCloud menu window within System Preferences

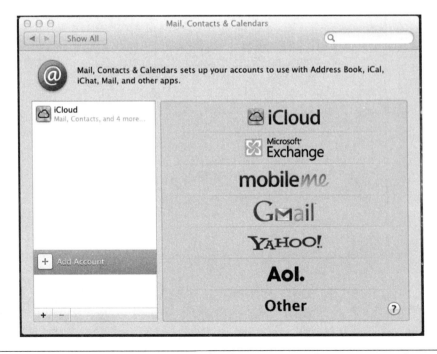

**FIGURE 12-4** The Mail, Contacts & Calendars option within System Preferences on a Mac

**FIGURE 12-5**   Enter your Apple ID and password when prompted.

4. On the right side of the Mail, Contacts & Calendars window, click the iCloud option.
5. When prompted, enter your existing Apple ID and password, and then click the Sign In icon (shown in Figure 12-5).

On a PC that's running Windows, do the following to set up your iCloud-related e-mail account to work with Microsoft Outlook 2010:

1. Launch Outlook, and choose File | Info.
2. Click the Add Account option.
3. Choose the Email Account option, and then enter your full name, along with your iCloud e-mail address (username@me.com) and iCloud e-mail account password.
4. Click the Next icon. Once the account information is verified, click the Finish icon. You will now see your iCloud Mail account details displayed within the left column of Microsoft Outlook.

If you're using Microsoft Outlook 2007 on a Windows-based PC, to set up your iCloud Mail account to work with this software, launch Outlook 2007, and then do the following:

1. Choose Tools | Account Settings.
2. Click the Email tab, and select the New option.
3. When prompted, click the Internet Email option, and then click Next.
4. When prompted, enter your full name, iCloud e-mail address, the server information, and your account username and password.
5. For the Account Type, select IMAP.
6. When asked for the Incoming Mail Server, enter **imap.mail.me.com**.

7. When asked for the Outgoing Mail Server, enter **smtp.mail.me.com**. At this point, make sure the Require Logon Secure Password Authentication (SPA) checkbox is not selected (no checkmark appears within the checkbox).
8. Click the More Settings option.
9. When the Outgoing Server tab is displayed, add a checkmark to the My Outgoing Server (SMTP) Requires Authorization and Use Same Settings As My Incoming Mail Server options, and then click the OK icon near the bottom of the window.
10. Click Next and then Finished. Your iCloud e-mail account will now function properly on your PC that's running Outlook 2007.

You can also set up your iCloud e-mail account to work with other versions of Microsoft Outlook, as well as Microsoft Exchange and/or Windows Vista Mail. To do this, follow the directions offered from Apple's web site (http://support .apple.com/kb/HT4864).

Once you turn on iCloud's Mail feature on your computer(s) and iOS device(s), everything pertaining to your iCloud-related e-mail account will automatically remain synchronized on all computers, the Web, and your iOS devices. Any changes made to the account will be updated almost instantly. Thus, if you delete a message from your Inbox on your iPhone, for example, it will automatically be deleted from your Inbox on all computers and devices.

E-mail messages (within your Inbox, for example) that are stored on iCloud's servers use some of your 5GB of free online storage space. So if you use this e-mail account a lot, and it stores e-mails with large attachments, your free allocated online storage space could get used up quickly, even if you're not using iCloud's other features.

## Syncing the Notes App on Your iOS Device with iCloud

The Notes app is a basic text editor. It does not offer the features of a word processor, such as the optional Pages app. However, using the Notes app, you can create and view text-based documents and then print or e-mail them to other people.

If you use the Notes app that comes preinstalled on any iPhone or iPad that's running iOS 5 (shown in Figure 12-6), you can set up this app to synchronize your notes with iCloud automatically, so they'll appear as e-mail messages sent to yourself within the Mail app on your Mac and/or as individual notes within the Notes app running on your other iOS devices.

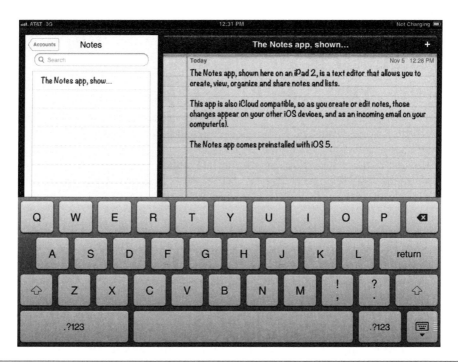

**FIGURE 12-6**   The Notes app that comes with iOS 5 is a text editor that allows you to create text-based notes, lists, and documents. It's shown here on an iPad 2.

**Note**   For the Notes app to sync with Outlook running on your Windows-based PC, load the iCloud Control Panel and place a checkmark next to the Mail & Notes option.

**How to...**   # Turn on iCloud Functionality for the Notes App

To turn on iCloud functionality for the Notes app on your iOS device, launch the Settings app. From the main Settings menu, tap the iCloud option. Then, from the iCloud menu screen, turn on the virtual on/off switch that's associated with the Notes option (refer back to Figure 12-1).

For the Notes app to sync with the Mail software on your Mac, from the iCloud window within System Preferences on your Mac (refer back to Figure 12-3), click the iCloud option. When the iCloud window appears, use the mouse to add a checkmark next to the Mail & Notes option.

# Configure Your iOS Device's Contacts, Calendars, and Reminders Apps to Work with iCloud

The Contacts, Calendars, and Reminders apps that come preinstalled with iOS 5 on the iPhone, iPad, and iPod touch are each powerful organizational tools that can be used on their own, exclusively on an iPhone, iPod touch, or iPad, for example. However, these three apps also offer data synchronization functionality, so you can share app-specific data with other iOS devices and/or your primary computer, either via iCloud or iTunes.

## Using the Contacts App with iCloud

Contacts is a contact manager that allows you to create and maintain a comprehensive and personalized database of people and/or companies you know and/or do business with (shown in Figure 12-7). On your iOS device, the information stored within your Contacts database is constantly used by a wide range of other apps, including Phone, Safari, Mail, Messages, and Maps.

When you turn on iCloud functionality for the Contacts app, the Contacts database you maintain on your iPhone, iPad, or iPod touch will automatically

**Did You Know?** **iCloud Offers an Alternative to iTunes Sync**

Using iCloud to sync your Contacts, Calendars, and Reminders data is an alternative to using the iTunes Sync feature that requires you to link your iOS device to your primary computer via the supplied USB cable or wirelessly link the computer and iOS device by connecting them to the same wireless home network. When you sync data with iCloud, the process is done wirelessly via the Web.

After this setup process is done once on each of your iOS devices and computers that are linked to the same iCloud account, all Contacts (iPhone/iPad), Calendars (iPhone/iPad), Reminders (iPhone/iPad), Address Book (Mac), iCal (Mac), and/or Outlook (PC) data will automatically remain synchronized, as long as your devices are connected to the Internet.

If one or more devices does not have an Internet connection, the necessary data will be transferred to or from iCloud when an Internet connection is reestablished.

**FIGURE 12-7** The Contacts app running on an iPhone 4S

remain synchronized not just with the Contacts app on your other iOS devices, but with the Address Book software that's running on your Mac and/or the Outlook software that's running on your PC.

 Remember that this feature needs to be turned on separately on each of your iOS device(s) and computer(s).

As changes are made to your Contacts database from your computer or any iOS device that's linked to the same iCloud account, they'll be reflected almost immediately within the Contacts app (on your iPhone, iPad or iPod touch), Address Book (on your Mac), or Outlook (on your PC).

To turn on iCloud functionality in relation to Contacts on your iPhone, iPad, or iPod touch, launch the Settings app from the Home Screen, and from the main Settings menu, tap the iCloud option. When the iCloud menu appears within Settings, tap the virtual on/off switch associated with the Contacts option to turn it on. Do this on each of your iOS devices.

 Once Contacts, Address Book, and/or Outlook data is being synchronized among your computers or devices, if you delete a contact from your iPhone, iPad, Mac, or PC, for example, that contact will almost instantly be deleted from all of the contacts-related databases with which iCloud is syncing.

**How to...** **View Your Address Book and Contacts Data on the Web**

Once you sync your Address Book (Mac) and/or Contacts (iPhone/iPad/iPod touch) database with iCloud, you can view those contacts from any computer, tablet, or mobile device that's connected to the Internet by pointing your web browser to www.iCloud.com/contacts.

After signing in using your Apple ID and password, your browser window will display a screen that looks and functions exactly like Address Book and Contacts. All data displayed is perfectly synchronized with your computer and/or mobile devices, even if changes are made online.

## Using the Calendar and Reminders App with iCloud

The Calendar app on the iPhone, iPod touch, and iPad (shown in Figure 12-8) is used to manage your schedule. On your iOS device's screen, you can display your personalized calendar in a variety of formats, including a daily, weekly, monthly,

**FIGURE 12-8** The Calendar app's Monthly view shown on an iPad 2

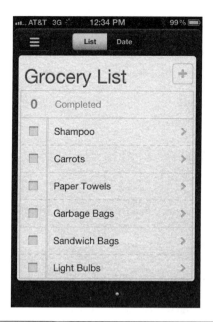

**FIGURE 12-9**   The Reminders app allows you to manage detailed to-do lists on your iPhone, iPad, or iPod touch. It's shown here on the iPhone 4S.

yearly (iPad only), and list-based format, plus associate alarms with each event or appointment added to your schedule.

Reminders is an advanced to-do list management app (shown in Figure 12-9) that was introduced in conjunction with iOS 5. Using this app, you can simultaneously create and maintain an unlimited number of separate to-do lists. Each item on each to-do list can have its own alarm(s) and/or notes associated with it.

Thanks to iCloud, your entire Calendar database, as well as your Reminders to-do lists, can be synchronized with iCloud and then made available to all of your other iOS devices, as well as the iCal app on your Mac and/or Outlook on your PC.

**How to...** **View Your iCal and Calendar App Data Online**

Once you sync your iCal (Mac), Outlook (PC), and/or Calendar (iPhone/iPad) database with iCloud, you can view your schedule, as well as to-do list items from the Reminders app, from any computer (PC or Mac) or any mobile device that's connected to the Internet.

Point your web browser to www.iCloud.com/calendar. Your browser window will display a screen that looks and functions exactly like the Calendar app, but it will also display your to-do list items from Reminders on the right side of the screen. All data displayed is perfectly synchronized with your computer and/or mobile devices, even if changes are made online.

To set up the Calendar and/or Reminders app to work with iCloud, from the iPhone, iPod touch, or iPad's Home Screen, launch the Settings app. Then, from the main Settings menu, tap the iCloud option. When the iCloud menu appears within Settings, turn on the virtual on/off switches associated with the Calendar and/or Reminders apps (refer back to Figure 12-1). By turning these switches on, each respective app will automatically sync data with iCloud.

# Access Contacts, Calendars, and Reminders via Address Book and iCal on Your Mac

To turn on iCloud functionality in relation to Address Book on your Mac, launch System Preferences, and then click the iCloud icon. When the iCloud window opens, use the mouse to add a virtual checkmark to the checkbox to the left of the Contacts option.

On your Mac, data from Calendar and Reminders are both used and displayed within the iCal software. To turn on iCloud functionality so your Mac will synchronize data with these two iOS apps running on your iPhone, iPod touch, and/or iPad, add a virtual checkmark within the checkbox for the Calendars option of the iCloud window within System Preferences (refer back to Figure 12-3).

# Set up Your PC to Access and Use Contacts, Calendars, and Reminders via Outlook

Data from Contacts, Calendars, and Reminders can be also be synchronized (via iCloud) with a PC that's running Microsoft Outlook 2007 or Outlook 2010. To do this, you'll first need to download and install the iCloud Control Panel onto your PC that's running Windows.

Once installed, open the Windows Control Panel, and select the iCloud Control Panel option. Add a checkmark next to the Contacts and Calendars options, and then click the Apply icon.

Now, when you launch Outlook on your PC, you should see data from your iPhone and/or iPad's Contacts, Calendars, and/or Reminders apps in conjunction with the data entered on your computer using the Outlook software.

---

**How to...** **Ensure that the iCloud Outlook Add-in Is Active with Outlook 2007**

To ensure that the iCloud Outlook Add-In is active when running Outlook 2007, launch the Outlook software from your PC and choose Tools | Trust Center. Click the Add-Ins option from the left column. Now look at the list of add-ins displayed under the Active Application Add-Ins heading, and make sure you see a listing for iCloud Outlook Add-In.

How to...

## Ensure that the iCloud Outlook Add-in Is Active with Outlook 2010

To ensure that the iCloud Outlook Add-In is active when running Outlook 2010, launch Outlook 2010 and choose File | Options. Click the Add-Ins option displayed in the left panel of the Outlook Options window. Below the Active Application Add-Ins heading, you should see a listing for iCloud Outlook Add-In.

# Configure Your iOS Device's Safari App to Work with iCloud

On your iPhone or iPad, Safari (shown in Figure 12-10) is the web browser used to surf the Web when your device is connected to the Web via a 3G or Wi-Fi connection. Likewise, on your Mac or PC, you have the option to use Apple's Safari web browser (on a Mac), Microsoft Internet Explorer (on a PC), as well as a handful of third-party web browsers, such as Firefox or Chrome.

**FIGURE 12-10**    The Safari web browser on an iPad 2

Each of these web browsers allows you to maintain a personalized Bookmarks menu containing your favorite or most frequented web site URLs, as well as a Bookmarks Bar that is typically displayed along the top of the web browser's screen. Safari also allows you to create and manage a personalized Reading List that includes articles you discover while surfing the Web that you want to refer back to later.

 Safari on the iPhone does not support a Bookmark Bar, but you can create a Bookmarks Menu with as many separate bookmark folders as you'd desire, as well as a separate Reading List.

Thanks to iCloud, all of your favorite web site–related bookmarks can be stored on iCloud and synchronized between your iOS devices, as well as the iCloud-compatible web browsers on your Mac or PC. Thus, as you add or delete bookmarks for your favorite or most frequented web sites from your Bookmarks menu, Bookmarks Bar, or Reading List (using Safari), they'll appear within the web browsers on all of the computers or iOS devices that are linked to the same iCloud account.

## Set up Your Computer to Use Safari Bookmarks and Reading List Data

The process for turning on iCloud synchronization functionality between Safari (or another compatible web browser) on your Mac is done from System Preferences. After launching System Preferences, click the iCloud option. When the iCloud window appears, add a checkmark to the checkbox associated with the Bookmarks option (refer back to Figure 12-3).

Now when you run Safari on your Mac, you should see all of your saved bookmarks from your iPhone and/or iPad displayed as part of your Bookmarks menu, Bookmarks Bar, and/or Reading List, in conjunction with the bookmarks you previously saved while surfing the Web on your Mac.

To configure Microsoft Explorer (or another compatible web browser) on your PC to synchronize bookmark-related data with iCloud, you'll need to download and install the iCloud Control Panel on your PC that's running Windows. Once it's installed, open the Windows Control Panel and select the iCloud Control Panel option. Then add a checkmark next to the Bookmarks option; then click the Apply icon.

 **Turn on iCloud Functionality for Safari on Your iOS Device**

To turn on iCloud functionality for Safari on your iOS device, launch the Settings app from the Home Screen. Then, from the main Settings menu, select the iCloud option. From the iCloud menu screen within Settings, turn on the virtual switch that's associated with the Bookmarks option (refer back to Figure 12-1).

Now when you launch Microsoft Explorer (or another iCloud-compatible web browser) on your PC, you should see bookmark-related data from your iPhone and/or iPad's Safari app when you view your Bookmarks menu and/or Bookmarks Bar.

# Configure iCloud to Synchronize Music, Apps, and eBooks Among Devices

Regardless of when or with which computer or device you purchase content from iTunes Store, App Store, or iBookstore, once you set up an iCloud account, as you know by now, all of your past and present purchases become available on all of your iOS devices. You'll never need to repurchase that content.

## Manually Install Purchased Apps from the App Store

At any time, you can manually install past app purchases on your iOS devices by launching the App Store app from your iPhone or iPad's Home Screen, tapping the Purchased command icon, selecting the Not On This iPhone/iPad option, and then tapping the iCloud icon associated with the already purchased app you want to install or reinstall on that iOS device. This applies to previously downloaded free apps as well.

## Manually Access Past iTunes Store Purchases via iTunes

If you have purchased music, TV show episodes, or movies through the iTunes Store and want to load any of those purchases on another computer or iOS device that's linked to your iCloud account, do the following: From the iTunes app on your iPhone or iPad, tap the Purchased icon. Then select what type of content you're looking for. On the iPhone, select Music, TV Shows, Movies, and so on, from the Purchased screen. Or, when using an iPad, tap the View icon in the upper-left corner of the screen, and then tap the option for Music, TV Shows, Movies, and so on.

On either an iPhone or iPad, tap the Not On This iPhone/iPad command tab, and then tap the iCloud icon for the already purchased content you want to download and enjoy on the iOS device you're currently using (shown in Figure 12-11).

 **Tip**   If you're running iTunes on a Mac or PC, click the iTunes Store option, and then click the Purchased option on the right side of the screen to view and manually download any of your past iTunes purchases.

**FIGURE 12-11** Manually download music from iCloud that you purchased from the iTunes Store on another computer or device.

## Manually Access Past iBookstore Purchases

If you've already acquired eBooks from Apple's iBookstore, you can read them on any of your iOS devices using the iBooks app. Plus, iCloud will automatically sync your virtual eBook bookmarks, so you can begin reading an eBook on one device, and then pick up exactly where you left off reading on another device.

To download or re-download an eBook you've already purchased from iBookstore, launch the iBooks app from the Home Screen. From the main Library screen (which looks like a virtual bookshelf), tap the Store icon near the top of the screen.

Once you've accessed iBookstore, tap the Purchased command icon near the bottom of the iBookstore screen. Select the previously purchased eBook you want to download, install, and read on the device you're using by tapping the iCloud icon associated with that eBook's listing.

# Set up Automatic App, eBook, and Music Synchronization

Instead of manually having to install your past and present iTunes Store, App Store, and/or iBookstore purchases on each of your iOS devices (as well as your Mac or PC), you can easily configure iCloud to download and install all new music, app, and eBook purchases automatically on all of your computers and/or iOS devices, regardless of from which device the content was actually purchased.

To set up this content synchronization feature on an iOS device, launch the Settings app from the Home Screen. From the main Settings menu, tap the iCloud option, and make sure the correct e-mail address that's associated with your iCloud account appears within the Account field near the top of the screen.

Return to the main Settings menu, and tap the Store option (shown in Figure 12-12). When the Store menu screen appears within Settings near the top of the screen, you'll see the Automatic Downloads heading. Below it are three options: Music, Apps, and Books. Each is associated with a virtual on/off switch.

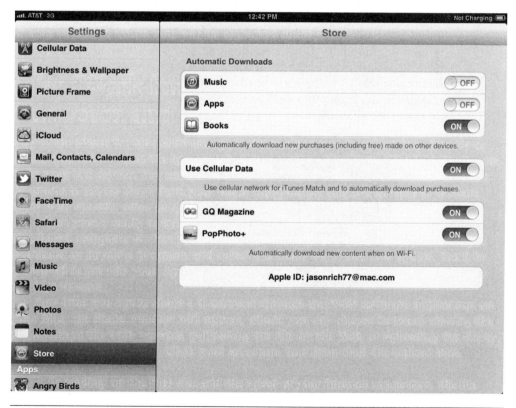

**FIGURE 12-12**   From the Store menu screen within Settings, you can set up iCloud functionality so all of your new music, app, and eBook purchases will automatically be downloaded to the iOS device you're currently using.

Based on the iTunes Store, App Store, or iBookstore content you want to download automatically to that device as new purchases are made, turn on the virtual switch associated with the Music, Apps, and/or Books option. Then decide if you want your iOS device to be able to use the 3G cellular network (as opposed to a Wi-Fi connection) to download purchases automatically.

 If you turn on the Use Cellular Data option, your iPhone or iPad will use a 3G Internet connection if no Wi-Fi connection is present to download new music (from the iTunes Store), apps (from the App Store), and/or eBooks (from iBookstore). This 3G data usage will be deducted from the monthly wireless data allocation provided by your wireless data provider. Unless you have an unlimited data plan, to avoid going over your monthly wireless data usage allocation and being charged accordingly, keep this Use Cellular Data option turned off.

On your Mac or PC computer, to turn on the auto-synchronization and downloading of new iTunes Store, App Store, and/or iBookstore purchases, launch the iTunes software (version 10.5 or later) on your computer, and then click the iTunes pull-down menu near the top-left corner of the screen. Select the Preferences option. When the Store Preferences window appears on your computer screen, click the Store option near the top-center of the window (shown in Figure 12-13).

Under the Automatic Downloads heading, you'll see three options: Music, Apps, and Books, each with a checkbox. Add a checkmark to the checkbox next to each of the options related to the content you want to download automatically as new purchases are made on other devices that are linked to the same iCloud account. Click OK to save your changes.

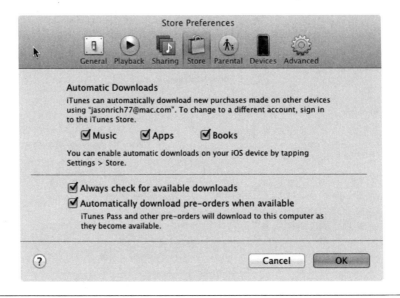

**FIGURE 12-13** Set up your Mac to auto-download all new music, app, and eBook purchases, regardless of from what computer or device it was purchased.

Although it is convenient to have all of your new music, apps, and eBook purchases automatically download and install on all of your computers and iOS devices, this content will take up internal storage space on the computers and devices on which they're stored. So if you're running low on storage space, you might want to download and install manually only the content that you want access to on each specific device, as opposed to downloading all new purchases automatically.

# The Benefits of Syncing App-Related Data via iCloud

Using the iTunes Sync process allows you to sync app-specific data between one iOS device and your primary computer. Then, to sync other iOS devices using that same data, the iTunes Sync process (using the same primary computer) needs to be performed again with the other devices. This data synchronization process does not occur in real-time, so the data on all of your devices will be up to date only after each manual iTunes Sync process is completed.

When you use iCloud to sync app-related data, however, as soon as changes are made to the data within an app, such as Contacts or Calendar, for example, that information is almost immediately uploaded to iCloud and then downloaded to all of the other computers and iOS devices that are linked to the same iCloud account. This process happens automatically, so all of your app-related data is always up to date, regardless of when or on which computer or device you're viewing it.

Plus, at any time, you can access your Contacts and Calendar databases online (from www.iCloud.com/contacts or www.iCloud.com/calendar) using any computer or mobile device that's connected to the Internet. When using this method to access your data, the computer or device you use does not need to be linked to your iCloud account. You can securely access the information using your Apple ID and password. So if something goes wrong with your iPhone or iPad while you're traveling, for example, you still have full access to your personal Contacts database and schedule, even if you need to access it from an Internet café or a friend's computer.

# 13

# Back Up Your iPhone and iPad with iCloud

**HOW TO...**

- Use iCloud to create a backup of an iOS device, such as your iPhone, iPad, and/or iPod touch.
- Use the iTunes Sync or Wireless iTunes Sync process to back up your iOS device.
- Restore your iOS device from a backup.

From the time Apple first released the original iPhone, users had to connect it to a Mac or PC running iTunes using the supplied USB cable to create a backup of the iPhone's entire contents, update the iOS, and synchronize other files, data, and (iTunes) content. With the release of the iOS 5 operating system in fall 2011, in conjunction with the launch of iCloud, you no longer need the USB cable connection for syncing and backing up data between your iOS device (including your iPhone, iPad, or iPod touch) and your primary computer.

 When you back up your iOS device using iCloud, that backup file is available to you from any Wi-Fi Internet hotspot. Should you need to restore data to your iPhone or iPad, you no longer need to connect it to your primary computer.

Thanks to iCloud, files, data, and content can easily be transferred and synced wirelessly between your iOS device and your primary computer. Plus, using iOS 5's "PC Free" functionality, if you have access to a Wi-Fi Internet connection, you can set up your iPhone, iPad, or iPod touch to back itself up each day automatically and wirelessly, and store the backup information on iCloud (linked to your password protected account).

Plus, once you have established an iCloud Backup of your iOS device, if something goes wrong with your iPhone, iPad, or iPod touch and you need to restore your device from a backup, you can do this from virtually anywhere with a Wi-Fi Internet connection, without having to connect your device to your primary computer manually using the supplied USB cable.

**Did You Know?**

## Your iOS Device Does an Automatic Backup to iCloud Every Day

Your iOS device will automatically back itself up to iCloud once per day when a Wi-Fi Internet connection is available. However, you can manually initiate a backup at any time. To save time, only new files and data, or revisions to existing files and data, are backed up. The end result, however, is a complete backup of your iOS device stored on iCloud.

To protect your actual iOS device, you should consider purchasing the AppleCare or AppleCare+ extended warrantee and/or third-party insurance, from a company such as Worth Avenue Group (www.worthavegroup.com). AppleCare covers certain types of hardware problems (but not loss or theft), while third-party insurance protection covers your iPhone or iPad against theft, loss, or any type of damage whatsoever. Having insurance for your device and maintaining a current backup of its data are two strategies that go hand-in-hand for saving yourself a lot of stress should something happen to your device.

In addition, if you want to back up your iOS device wirelessly, but you want that backup data to be stored on your primary computer as opposed to on the iCloud service, you can use the new Wireless iTunes Sync process (assuming your primary computer and iOS device are connected to the same Wi-Fi network).

Thus, when it comes to maintaining a backup of your iPhone, iPad, or iPod touch, you now have three viable options:

- Use the traditional iTunes sync process, which involves connecting the iOS device to your primary computer using the supplied USB cable and initiating the sync using the iTunes software that's running on your Mac or PC.
- Wirelessly back up your iOS device to your primary computer using the new iTunes Wireless Sync process, as long as both the computer and device have access to the same Wi-Fi network. The backup and sync process requires that the latest version of iTunes be running on your Mac or PC.
- Forego connecting your iPhone, iPad, or iPod touch to your primary computer altogether, and back up your iOS device wirelessly from anywhere using iCloud, assuming your iOS device has access to a Wi-Fi Internet connection.

# Back Up Your iOS Device to iCloud

To create and then maintain a backup of your iOS device on iCloud, your device must be running iOS 5 and have access to a Wi-Fi Internet connection, and you'll need to have a free iCloud account already established. The backup file from your iPhone, iPad, and/or iPod touch will use some of your allocated 5GB of online storage space on iCloud (which is provided free of charge with the iCloud account).

> **How to...**
>
> ## Keep Tabs on How Your iCloud Online Storage Space Is Being Utilized
>
> To determine how much of your allocated online storage space on iCloud is currently being used, from the Settings app, tap the iCloud option under the main Settings menu, and then tap the Storage & Backup option near the bottom of the iCloud screen within Settings. Near the top of the Storage & Backup screen (shown later in Figures 13-6 and 13-8), look under the Storage heading to see your Total Storage and Available Storage. Tap Manage Storage to see exactly how the storage space is being used. If necessary, tap the Buy More Storage option to expand your iCloud online storage capacity for an annual fee.

Once your iCloud account is set up and functional, make sure your iOS device is connected to a Wi-Fi Internet connection, and then launch the Settings app. To do this, tap the Wi-Fi option under the Airplane Mode virtual switch on your iPhone or iPad (if it's a Wi-Fi + 3G model). When the Wi-Fi Networks window appears within Settings, select the available Wi-Fi network you want to use (as shown in Figure 13-1 on an iPad 2).

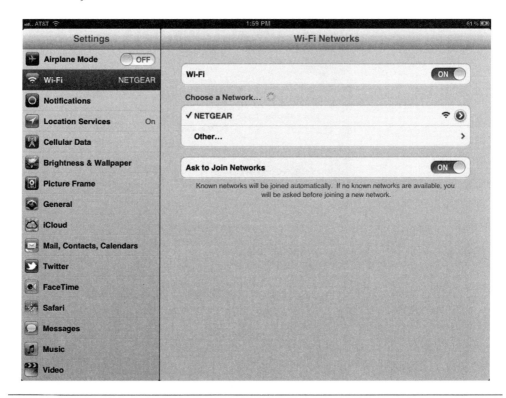

**FIGURE 13-1**   Connect your iOS device to a Wi-Fi network or hotspot from the Settings app.

The menus and specific commands needed to use iCloud and to initiate an iCloud backup or restore from an iCloud Backup are virtually the same on the iPhone, iPad, and iPod touch. Although the commands and menus are the same, their appearance on the various devices will vary slightly due to screen size issues.

As you attempt to connect to a Wi-Fi network or hotspot, from the Wi-Fi Networks screen within Settings, if you notice a lock icon displayed to the right of a network's listing (under the Choose A Network heading), this means you will require a password to access that particular Wi-Fi hotspot or network. When you attempt to select a locked Wi-Fi network and connect to it, a password prompt will be displayed.

 You can tell that your iOS device is connected to a Wi-Fi network when the Wi-Fi signal indicator is displayed in the upper-left corner of the screen.

After your iOS device is connected to a Wi-Fi network, from the Settings app, tap the iCloud option. The iCloud option also appears in the main Settings menu. When the iCloud screen appears within Settings, scroll down to the Storage & Backup option and tap it (as shown in Figure 13-2 on an iPad 2). On the iPhone, tap the iCloud option

**FIGURE 13-2** Tap the iCloud option from within Settings after the device is connected to a Wi-Fi network.

**FIGURE 13-3**   On the iPhone, the iCloud option is displayed on the main menu within Settings screen.

from the Settings screen within the Settings app (shown in Figure 13-3), and from the iCloud screen (shown in Figure 13-4) tap the Storage & Backup option.

From the Storage & Backup screen (shown in Figure 13-5 on the iPad 2 or Figure 13-6 on the iPhone), tap the virtual switch associated with the iCloud Backup option to set

**FIGURE 13-4**   Also on the iPhone, from the iCloud screen, tap the Storage & Backup option.

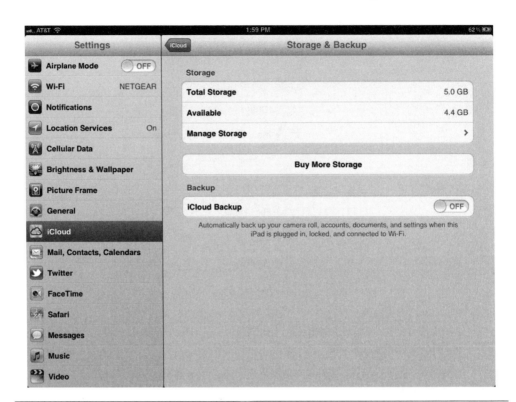

**FIGURE 13-5** To begin using the iCloud Backup feature, turn it on from the Storage & Backup screen.

**FIGURE 13-6** On the iPhone, the Storage & Backup screen within Settings is shown here.

it to the On position. If this is the first time you're creating an iCloud backup, a pop-up window will appear (shown in Figure 13-7) that says, "Start iCloud Backup: Your iPad [iPhone or iPod touch] will no longer back up to your computer automatically when you sync with iTunes." To continue, tap OK.

Another pop-up window will briefly appear that says, "Turning On Backup." Below the iCloud Backup option displayed on the Storage & Backup screen within Settings, a new option will appear: Back Up Now (shown in Figure 13-8). Just below this option, the Settings app will tell you when the last backup was created. Since the option was just turned on for the first time, the message will say, "Last Backup: Never."

 Once the iCloud Backup feature is turned on, a backup will automatically be made once per day (when your iOS device is not in use, but is connected to a Wi-Fi network). At any time, however, you can create an updated backup by tapping the Back Up Now option on the Storage & Backup screen of the Settings app (see Figure 13-8).

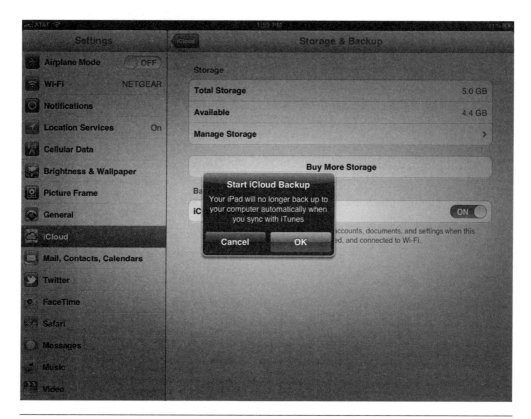

**FIGURE 13-7**   Tap the OK icon when this pop-up window appears telling you iTunes Sync will no longer automatically activate.

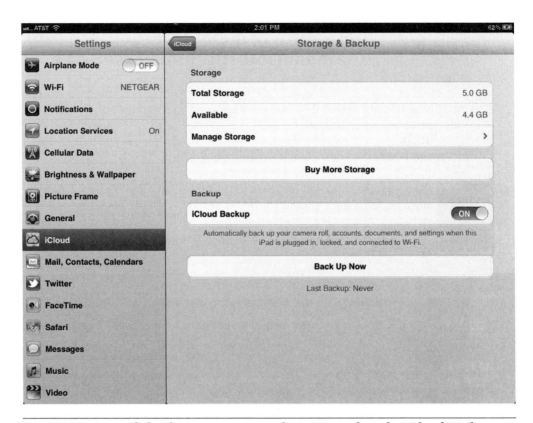

**FIGURE 13-8** Look for the new option, Back Up Now, when the iCloud Backup feature becomes accessible.

Because this is your first time creating a backup using iCloud, tap the Back Up Now option. Your device will begin the backup process by determining how long the process will take. The message "Backing Up…" and a progress bar will be displayed at the bottom of the Storage & Backup screen within Settings (as shown within Figure 13-9).

The first time you initiate a backup via iCloud, expect the process to take from 15 to 60 minutes (or longer), depending on how much data, the number of apps, and what content you have stored on your device. Subsequent daily backups, however, will take much less time, as only newly created or revised files, data, and content are backed up.

During the initial backup procedure to iCloud, once you initiate the backup, refrain from using your iOS device until the backup is completed. In the future, the backup process will be automatically initiated when your iOS device is not in use.

When the backup process is done, the Last Backup message displayed at the bottom of the Storage & Backup screen will be updated. As the wireless backup process is underway, you can cancel it at any time by tapping on the Cancel Backup option, which replaces the Backup Now option on the Storage & Backup screen within Settings (see Figure 13-9).

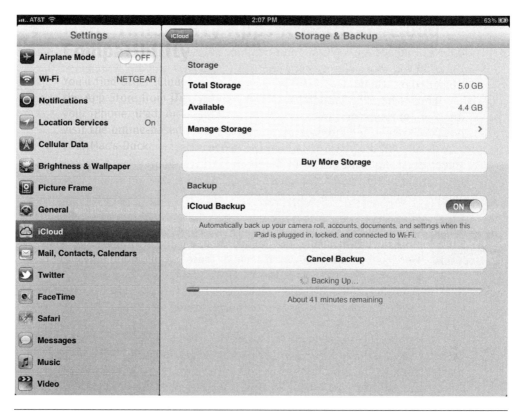

**FIGURE 13-9**   Once an iCloud Backup is initiated for the first time, it could take an hour or longer to complete.

Once you turn on the iCloud Backup feature, if you opt later to connect your iOS device to your primary computer to initiate an iTunes Sync (either using the supplied USB cable or wirelessly), nothing will happen until you first turn off the iCloud Backup feature from within the Settings app.

# Use iCloud to Back up App-Related Documents, Files, and Data

In addition to data and information that is backed up using the iCloud Backup feature, you can set your iOS device to use iCloud for specific file/data/document backup purposes, which can happen automatically and in real-time as you're using specific apps, such as Calendar, Contacts, Safari, Camera, and Photos, or optional apps, such as Pages, Numbers, Keynote, and many others. You must set up this feature with each compatible app from within Settings.

For example, if you frequently use the Pages word processing app, you can access the Settings app on your iOS device to turn on the iCloud option for Pages. Once you do this, any time you access a Pages document on your iOS device, it will check to see if you're viewing the most recent version of that document, based on what's stored on your iCloud account. When you update or change the Pages document in any way, not only will those changes automatically be saved on your iOS device, they'll also be uploaded on iCloud.

Thus, when you launch Pages and start viewing or editing that same document on another computer or device, you'll always be working with the most recent version, but you'll never need to back up or transfer the document file manually.

To turn on this feature, launch the Settings app from your iOS device, and then select Pages, for example, from the main Settings menu. You'll find it listed in the section of the Settings menu where optional Apps that you've installed on your iPhone, iPad, or iPod touch are listed.

The Pages, Numbers, and Keynote apps also allow you to import and export files or documents manually from within the app using e-mail, WebDAV, iTunes Sync, iWork.com, or iDisk. However, some of these options may be removed or replaced after June 30, 2012, when the MobileMe service is discontinued. Other apps are also compatible with other cloud-based file sharing services, such as DropBox. Chapters 10 and 11 focus on other cloud-based services.

When the Pages screen appears within Settings, turn on the Use iCloud virtual switch near the top of the screen, below the Pages heading. You can then exit out of the Settings app by tapping the Home button. From this point forward, every time you launch Pages from your Home Screen, if the device is connected to the Web (using a 3G or Wi-Fi connection), all of your Pages documents will automatically be updated with the latest versions.

This app-specific document backup and retrieval feature now works with several other apps in addition to Pages, including Numbers and Keynote. This topic is covered in greater detail within Chapter 8.

# Restore Your iOS Device from an iCloud Backup

All of Apple's iOS-based mobile devices are designed to be durable and reliable. However, for a wide range of reasons, things can sometimes go wrong. As long as you have a reliable and current backup of your iPhone, iPad, or iPod touch data, you can restore your device within a matter of minutes. Or, if you wind up having to replace the device, you can use the Restore feature to load all of your apps, data, files, and personalized settings, so the new device will become a duplicate of the old one in terms of what's stored on it.

If things do go wrong and you need up restore your iOS device from an iCloud backup, the process is relatively straightforward. However, once again, the device will need access to a Wi-Fi Internet connection.

When you turn on an iPhone or iPad that has been erased, or that's brand new, you'll first need to initialize it before restoring your data. To do this, turn on the iOS device and follow the on-screen prompts. As soon as the device is turned on, you will see a slate-colored screen with the word "iPhone" or "iPad 2," for example, displayed (shown in Figure 13-10 on an iPhone 4). At the bottom of this screen is a Slide To Set Up slider. Using your finger, move this slider from left to right. Then choose the default language for the device by tapping your selection, and then tap the blue-and-white arrow icon in the upper-right corner of the screen to continue.

When the Country or Region screen appears (shown in Figure 13-11), make a selection (the default option is the United States), and then tap the Next icon in the upper-right corner of the screen. From the Location Services screen, tap either the Enable Location Service or Disable Location Services, based on whether you want your iOS device to be able to access its GPS capabilities and pinpoint (and potentially share) your location. Tap the Next icon at the upper-right corner of the screen to continue.

From the Wi-Fi Networks screen, you'll be asked to Choose A Network from a list of available Wi-Fi networks. At this point, your iPhone, iPad, or iPod touch must have access to a Wi-Fi network to continue the setup process wirelessly. The alternative is to connect the device to your primary computer using the supplied USB cable. However, if you select this option, you will not be able to restore your iOS device from an iCloud backup.

Tap the Wi-Fi network of your choice (shown in Figure 13-12) and, once again, tap the Next icon. Your iOS device will now be activated. From the Set Up iPhone [or iPad] screen that appears next, you're given three options (shown in Figure 13-13): Set Up

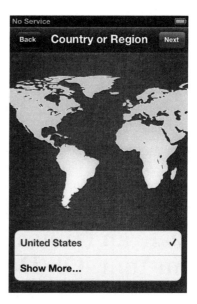

**FIGURE 13-10**   Your newly reset or brand new iOS device will need to be initialized and set up before data can be restored.

**FIGURE 13-11**   Part of the setup process involves selecting a home country or region for the device.

**FIGURE 13-12** Choose from the available list of Wi-Fi networks which one to connect to, as you restore or set up your new iOS device.

**FIGURE 13-13** Choose the iCloud restore option to reload all of your data from the backup stored on iCloud.

As New iPhone [iPad], Restore from iCloud Backup, or Restore From iTunes. To restore from your most recent iCloud backup, tap the second option, and then tap Next.

The wireless restore process will begin. It can take up to an hour for all of your apps, data, files, and personalized settings to be restored, based on how much information needs to be downloaded and restored to the device. Once the process begins, sit back and be patient. When the restore process is complete, the iOS device will be exactly as it was when the last backup was made.

 You can restore an iPhone backup to your iPhone (or a new iPhone), or an iPad backup to your existing or a new iPad, but you cannot restore an iPhone using an iPad backup or vice versa.

# Create an iTunes Sync Backup from Your iOS Device

By connecting your iOS device to your primary computer using the supplied USB cable, you can create and maintain a backup of your device, plus transfer any content, apps, or data from your primary computer to your device using the iTunes sync process. This requires that you run the latest version of iTunes on your primary computer.

When you use the traditional iTunes Sync backup process, this in no way uses iCloud. A direct connection is made between your primary computer and your iOS

## You Can Still Create Backups Using iTunes Sync

When you create an iTunes Sync backup of your iOS device, all apps, audio content (music), Safari bookmarks, eBooks, Contacts data, Calendar data, movies and TV shows (iTunes content), photos, notes, documents, and ringtones are backed up and stored on your primary computer's hard drive. This is more information that is stored when you use the iTunes backup process, because all of your iTunes purchased content (apps, music, TV shows, movies, eBooks, and so on) automatically get stored within your iCloud account and are always readily accessible from iCloud.

device, and the backup data is stored directly on your primary computer's hard drive. For detailed instructions on how this process works, access this page of Apple's web site: http://support.apple.com/kb/HT1386.

When and if you need to restore your iPhone, iPad, or iPod touch from an iTunes backup, follow the initial steps outlined previously in the section "Restore Your iOS Device from an iCloud Backup." But when you get to the Set Up screen that has three options (refer to Figure 13-13), select the Restore from iTunes option, connect your iOS device to your primary computer via the supplied USB cable, and then follow the on-screen prompts.

# Create a Wireless iTunes Sync Backup from Your iOS Device

At the same time iOS 5 was released for your iPhone, iPad, and iPod touch and Apple launched the iCloud service, it also added a new Wireless iTunes Sync option to the iTunes software on your Mac or PC. Now you can back up and transfer your iOS device data wirelessly and have it stored on your primary computer's hard drive (just like when you use the traditional iTunes Sync process). However, when you opt to do this wirelessly, the supplied USB cable is not required. Instead, your iOS device and primary computer (a Mac or PC) must be able to connect to the same Wi-Fi network, which means that depending on the strength of your wireless Internet router, the iPhone, iPad, or iPod touch must be within 150 feet or so from your primary computer.

To use this wireless sync feature, which also bypasses the need to use iCloud for iOS device backup purposes, turn on the Sync Over Wi-Fi Connection option displayed within iTunes on your primary computer. You'll find this option under the Options heading on the Summary screen of iTunes (running on your primary computer). To set up this feature the first time, your iOS device and computer must be connected via the supplied USB cable. Once the feature is turned on, the USB cable connection is no longer required.

**FIGURE 13-14** Once iTunes on your Mac or PC establishes a wireless link with your iOS device via Wi-Fi, tap the Sync Now icon on your iPhone or iPad to start the sync process.

On your iOS device, launch the Settings app and select the General option from the main Settings screen. Scroll down to the iTunes Wi-Fi Sync option, and if both devices are connected to the same Wi-Fi network, tap the Sync Now icon (shown in Figure 13-14).

 For the Wireless iTunes Sync process to work, your iOS device must also be connected to an external power source.

When and if you need to restore your iPhone, iPad, or iPod touch from an iTunes backup, follow the initial steps outlined earlier in this chapter in the section called, "Restore Your iOS Device from an iCloud Backup." Then, when you get to the Set Up screen that has three options (refer back to Figure 13-13), select the Restore from iTunes option, and then follow the on-screen prompts.

# Use iTunes Sync and iCloud Together

This is where things get a little bit confusing. You can have the iCloud Backup option turned off (which means you'll need to create and maintain primary backups of your iOS device by connecting it to your primary computer and use the iTunes Sync or Wireless iTunes Sync process), but still use iCloud to back up, sync, and/or transfer specific types of data files or documents that are related to specific apps.

For example, the iCloud Photo Stream feature or the ability to download iTunes content you've already purchased to your iOS device from iCloud is separate from the iCloud Backup feature. The feature that allows apps such as Pages, Numbers, and Keynote to keep all of those related documents and related files up to date on all of your iCloud connected computers and iOS devices is also separate from the iCloud Backup feature. So is the feature that allows your iOS device to keep your Contacts data, Calendars data, and Safari bookmarks automatically synced between your computer(s) and other iOS devices via iCloud.

If you want to maintain a backup of your iOS device on iCloud *and* on your primary computer, you can do this using a two-step process. After the backup is created on iCloud (either automatically or by your tapping the Back Up Now option from the Storage & Backup screen of the Settings app), you'll need to turn off the iCloud Backup feature and then connect your iOS device with your primary computer and manually initiate an iTunes Sync or Wireless iTunes sync. Or, if you typically use iTunes Sync but want to create a one-time iCloud backup, turn on the iCloud Backup feature within the Settings app, manually create the backup, and then turn off the feature once the backup to iCloud is completed.

# 14

# iCloud and Apple TV: The Perfect Entertainment Combination

**HOW TO...**

- Enhance your home theater system with an Apple TV device.
- Use Apple TV to view iTunes content retrieved from iCloud.
- Access iCloud's Photo Stream to view your photos via Apple TV on your television set.

Thus far in *How to Do Everything with Apple iCloud,* you've learned all about how Apple's iCloud service can be used in conjunction with your Mac, iPhone, iPad, and iPod touch. With the introduction of iOS 5 for Apple's mobile devices, the company also updated the operating system used within its Apple TV console, allowing for it, too, to be compatible with iCloud.

When an Apple TV device is connected to your high-definition television set and/ or home theater system, through iCloud, you can access all of your iTunes purchases, past and present, including music, music videos, TV episodes, and movies, and instantly watch (or listen to) them on your high-definition television (HDTV) and home theater system with surround sound. You can also access your iCloud Photo Stream using Apple TV to view your digital images on a big screen television as either individual still photos, as part of an animated slide show, or as Apple TV's screen saver (when the device isn't otherwise in use or while music is playing).

**Did You Know?**

## Use AirPlay to Transfer Movies from Your iOS Device to Apple TV

Purchased movies won't stream from iCloud to Apple TV, but TV episodes will. Getting a purchased movie to an Apple TV requires first downloading the movie to a device (iPad, iPhone, iPod touch, or computer) and then using AirPlay to stream it over to Apple TV.

In conjunction with the AirPlay feature that's built into your iPhone, iPad, or iPod touch (and iCloud), you can also stream content directly from your iOS device to Apple TV to experience it through your home entertainment system.

**Note** To use Apple TV in conjunction with AirPlay, and to use some other new features, the Apple TV device must be connected to your home network via a Wi-Fi connection, and your Mac, iPhone, iPad and/or iPod touch must also be connected to that same wireless home network.

# What Is Apple TV and How Does It Work?

Unlike TiVo, for example, Apple TV is not a digital video recorder (DVR). It is not designed to record and play back programming from television broadcasts. One of its uses, however, is to grant you access to your iTunes account from your television set or home theater system, so you can purchase (or in some cases rent) and *stream* television show episodes, music videos, or movies to watch whenever you want. Thanks to iCloud, after any content is purchased through the iTunes Store, it becomes accessible any time via your Apple TV device as well as on your Mac(s) and/or iOS mobile devices that are linked to your iCloud account.

Apple TV ($99.00) is a device that connects to both the Internet (via a Wi-Fi or Ethernet connection), as well as directly to the High Definition Multimedia Input (HDMI) port of your HDTV or home theater system. Once it's connected, here are some of Apple TV's key features:

- You can watch television shows, music videos, or movies that have been rented from the iTunes Store.
- You can access and stream movies and TV episodes from Netflix, YouTube, and several other services. (A paid subscription is required to access some of these Apple TV–compatible services.)

## Purchasing an Entire Season of a TV Series Saves You Money, and Other Facts

TV show episodes can be purchased from iTunes for $1.99 each (Standard definition) or $2.99 each (HD). However, you'll receive a discount if you purchase an entire season's worth of a television series. Television show episodes can no longer be rented from iTunes. New TV show episodes are typically made available on iTunes the day after they air on network or cable TV. So, for example, an episode of *The Office* that airs on NBC on a Thursday will be available for purchase on the iTunes Store the next day, on Friday.

## You Can Also Rent Movies from iTunes

You can purchase or rent movies from iTunes. The rental price is typically $3.99 (Standard definition) or $4.99 (HD). Once you rent a movie, it will remain available to you for 30 days. However, once you begin playing the movie, you will have 24 hours to watch it as often as you'd like before it will be automatically deleted. The price to purchase a movie via iTunes varies but is typically slightly cheaper than purchasing a DVD or Blu-Ray version of that movie.

- You can stream content directly from your iPhone, iPad, or iPod touch to your HD television set or home theater system, wirelessly via Apple TV (if all of the devices are connected to the same wireless home network). So if you want to listen to a song you downloaded on your iPhone using the speakers of your home theater system, you can stream it with a touch of the iPhone's screen using the AirPlay feature, or you can access that music from iCloud if it was purchased from the iTunes Store.
- You can access your iCloud Photo Stream from your Apple TV device to view your digital images on an HDTV.

When you purchase an Apple TV device from the Apple Store, Apple.com (as shown in Figure 14-1), or any authorized Apple reseller, you'll receive the Apple TV console, a power cord, and a remote control. An HDMI cable is also required to connect your Apple TV to the HDMI port of your television or home theater system. Apple TV can be connected to a television or home theater system via HDMI only. Composite or component cable connections or adapters are not available.

You can also use an optional digital optical audio cable (sold separately) to connect the Apple TV console directly to your home theater system (for an enhanced audio experience), as opposed to experiencing the audio sent to the TV via the HDMI cable.

**Note** The Apple TV console itself measures about 4 by 4 by 1 inch, and it weighs 0.6 pound. It comes with a handheld remote control device.

Apple TV must also be connected to the Internet via a high-speed connection. To use any of the AirPlay features, a Wi-Fi connection is necessary. However, Apple TV can also be connected to the Web via a standard Ethernet cable (also sold separately).

To access the iTunes Store via Apple TV and/or your iCloud account, you must first establish both a free iTunes and iCloud account using your Apple ID and by linking a major credit card to the Apple ID account. When you set up your Apple TV console for the first time, you will be prompted to enter your iTunes Store account and iCloud account information separately, even though, for many people, this information is the same and comprises your Apple ID and password.

**FIGURE 14-1**    You can order an Apple TV device directly from Apple.com.

## Use the Apple AV Digital Video Cable to View Content on TV

Although you can circumvent using Apple TV to display your iPad's screen on your HDTV using the optional Apple AV Digital Video Cable ($39.00), this cable and the "mirroring" feature built into iOS 5 do not work with copyrighted video content such as TV show episodes, movies, or music videos purchased from the iTunes Store or streamed from Netflix. An Apple TV device is needed to stream this content wirelessly from your iPad to your TV using the AirPlay feature.

**How to...** **Make Sure Your Apple TV's OS Is Up to Date**

Before attempting to use your Apple TV with iCloud or use the AirPlay feature in conjunction with your iOS device, make sure your Apple TV has the latest version of its operating system installed. Here's how to update the operating system, if necessary, within your Apple TV device:

1. From the Apple TV Main Menu, which you can access by pressing the Menu button on the Apple TV's remote control, press the right directional arrow to highlight and select the Settings option.
2. From the Settings pull-down menu that appears on the TV screen, select the General option.
3. When the General menu appears (shown in Figure 14-2), scroll down to the Update Software option and select it with the remote.
4. If your Apple TV's operating system is up to date, the message, "Your Apple TV is up to date" will be displayed. If an operating system update is required, follow the onscreen prompts.

**Tip** In addition to streaming content directly from your iPhone, iPad or iPod touch to your Apple TV using AirPlay (when the devices are connected to the same home wireless network via Wi-Fi), you can use your Apple mobile device as a feature-packed remote control unit for your Apple TV. To do this, download the free Remote app from the Apple Store.

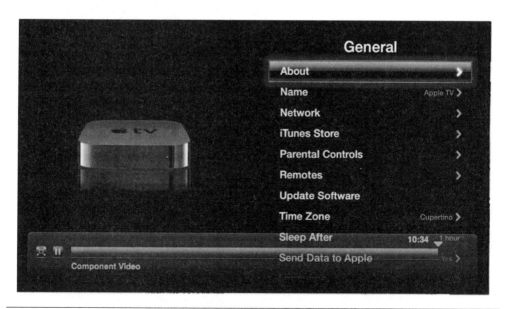

**FIGURE 14-2**    The General menu options available from the Settings pull-down menu of Apple TV

# Using Apple TV to Access iTunes Content via iCloud

Once you get your Apple TV connected to your HDTV and/or home theater system, the Main Menu (accessible by pressing the Menu button on the Apple TV remote control) will display five main options:

- **Movies** From here, you can access any movies stored on your Apple TV that were purchased from iTunes and that you own. You can also shop for movies to rent or purchase directly from the iTunes Store, and these can be watched almost instantly. The Movies Main Menu option reveals a pull-down menu that allows you to shop for Top Movies, search by movie genre (action/adventure, classics, comedy, drama, horror, and so on), use a general Search feature (which allows you to find movies based on any keyword), or access an In Theaters option (which offers free previews of movies currently playing in theaters, as well as other features).
- **TV Shows** From this pull-down menu, you can access Purchased TV show episodes (via your iCloud account or that are stored on your Apple TV device), or shop for new TV show episodes or entire seasons of shows from the iTunes Store. You can search for TV shows based on what's popular, genre, TV network, or using a general keyword search.
- **Internet** Use this feature to stream video and audio content from the Internet via your Apple TV device to your TV or home theater system. If you subscribe to Netflix, for example, select the Netflix option to stream movies from Netflix (a monthly fee applies). You can also access Apple TV–specific programming from the National Basketball Association (NBA) and Major League Baseball, or access YouTube, Vimeo, podcasts, your iCloud Photo Stream, Flickr, and a variety of Internet-based radio stations. Content that is streamed from the Internet does not get saved (or stored) on your Apple TV device.
- **Computers** This feature allows you to access iTunes content that is stored on your Mac, assuming the computer is connected to the same home network via Wi-Fi as your Apple TV. To use this feature, turn on Home Sharing within iTunes on your Mac. From iTunes on your Mac, select the Home Sharing option from the Advanced pull-down menu. When prompted, enter your Apple ID and password, and then click the Create Home Share icon. When a connection with Apple TV is established, the message, "Home Sharing Is Now On" will be displayed on your Mac's screen. Click the Done icon and return to using your Apple TV. You will

### All of Your Past iTunes Purchased Are Accessible via iCloud

If you have purchased movies in the past via iTunes, but they're not currently stored on your Apple TV device, select the Purchased option from the Movies pull-down menu to access your iTunes movie library stored on iCloud (which includes movies you've already purchased and own).

now have access, via Apple TV, to movies, TV show episodes, music videos, music, photos, and other content saved on your Mac. This content will be streamed from your computer to Apple TV but will not be stored on your Apple TV device.

- **Settings**   From the Settings pull-down menu, you can customize a handful of options relating to the operation of your Apple TV device. For example, in terms of iCloud-related options, you can set the screen saver to access your Photo Stream and display an animated slide show of your digital images.

## Access Movies Rented on iTunes Using Another Computer or Device

From the Movies Main Menu option of Apple TV, you can search for and rent movies directly from your Apple TV console. The downloaded content will then be streamed to the Apple TV and made available for you to watch on your TV.

 When using the Search feature to find a TV show or movie, you can enter a show or movie title, part of a title, an actor's name, or any other keyword that will help you find what you're looking for.

However, if you have previously rented a movie from iTunes using your Mac or an iOS device (such as your iPhone or iPad), and you haven't yet watched it, or you're still within the 24-hour viewing period, you can access that movie on your Apple TV from iCloud (via iTunes) and watch it on your TV. Here's how to do this:

1. From the Apple TV Main Menu (shown in Figure 14-3), select the Settings option at the far right.

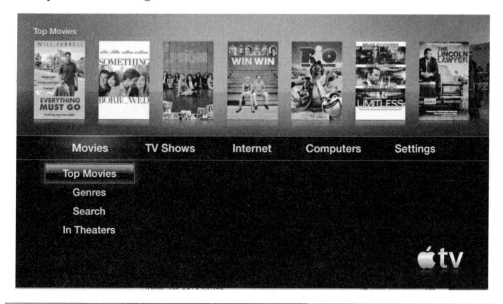

**FIGURE 14-3**   The Apple TV Main Menu

2. From the Settings pull-down menu, select the General option.
3. When the General menu appears, select the iTunes Store option.
4. Scroll down toward the bottom of the iTunes Store menu screen and select the Check For Rentals option. If any iTunes movie rentals are available to you, listings for them will be displayed and you will be able to load those rented movies from iTunes to your Apple TV to watch on your TV.

## Use AirPlay to Stream Content from an iOS Device to Apple TV

If you have the rental movies already loaded on your iPhone, iPad, or iPod touch, and the devices are linked to the same home network as your Apple TV console, you can use the AirPlay feature to stream your rented movie(s) or any iTunes content from your iOS device to your Apple TV, and then watch that content on your TV or home theater system.

To do this, connect your iOS device to your home network via a Wi-Fi connection (a 3G connection will not work), and then follow these steps:

1. Launch the Video app on your iOS mobile device.
2. Select the TV show episode, movie, or music video you want to watch, and begin playing it on your iPhone, iPad, or iPod touch's screen.
3. As soon as the video content begins playing, tap anywhere on the screen to access the on-screen controls.
4. Near the bottom of the screen, to the right of the Rewind, Play/Pause, and Fast Forward icons, the AirPlay icon appears (shown in Figure 14-4). This icon appears only when your iOS device and Apple TV have a connection established through your wireless home network. Tap the AirPlay icon.
5. When the AirPlay pop-up menu appears on your iOS device's screen, select the Apple TV option.
6. Within a few seconds, the video content will be sent wirelessly from your iOS device to your Apple TV and will appear on your TV or home theater system.
7. Use the on-screen control options on your iPhone, iPad, or iPod touch to rewind, fast forward, pause, or resume playing the movie. Or you can use the Apple TV's remote control to do this.

**Note** When you use the AirPlay feature to stream video content between your iOS device and Apple TV, that content will not be stored on your Apple TV. If you want to access other iTunes Store purchases (made from other devices or computers), you will need to access it via iCloud from the Apple TV's Main Menu. From the Movies or TV Shows menu options on your Apple TV, select the Purchased option to access content from your iCloud account.

**FIGURE 14-4**    The AirPlay icon appears on your iOS device when content can be shared with Apple TV via a Wi-Fi connection to your wireless home network.

## Access Purchased TV Shows from iCloud to Watch via Apple TV

If you've already purchased TV show episodes via iTunes using your Mac, iPhone, iPad, or iPod touch, those purchases (past and present) automatically get stored within your iCloud account. To access TV show episodes you've already purchased, but that are not yet stored on your Apple TV device, follow these steps:

1. From the Apple TV Main Menu, select the TV Shows option using the Apple TV remote control.
2. From the TV Shows pull-down menu, select the Purchased option.
3. The Purchased TV Shows screen will display thumbnail images representing every TV series for which you have previously purchased episodes. Whether you have purchased just one or two episodes of *Glee*, or an entire season of *Grey's Anatomy*, for example, each TV series will be represented by a single thumbnail (as shown in Figure 14-5).
4. Using the Apple TV's remote control, highlight and select a TV series icon.

**FIGURE 14-5** Each separate TV series is represented on the Purchased TV Shows screen.

5. On the right side of the TV screen, a listing of all episodes from that TV series will be displayed (as shown in Figure 14-6). To the right of each listing, if you see a cloud icon, this means the episode is currently stored within your iCloud account, not on your Apple TV device.

**FIGURE 14-6** Select an episode of a TV series and stream it to your Apple TV device to watch it on your TV set or home theater system.

**Did You Know?**

## You Can Always Purchase More Episodes of Your Favorite TV Series

From the Apple TV screen that lists the specific episodes of a TV series that you own, you'll also see an option to find and purchase additional episodes from the iTunes Store. If you opt to purchase additional episodes, they will be streamed directly to your Apple TV device and will become viewable within seconds after they're purchased. Those newly purchased episodes will simultaneously be stored within your iCloud account and also become accessible on your Mac or iOS mobile devices via iCloud.

6. Again, using the Apple TV's remote control, highlight and select a specific TV series episode that you currently own and that you want to watch.

7. When the TV episode's Description screen appears, select the Play option. That TV episode will be downloaded from your iCloud account to your Apple TV device and will begin playing on your TV screen or home theater system within a few seconds.

**Tip**   Just as you can with movies, you can also use the AirPlay feature to wirelessly stream iTunes-purchased TV show episodes and music videos to your Apple TV that are currently stored on an iOS device. To do this, follow the directions outlined in the earlier section, "Use AirPlay to Stream Content from an iOS Device to Apple TV."

**Did You Know?**

## Catch up on Past Seasons of Your Favorite Shows

One of the great features of Apple TV (and the iTunes Store in general) is that in addition to purchasing TV show episodes from the current season, you can often download episodes from past seasons of your favorite shows, plus purchase and watch classic TV shows. In some cases, you can also preview a full episode of a brand-new television show before it premiers on network or cable television.

# Using Apple TV to Access Your iCloud Photo Stream

You already know from Chapter 7 that iCloud offers its Photo Stream feature that allows you to synchronize, view, and access up to 1000 of your most recent (or favorite) digital images on any computer or iOS mobile device that is linked to your iCloud account.

This same Photo Stream can also be accessed from your Apple TV device and displayed on your TV in two ways :

- You can view the images or create a slide show of those images by selecting the appropriate option from the Main Menu of your Apple TV. How to do this will be explained shortly.
- You can use your Photo Stream images as your Apple TV's screen saver (which can also be displayed as you're listening to music or audio content but not watching video supplied by your Apple TV device to your TV or home theater system).

To access your iCloud Photo Stream from Apple TV's Main Menu, select the Internet option, and then choose the Photo Stream option from the pull-down menu. Thumbnails for all images within your Photo Stream will be displayed on the TV screen.

In the upper-left corner of the screen are the Slideshow and Settings options. Select Slideshow to view an animated slide show of your Photo Stream images.

To customize the appearance of the slide show, select the Settings option. From the Slideshow Settings screen (shown in Figure 14-7), you can customize the following options:

- **Shuffle Photos**  Turn on this option to display the photos from your Photo Stream in a random order. When the option is turned off, the photos will be displayed in the order in which they were saved in your Photo Stream.
- **Repeat Photos**  Turn on this option and photos from your Photo Stream can be repeated within the slide show presentation.
- **Default Music**  This option allows you to select music that will be played in the background when you're viewing a slide show of your Photo Stream images. You can select any music from an iTunes Playlist that is stored on your Apple TV or that's being shared from your Mac.
- **Shuffle Music**  Use this option to select songs randomly from your selected iTunes Playlist, as opposed to playing them in order.
- **Themes**  Your animated slide show that features your digital images from your iCloud Photo Stream can be displayed using a variety of animated special effects and transitions. Under the Themes heading, you'll discover 12 Theme options, such as Origami, Scrapbook, Holiday Mobile, Flip-Up, and Ken Burns.

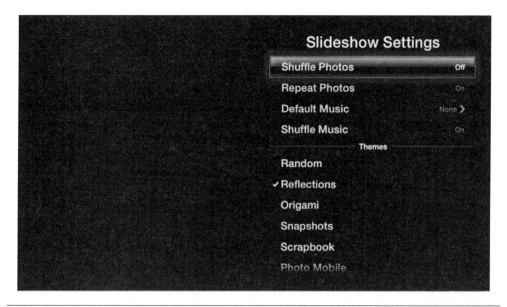

**FIGURE 14-7**   Customize the Slideshow Settings before watching the images stored within your iCloud Photo Stream on your television set or home theater system.

As you use the Apple TV's remote to highlight an option, it will be previewed on the TV screen so you can see what it will look like before selecting it.

After selecting a theme, customize the theme-specific options, such as how long each slide will be displayed for (in seconds), as well as the transition effect that will be used between images. When you're done making your Theme and Transition selections, press the Menu button on the Apple TV's remote control to return to the Photo Stream menu. Then select the Slideshow option to view your slide show.

## Photo Stream Has a Few Limitations

When iCloud first launched, it was not possible to select specific images from your iCloud Photo Stream to include within your Apple TV slide show. All images stored within your Photo Stream (up to 1000 of them) are automatically displayed, either in order or randomly, based on the Slideshow Settings option you select. The iOS 5.1 operating system will offer a feature that allows you to remove individual images from your Photo Stream.

## View Individual Photo Stream Images on Your Television Set via Apple TV

To view individual images in full-screen mode on your television set and manually scroll through the images stored as part of your iCloud Photo Stream (as opposed to viewing the images as part of an animated slideshow), follow these steps:

1. From the Apple TV Main Menu, select the Internet option using Apple TV's remote control.
2. When the Internet pull-down menu appears, select the Photo Stream option.
3. The Photo Stream screen will be displayed. It will include thumbnails of all individual photos stored within your iCloud Photo Stream. Using the directional arrows of your Apple TV's remote control, select and highlight one image thumbnail that you want to view in full-screen mode.

 Next to the Photo Stream heading in the upper-left corner of the screen, in parentheses, is the number of photos currently stored within your iCloud Photo Stream.

4. When the image thumbnail is highlighted and has a blue box around it, press the Select button on the Apple TV's remote control (in the center of the directional arrows). Your selected image will be displayed in full-screen mode on your TV set.
5. Again, using the Apple TV remote control, press the Left or Right directional arrow to advance or move back and view another image within your Photo Stream. This allows you to create a manually controlled slide show, but with no special effects or transitions.

## Set up the Screen Saver to Display Photo Stream Images

The second way to enjoy looking at the digital images stored as part of your iCloud Photo Stream is to adjust the Apple TV's Settings to use your Photo Stream as an animated screen saver.

This screen saver appears when the Apple TV's Main Menu is dormant for a predetermined amount of time (the default is 5 minutes), or when music is being played using your Apple TV device.

To set up Apple TV's Screen Saver option to showcase your iCloud Photo Stream digital images, follow these steps:

1. From the Apple TV Main Menu, use Apple TV's remote control to select the Settings option.
2. When the Settings pull-down menu appears, choose the Screen Saver option.

3. The Screen Saver screen (shown in Figure 14-8) allows you to adjust a handful of options relating to how your Apple TV's screen saver will appear. Start by adjusting the Start After option, which determines how long the Apple TV device will remain dormant before displaying the screen saver. The default is 5 minutes. Your options include Never, or 2, 5, 10, 15, or 30 minutes.

4. Also from the Screen Saver menu screen, you can choose whether or not the screen saver will be displayed while music is being played. Turn on the Show During Music feature by selecting the Yes option.

5. Next, from the Photos option that appears within the Screen Saver menu screen, select the Photo Stream option.

6. You can now use the Apple TV's remote control to select the preview option to see how your screen saver will look. Or you can scroll down on the Screen Saver menu screen to select a Screen Saver theme. You can choose from among a dozen different themes, including Floating, Reflections, Scrapbook, Photo Wall, and Shifting Tiles. Make your selection, and then press the Menu button on the Apple TV's remote control to save your changes and return to the Main Menu. The Screen Saver option is now programmed and will launch at the designated times.

If your Photo Stream will be displayed on a TV screen that's viewable by the public or anyone other than yourself, make sure only the photos you want seen will appear within your iCloud Photo Stream. You cannot currently select specific photos to view as part of the Apple TV Screen Saver from your Apple TV device. All photos from your iCloud Photo Stream will be displayed. See Chapter 7 for more information about selecting images that get included within your iCloud Photo Stream from your Mac or PC.

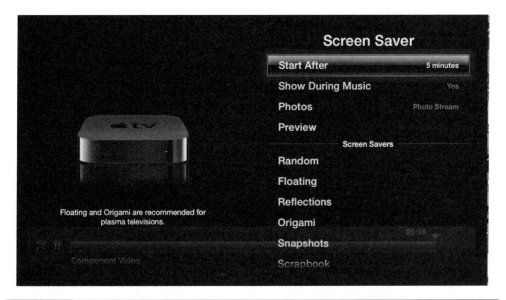

**FIGURE 14-8**   Use the Screen Saver screen accessible from the Settings menu option to customize the Apple TV Screen Saver feature and display Photo Stream images.

Apple TV's integration with iCloud and the AirPlay feature that's built into the iOS operating system are just the initial steps in making the programming and content you want to experience available to you whenever and wherever you want it. As this book was being written, rumors were circulating about Apple launching a line of HDTVs in 2012 that would have Apple TV–like functionality built in.

# iCloud's Evolution Continues...

Well, there you have it—a comprehensive introduction to cloud-based computing using Apple's iCloud. As you can see, iCloud is an extremely powerful and versatile online-based service that can change the way you manage your files, documents, data, photos, videos, and iTunes content. However, what you've read about within *How to Do Everything with Apple iCloud* is only the beginning.

 To learn about new iCloud-related features and functions as they're introduced, be sure to visit Apple's web site at www.Apple.com/icloud.

Apple will, no doubt, continue to introduce new features and functionality to the iCloud service, plus improve upon features already incorporated into the service. Over time, it will evolve. Plus, Apple has made iCloud functionality accessible to its third-party Mac software and iOS app developers to include within their software and apps. As you read this, some of the best programmers in the world are actively developing and introducing new ways to use iCloud in conjunction with software and apps running on Macs, PCs, Apple TV, and iOS mobile devices.

Thanks to iCloud, it's never been easier to access your purchased (or rented) iTunes content, or to share data, documents, files, and information easily and wirelessly between computers and mobile devices linked to the same iCloud account. Out of all of the cloud-based services currently available for Apple users, none offer the versatility of iCloud.

Now that you know what iCloud is capable of, decide which features and functions can be most useful to you, based on how you use your Mac computer(s) and iOS device(s), and then initially activate only those features within your iCloud account.

 Remember that the free or purchased online storage space you have available within your iCloud account is for your personal data and content only. Whatever additional online storage space is required for your iTunes, iBookstore, Newsstand, Mac App Store, or iOS App Store purchases is provided free of charge by Apple. However, if you are using iCloud to back up multiple iOS devices or large files from your Mac, you might need to purchase additional online storage, beyond the 5GB that is provided for free.

# A

# Troubleshoot iCloud-Related Problems

Apple's iCloud service is designed to make seamless connectivity between computers and devices easy via the Internet, allowing for data, files, documents, photos, and other content to be synchronized behind the scenes without user intervention. Like anything else that's technologically complex, when iCloud works, it works well. But, when something isn't set up correctly, it doesn't work as expected (or not at all).

## What to Do if iCloud Doesn't Work as Expected

Perhaps the most common reason why iCloud doesn't function as expected is because the user didn't properly set up iCloud to work on each of his or her computers and iOS devices. Remember that you need to set up an iCloud account on the Internet, and then turn on iCloud connectivity on each of your computers and mobile devices separately. As you do this, the same Apple ID and password need to be used on each computer.

Then, in many cases, you also need to turn on iCloud functionality for specific software or applications and for specific iCloud features and functions to work. Plus, each of your computers and iOS devices needs access to the Internet. So if you're experiencing problems with iCloud, ask yourself the following questions:

- Did I set up an iCloud account correctly using my Apple ID and password?
- Did I turn on iCloud functionality on each of my Mac(s) and/or PCs using the same Apple ID and password (that is, the same iCloud account information) that I used on my primary computer?
- Did I turn on iCloud functionality on my iPhone, iPad, and/or iPod touch using the same Apple ID and password (that is, the same iCloud account information) that I used on my primary computer?

- On each computer and iOS device, did I turn on the iCloud features or functions that I want to use?
- On each computer and iOS device, is the same assortment of iCloud features and functions turned on? (If Contacts or Documents & Data is activated only on your Mac and not on your iPhone, for example, those two devices will not be able to sync contacts and/or iWork file and document information via iCloud.)
- On each computer and iOS device, did I turn on iCloud functionality for specific software applications and/or apps? (Remember that, in addition to turning on the Documents & Data feature within Settings on your iOS device, you also need to turn on iCloud functionality for Pages, Numbers, and Keynote, for example, from within the app-specific menus of the Settings app.)
- Are my computers and/or iOS devices currently connected to the Internet?
- Am I using a Wi-Fi Internet connection on my iOS device(s) for iCloud-related tasks that do not work with a 3G connection, such as Photo Stream and iCloud Backup? (Even if everything is set up correctly, your iPhone or iPad will not access your Photo Stream or perform an iCloud Backup (or allow you to restore from a backup) if no Wi-Fi connection is available. Likewise, iCloud Backup will not work unless your iOS device is also plugged in to an external power source.)

Chances are, if you're experiencing a problem with iCloud or iCloud's ability to transfer, share, or synchronize data, documents, files, photos, or content among computers and devices via the Web, you answered "no" to at least one of these questions.

However, if after addressing these issues, you're still experiencing a problem, make sure you're running the most recent versions of the OS X Lion operating system on your Mac; the most recent version of iOS 5 on your iPhone, iPad, or iPod touch; the latest version of the operating system on your Apple TV; version 10.5 or later of the iTunes software on your Mac or PC; the latest version of the iCloud Control Panel on your Windows-based PC; and the latest versions of whatever apps you're trying to use iCloud with (such as Pages, Keynote, or Numbers).

If iCloud still isn't functioning as expected, call AppleCare's toll-free phone number for technical support at (800) APL-CARE (800-275-2273) or make an appointment with an Apple Genius at any Apple Store. You might also find the answers you need from Apple's Support web site (www.apple.com/support).

# Avoid Accidently Overwriting One File Version with Another

With so much syncing going on between your computer(s) and iOS device(s), the goal is for you to have access to the most recent versions of your data, documents, files, photos, and/or content any time and from any computer or device you're using.

Especially if you're using iCloud's "Documents in the Cloud" capabilities to sync Pages, Numbers, and Keynote files, for example, as soon as you make any change to any file or document, it will impact that file on all of your computers and devices, almost instantly. Or, if you delete a Pages, Numbers, or Keynote file, it will be erased from all of your computers and devices almost instantly (not just from the computer or device you're presently using). This is also true with Contacts and Calendar entries, as well as with Safari bookmarks, for example.

 If you're running Time Machine on your Mac, or you've recently performed a backup of your iOS device via iTunes Sync, Wireless iTunes Sync, or iCloud Backup, you can always revert back to an older version of a file from the backup data.

One way to prevent a file from accidently being modified or deleted is to create a copy of that file on the computer or device you're using, before you start working with it. This will result in the original file remaining intact on iCloud and on all of your computers and devices. However, the copy of the file you make and ultimately work with will be synchronized and shared with your other computers and/or devices as well. You can delete the original version of the file later if you want.

To make a copy, do the following:

1. As you're using Pages, Numbers, or Keynote, for example, from the Document Manager screen of these apps when you're using them on an iPhone, iPad, or iPod touch, tap the Edit icon in the upper-right corner of the screen.
2. Then, when all of the thumbnails (representing your documents or files) start to shake, tap the thumbnail for the document or file you want to edit or work with. A yellow frame will appear around it.
3. Next, tap the Copy command icon near the upper-left corner of the screen. A duplicate of the original file or document will be created and displayed on the Document Manager screen. It will have the same filename as the original file, but the word "copy" will be added to the filename. (You can always modify the filename from the Document Manager screen.)

 If you're concerned about accidently erasing a file or document, or making changes that you don't want applied to all versions of a file or document that are accessible on all of your computers and/or iOS devices via iCloud, consider temporarily turning off iCloud functionality for that app or on that device, and then turning it back on when you're ready for the files or documents to synchronize.

# What to Do if You Forget Your iCloud Account Information

Apple strongly advises you to use your Apple ID and password when creating and using an iCloud account, and to maintain just one Apple ID to use all of Apple's services that require your Apple ID information.

If you've forgotten your Apple ID altogether, visit https://appleid.apple.com. For information about how to manage your Apple ID account (and retrieve your Apple ID and/or password), visit http://support.apple.com/kb/HE34. Once you rediscover your Apple ID, you can use the Reset Your Password option to retrieve or change the related password as well.

If you forget your Apple ID or iCloud log-in information, you have a variety of options for retrieving that information, as long as you have access to the Web. For example, you can visit www.iCloud.com. In small type near the bottom-left corner of the screen, you'll see the Forgot ID Or Password? option. Click it. This will take you to a specific page of Apple's web site, called My Apple ID, where you can get help retrieving your forgotten Apple ID and/or password (one at a time).

 The My Apple ID web page can also be accessed directly by pointing your web browser to https://iforgot.apple.com.

When prompted, enter your Apple ID, and the web site will help you retrieve the related password. Or, if you've forgotten your Apple ID, click the Forgot Your Apple ID option below the Apple ID field. Follow the on-screen prompts to retrieve your Apple ID and/or password.

 You can also access the My Apple ID web page to change your Apple ID password, which is something you should do periodically for security purposes.

From your Mac, if you know your Apple ID but can't remember the password, do the following:

1. Launch System Preferences from the Dock or Applications folder.
2. Click the iCloud option. From the iCloud window within System Preferences, click the Manage icon near the lower-right corner of the window.
3. Next, click the View Account icon near the lower-left corner of the Manage Storage window. Your Apple ID will be displayed, but next to the Password field will be a Forgot? option. Click it to retrieve your forgotten Apple ID or iCloud password.

 If you're a Windows-based PC user, the preceding Apple ID/iCloud password retrieval method also works from the iCloud Control Panel, as long as the computer is connected to the Internet.

# Index

## Numbers

3G, iOS mobile devices, 14

## A

AAC format, 82
accounts, Amazon.com. *See* Amazon Cloud Drive
accounts, Dropbox
    managing, 152
    setting up, 141–143
accounts, iCloud
    Apple ID and, 54
    creating, 30–31
    customizing, 52–53
    downloading songs, 90–91
    linking mobile devices to, 54–55
    troubleshooting, 241
    what to do if you forget account info, 243–244
accounts, iWork.com, 117–118
accounts, Spotify, 173
Address Book
    backing up, 48
    configuring to work with iCloud, 197–198
    turning on iCloud functionality for, 200
address books
    accessing via iCloud, 18
    syncing on iOS devices, 18
    transferring from MobileMe to iCloud, 41
AirDrop, 27
AirPlay, streaming content and, 226, 229, 232–233
AirPort Extreme card, 27
Album Title, iTunes View options, 92
albums
    Complete My Album feature, 66–68

downloading album artwork, 93
Photo Stream, 102
sharing/storing Photo Albums with Dropbox, 150
shopping for music, 62
star-based rating system, 64
Amazon Cloud Drive
    accessing, 163
    comparing with Dropbox, 169
    file sharing with, 5
    integration of Amazon.com online services, 168
    managing, 162–164
    overview of, 160
    setting up, 161–162
Amazon Cloud Player
    integration of Amazon.com online services, 168
    overview of, 160
    playing MP3s, 165–166
Amazon MP3 store
    Google Music compared with, 170
    integration of Amazon.com online services, 168
    listening to MP3s, 164
    listening to MP3s on iOS devices, 165
    overview of, 160
    purchasing and managing music not bought from iTunes, 81
    purchasing music from, 167
Amazon.com
    accessing Cloud Drive account, 163
    Amazon Cloud Player, 165–166
    features of, 160–161
    iCloud compared with, 167–169
    listening to Amazon MP3s on iOS devices, 165

managing Cloud Drive account, 162–164
    overview of, 159–160
    purchasing additional storage space, 164
    purchasing music, 167
    setting up Cloud Drive account, 161–162
Android devices
    Amazon's music service and, 168
    Dropbox apps for, 141
    Google Music service and, 172
Aperture 3
    deleting Photo Stream images from Mac computers, 112
    downloading latest version, 98
    setting up on Macs, 101
App Store
    Apple ID required, 68–69
    download preferences, 72
    manually installing apps from, 203
    purchasing and downloading from, 59
Apple ID
    accessing iCloud accounts, 8, 189
    changing, 55
    iCloud account info and, 54
    for iTunes on Mac computers, 70
    for iTunes on Windows PCs, 72
    linking mobile devices to iCloud, 54–55
    overview of, 15
    requirements for, 68–69
    transferring from MobileMe to iCloud, 42
    what to do if you forget account info, 243–244

Apple TV
  accessing content via iCloud
    account, 9
  accessing iTunes content,
    230–231
  accessing Photo Stream from,
    113–114, 236–237
  accessing rented movies,
    231–232
  accessing TV shows, 233–235
  combining with Photo
    Stream, 97
  HDTV and, 95
  overview of, 225
  purchasing TV season
    series, 226
  renting movies, 227
  setting up screen saver with
    Photo Stream images,
    238–240
  streaming content to,
    232–233
  transferring from MobileMe
    to iCloud, 42
  transferring movies from iOS
    device to, 225–226
  viewing Photo Stream
    images, 107, 238
  what it is/how it works,
    226–229
AppleCare extended
  warranties, 210
apps
  accessing iTunes purchases
    on Macs, 19
  automatic sync, 205–207
  benefits of iCloud, 6–7
  manually installing, 203
  purchasing, 61
  sharing, 9
  syncing, 207
  third-party apps compatible
    with iCloud, 136–137
  third-party apps supporting
    Dropbox, 147
artist
  iTunes View options, 92
  shopping for music by, 62
audio CDs, ripping, 74
audiobooks, 60
automatic backup, 210
Automatic Downloads, iTunes
  Store, 70, 73
auto-update service, iTunes
  Match, 93

**B**

Back to My Mac feature, 40
Backup Software, deactivating, 55

backups
  of app-related documents,
    files, and data, 217–218
  benefits of iCloud for, 7
  cloud-based, 5, 140
  combining iTunes Sync and
    iCloud Backup, 222–223
  creating iTunes Sync backup,
    220–221
  creating Wireless iTunes
    Sync backup, 221–222
  of iOS devices to iCloud,
    210–217
  overview of, 209–210
  restoring iOS device from,
    218–220
  tasks iCloud can perform
    in conjunction with iOS
    devices, 30
  using iCloud account, 9
  while transitioning from
    MobileMe to iCloud,
    48–52
Blackberry devices
  Amazon's music services
    and, 168
  Dropbox apps for, 141
blogs, embedding presentation
  into, 27
bookmarks
  backing up, 50–51
  setting up computer to use,
    202–203
  tasks iCloud can perform
    in conjunction with iOS
    devices, 30
  transferring from MobileMe
    to iCloud, 40
books. See ebooks
broadband, Photo Stream
  requirements, 96
bugs, fixing, 31

**C**

calendars
  accessing via Address Book
    and iCal, 200
  accessing via iCloud, 20, 37
  accessing via Outlook,
    200–201
  activating iCloud for, 188
  backing up Outlook data, 51
  backing up while
    transitioning to iCloud,
    48–50
  benefits of iCloud, 6–7
  configuring Calendar and
    Reminders apps to work
    with iCloud, 198–200

  New MobileMe Calendar
    feature, 43
  syncing, 8
  syncing on iOS devices, 18
  system preferences, 192
  tasks iCloud can perform
    in conjunction with iOS
    devices, 30
  transferring from MobileMe
    to iCloud, 40–41, 44–46
  viewing schedules online, 199
  Windows PCs and, 200
Camera Connection Kit, 96
Camera Roll
  accessing/backing up photos
    in, 7
  album in Photos App, 96
  saving images in albums,
    105–106
CDs, ripping, 74
cloud-based file-sharing
  alternatives to iCloud,
    139–140
  backing up important data,
    140–141
  benefits of iCloud, 6–8
  costs of, 9–10
  with Dropbox. See Dropbox
  finding/locating lost or stolen
    computers or devices,
    11–12
  overview of, 3–5
  requirements for using
    iCloud with iPhone or
    iPad, 13–14
  requirements for using
    iCloud with Mac
    computers, 10–11
  with WebDAV. See WebDAV
  what it is, 5
Complete My Album feature,
  iTunes Store, 66–68
computers
  Apple TV options, 230
  benefits of iCloud, 6–7
  finding/locating lost or
    stolen, 11–12
  Macs. See Mac computers
  transferring Office
    documents to iOS devices,
    124–125
  Windows PCs. See
    Windows PCs
confidentiality, Apple ID and, 15
contacts
  accessing via Address Book
    and iCal, 200
  accessing via iCloud, 20, 37
  accessing via Outlook on
    PCs, 200–201

activating iCloud for, 188
backing up Outlook data, 51
backing up while
    transitioning to iCloud,
    48–50
configuring to work with
    iCloud, 196–198
syncing, 8
syncing on iOS devices, 18
system preferences, 192
tasks iCloud can perform
    in conjunction with iOS
    devices, 30
transferring from MobileMe
    to iCloud, 40
turning on app-specific
    syncing, 34–35
costs, of cloud-based file-sharing,
    9–10
credit cards, linking to Apple ID, 68

## D

data
    backing up to iCloud, 217–218
    benefits of iCloud for
        managing, 6–7
    when to share, 36–37
debit cards, linking to Apple ID, 68
digital images. *See* images
digital music. *See* music
digital photos. *See* photos
digital publications, making
    purchases from iTunes
    Store, 60
digital video recorders (DVRs), 226
documents
    backing up to iCloud,
        217–218
    benefits of iCloud for
        managing, 6–7
    compatibility of iWork with
        Microsoft Office, 119
    copying from computer
        to iPhone or iPad using
        WebDAV, 154–155
    Google Docs, 182–184
    management capabilities of
        iCloud, 175
    manually exporting from
        iWork apps, 131–132
    password-protection and,
        120–123
    sharing via cloud, 26–28
    sharing via e-mail, 132–135
    tasks iCloud can perform
        in conjunction with iOS
        devices, 30
    transferring Office and iWork
        documents to iWork.com,
        119–120

transferring Office
    documents to iOS device,
    124–125, 147–150
transferring/sharing files or
    documents from iPhone or
    iPad, 156
when to share content with/
    without iCloud, 36–37
Documents & Data option
    enabling on Macs, 27
    turning on iCloud
        functionality for specific
        apps, 35
Documents in the Cloud feature
    iCloud, 175
    for sharing files, 26–28
    updates for, 31
downloading
    iPhoto or Aperture, 98
    purchased music to multiple
        devices, 72–73
drop box, using iCloud as virtual
    drop box for file sharing, 26–28
Dropbox
    accessing files from Internet-
        connected devices, 141–142
    backing up important
        data, 140
    choosing as file sharing
        service, 156
    for collaboration or
        sharing, 140
    creating folders using Macs,
        145–146
    as file sharing service, 37
    file sharing with, 5
    getting started with, 142–145
    iCloud compared with,
        152–153
    iCloud or Amazon.com
        compared with, 169
    managing files from
        Dropbox.com, 151–152
    overview of, 141
    setting up account, 141–143
    storing/sharing photos and
        videos, 150
    third-party apps
        supporting, 147
    transferring Word document
        to iPad, 147–150
    using with iPhones or iPads,
        146–147
DVRs (digital video recorders), 226

## E

ebooks
    accessing previous iTunes
        purchases on Macs, 19
    benefits of iCloud, 6–7

configuring iCloud to
    synchronize among
    devices, 203
Kindle reader, 159–160
manually accessing past
    purchases, 204
purchasing, 60
setting up automatic sync,
    205–207
editing photos, in Photo Stream,
    108–109
educational programming, 61
e-mail
    activating iCloud for Mail
        app, 188
    iCloud account for, 189
    importing/exporting files and
        documents vi, 218
    managing via iCloud, 8
    Microsoft Office 365 account
        for, 176, 182
    MobileMe services, 39
    setting up iCloud account for,
        189, 193–194
    sharing content with, 37
    sharing documents with,
        132–135
    Spotify integration
        with, 172
    system preferences, 192
    transferring from MobileMe
        to iCloud, 40–41
    transferring from MobileMe
        to iCloud and, 43–46
    turning on iCloud sync
        feature for, 190
exports
    files and documents, 218
    files to iTunes, iDisk, or
        WebDAV, 136
    files to iWork.com, 135
    manually exporting iWork
        documents, 131–132

## F

Facebook
    sharing content from iOS 5
        apps, 37
    Spotify integration with, 172
files
    accessing using Dropbox,
        141–142
    avoiding file overwrites,
        242–243
    Back to My Mac feature for
        sharing, 24–25
    backing up to iCloud,
        217–218
    cloud-based file-sharing. *See*
        cloud-based file-sharing

files *(cont.)*
 copying from computer
  to iPhone or iPad using
  WebDAV, 154–155
 managing files from
  Dropbox.com, 151–152
 sharing. *See* sharing
  documents and files
 syncing, 6
 transferring/sharing from
  iPhone or iPad, 156
Find My Friends app, iPhone or
 iPad, 13
Find My iPad, 39–40
Find My iPhone, 8, 11–12, 39–40
Find My Mac, 8, 11–12, 21–22
Firefox, 201–202
flickr.com, 37
folders
 creating Dropbox folders
  using Macs, 145–146
 locating Library/Mobile
  Documents folder, 28
 shared folders in Dropbox,
  151–152
Free Music option, iTunes, 65

**G**

Galleries, transferring photos
 from MobileMe to iCloud, 48
Genius feature, iTunes, 62
genre
 browsing iTunes Store by, 66
 iTunes View options, 92
 shopping for music by, 62
Gift Cards, iTunes, 68–69
Google Chrome, 201–202
Google Docs
 alternatives to iCloud,
  175–176
 compared with Microsoft
  365, 184
 overview of, 182–183
 third-party apps
  supporting, 183
Google Music Player, 171
Google Music service, 169–172

**H**

hardware update, requirements
 for using iCloud with Mac
 computers, 10
HDMI (High Definition
 Multimedia), Apple TV and, 226
HDTV (high-definition television)
 Apple TV and, 225, 226
 viewing digital images on, 227
 viewing Photo Stream images
  on HD TV, 107

High Definition Multimedia
 (HDMI), Apple TV and, 226
high-definition television.
 *See* HDTV (high-definition
 television)

**I**

iBooks app
 accessing iBookstore, 60
 reading PDFs with, 146
iBookstore
 accessing, 60
 Apple ID required, 68–69
 download preferences, 72
 manually accessing past
  purchases, 204
 purchasing and downloading
  from, 59
iCal
 accessing calendars, 20
 backing up database, 50
 viewing schedules, 199
iCloud
 account. *See* accounts, iCloud
 Amazon.com compared with,
  167–169
 benefits of syncing
  with, 207
 choosing file sharing
  services, 156
 compatible with WebDAV, 154
 configuring iCloud to
  synchronize among
  devices, 203
 Control Panel, 188–189
 Dropbox compared with,
  152–153, 169
 limitations for
  collaboration, 140
 Microsoft Office 365
  and Google Docs as
  alternatives to, 175–176
 music services compared
  with, 158
 ongoing evolution of, 240
iCloud Backup
 accessing from iPhone,
  213–214
 automating backups, 215
 Back Up Now option, 216
 backing up documents, files,
  and data, 217–218
 establishing on iOS
  devices, 209
 initiating backups, 212
 restoring from backups,
  218–222
 time required for
  backups, 217
 turning off, 222–223

iDisk
 exporting to/from iWork
  app, 135
 transferring files to iCloud,
  46–47
IE (Internet Explorer)
 backing up bookmarks, 51
 configuring web browsers to
  work with iCloud, 201–202
images. *See* photos
instant messaging, in Office
 365, 176
insurance, third-party, 210
Internet
 Apple TV options, 230
 connection for syncing, 187
 iCloud requirements, 4, 11
 Photo Stream requirements, 96
Internet Explorer (IE)
 backing up bookmarks, 51
 configuring web browsers to
  work with iCloud, 201–202
iOS 5
 file-sharing services in, 5
 iCloud integration with, 5
 QuickLook feature in, 146
 transferring from MobileMe
  to iCloud, 42
 updates, 13, 31–33
 upgrading to, 46, 48–49
 Wi-Fi requirements in mobile
  devices, 14
iOS App Store, 61
iOS devices
 accessing movies rented
  from iTunes, 231–232
 accessing Photo Stream from,
  113–114
 adding images to Photo
  Stream, 96
 app-specific syncing, 34–35
 backing up to iCloud, 210–217
 deleting images from Photo
  Stream, 111
 downloading music to, 72–73
 editing photos in Photo
  Stream, 108–109
 e-mail sync feature, 190
 enabling/turning on, 53
 exporting iWork documents,
  131–132
 exporting iWork files to
  iWork.com, 135
 iCloud sync vs. iTunes
  Sync, 196
 iPads. *See* iPads
 iPhones. *See* iPhones
 iPod Touch. *See* iPod Touch
 iTunes Sync from, 220–222
 iWork used with, 129–131
 listening to Amazon MP3s, 165

Mac computers. *See* Mac computers
movies transferred to Apple TV, 225–226
music management, 17–18, 158
notes synced to iCloud, 194–195
Office documents transferred to, 124–125
password-protecting files, 121–123
requirements for syncing to iCloud, 187
restoring from backup or sync, 218–221
Safari app for, 201–202
setting up iCloud for, 4, 30–31
sharing iWork documents, 132–135
streaming content to Apple TV, 232–233
tasks iCloud performs in conjunction with, 29–30
troubleshooting, 241–242
turning on iCloud functionality, 33–36
turning on iCloud functionality for iWork apps, 126–129
updates, 31–33
upgrading to iOS 5, 31
viewing Photo Stream images, 104–106
when to share content with/without iCloud, 36–37
iOSX Lion
file-sharing services in, 5
iCloud integration with, 5
requirements for using iCloud with Mac computers, 10
iPads. *See also* iOS devices
accessing previous iTunes purchases, 78–80
activating iTunes Match service, 89–90
adding Photo Stream images, 108
AirPlay feature for streaming content, 226
backing up, 209–210
Calendar and Reminders apps, 200
checking for iOS 5 updates, 31
Complete My Album feature, 67
copying files/documents to using WebDAV, 154–155

downloading purchased music, 72–73
downloading songs from iCloud account, 90–91
Dropbox apps for, 141
Dropbox for storing photos and videos, 150
files or documents transferred to or shared with, 156
password-protecting files, 121–123
restoring, 218–220
Safari app configured for, 201–202
sharing documents created in Office 365, 182
Spotify app for, 173
turning on Photo Stream, 102–103
using with Dropbox, 146–147
Word documents transferred to, 147–150
iPhones. *See also* iOS devices
accessing content via iCloud account, 9
accessing previous iTunes purchases, 77–78
activating iTunes Match service, 87–89
adding Photo Stream images, 108
AirPlay feature for streaming content, 226
backing up, 209–210
browsing iTunes Store by genre, 66
Calendar and Reminders apps, 200
checking for iOS 5 updates, 31
Complete My Album feature, 67
copying files/documents to using WebDAV, 154–155
downloading purchased music, 72–73
Dropbox apps for, 141
Dropbox for storing photos and videos, 150
files or documents transferred to or shared with, 156
Find My Friends app, 13
finding/locating lost or stolen, 11–12
iCloud backup option, 213–214
password-protecting files, 121–123
restoring, 218–220
Safari app configured for, 201–202

shopping for music, 64
Spotify app for, 173
syncing with linked devices, 4
syncing with other iOS devices, 18
turning on Photo Stream, 102–103
upgrading online storage, 9
using with Dropbox, 146–147
Word documents transferred to, 147–150
iPhoto
deleting Photo Stream images from Macs, 112
downloading latest version, 98
software requirements for using iCloud with Macs, 11
turning on Photo Stream, 100–101
iPod Touch. *See also* iOS devices
accessing content via iCloud account, 9
accessing previous iTunes purchases, 78–80
activating iTunes Match service, 87–89
adding Photo Stream images, 108
AirPlay feature for streaming content, 226
backing up, 209–210
Calendar and Reminders apps, 200
checking for iOS 5 updates, 31
Find My Friends app, 13
finding/locating lost or stolen, 11–12
restoring, 218–220
Spotify app for, 173
syncing with linked devices via iCloud, 4
syncing with other iOS devices, 18
turning on Photo Stream, 102–103
upgrading online storage, 9
iTunes
accessing iTunes content via iCloud, 36, 230–231
accessing previous purchases, 19, 203–204
benefits of iCloud, 6–7
exporting to/from iWork apps, 135
Genius feature, 62
iCloud sync vs. iTunes Sync, 196
installing and using on Macs, 70–72
installing and using on Windows PCs, 72

iTunes (cont.)
managing music library
with, 69
managing music not acquired
from, 157
managing music on Macs,
17–18
overview of, 59
renting movies with, 227
software requirements for
using iCloud with Macs,
10–11
tasks iCloud can perform in
conjunction with, 29–30
Top Charts feature, 62
updating, 48
uploading music library to
Google Music Player, 171
View options, 92
iTunes Gift Cards, 68–69
iTunes Match service
activating on another
computer, 91–93
activating on iPad, 89–90
activating on iPhone or iPod
Touch, 87–89
auto-update service for
syncing music to all
devices, 93
canceling auto-renewing
subscription, 86–87
cost of, 9
managing music library with,
17–18, 157
overview of, 6, 81–82
quality and, 82
signing up for/activating,
82–85
syncing music from all
sources, 74
iTunes Store
accessing previous iTunes
purchases, 19–20, 77–80,
203–204
Apple ID required, 68–69
benefits of managing music
with iCloud, 158
browsing by genre, 66
Complete My Album feature,
66–68
limitations on movie
rentals, 61
making purchases from, 60–61
Purchased option, 75–77
purchasing and downloading
from, 59
system preferences, 70–72
iTunes Sync
backup options, 210
checking for iOS 5 updates,
31–32

combining iTunes Sync and
iCloud Backup, 222–223
creating iTunes Sync backup,
220–221
creating Wireless iTunes
Sync backup, 221–222
iCloud sync compared with,
18, 196
importing/exporting files and
documents, 218
restoring from, 221
iWork
accessing files via iCloud, 20
backing up and syncing, 175
iCloud compatibility of, 4
importing/exporting files
and documents, 131–132,
135, 218
sharing document and files
with iCloud, 117
sharing documents via
e-mail, 132–135
software requirements for
using iCloud with Mac
computers, 11
tasks iCloud can perform
in conjunction with iOS
devices, 30
transferring documents to
iWork.com, 119–120
transferring iWork for Mac
files to iWork.com,
125–126
turning on iCloud
functionality for specific
apps, 35
turning on iCloud
functionality on iOS
devices, 126–129
using for iOS apps with
iCloud, 129–131
using iCloud as virtual drop
box for file sharing, 26–28
WebDAV compatibility, 154
when to share content with/
without iCloud, 37
iWork.com
embedding presentation into
web site or blog, 27
exporting files to, 135
password-protecting files that
are uploaded to, 120–123
setting up account, 117–118
transferring iWork for Mac
files to, 125–126
transferring Office and iWork
documents to, 119–120

**J**

JPEGs, 107

**K**

Keynote app (presentations/slide
shows). See also iWork
avoiding file overwrites, 243
embedding presentation into
web site or blog, 27
iCloud compatibility of, 4
importing/exporting files and
documents, 218
sharing document and
files, 117
software requirements for
using iCloud with Mac
computers, 11
transferring/sharing files or
documents, 156
turning on iCloud
functionality for specific
apps, 35
using iCloud as virtual drop
box for file sharing, 26–28
WebDAV compatibility, 154
when to share content with/
without iCloud, 37
Kindle, 159–160

**L**

language settings, creating iCloud
accounts, 52–53
libraries, locating Library/Mobile
Documents folder, 28
libraries, music. See music library
log-in problems, 244

**M**

Mac App Store, 61
Mac computers. See also iOS
devices
accessing iTunes content
with Apple TV, 230
accessing Photo Stream from,
113–114
accessing previous iTunes
purchases, 19, 75–77
adding Photo Stream
images, 108
addressing files stored on
Dropbox, 141
AirDrop support and, 27
Back to My Mac feature,
24–25
creating Dropbox folders,
145–146
deleting Photo Stream
images, 110–112
Find My Mac feature, 22–23
installing iTunes on, 70–72
iTunes Match service on,
91–93

iWork for Mac files, 125–126
managing music on, 17–18
requirements for using
    iCloud with, 10–11, 60
sharing photos, 18
syncing with iPhone, iPad, or
    iPod touch, 18
third-party options related to
    iCloud, 27
turning off Photo Stream
    without deleting photos, 113
turning on mail
    synchronization, 191
turning on Photo Stream,
    98–101
viewing Photo Stream
    images, 104
what to do if you forget
    account info, 244
Mail app. *See* e-mail
Microsoft Excel
    apps, 180–181
    Numbers compatibility
        with, 26
    in Office 365, 176
    sharing document and
        files, 117
    transferring documents from
        computer to iOS device,
        124–125
    transferring spreadsheets to
        iPad, 148–150
Microsoft Office
    iWork compatibility with, 119
    sharing document and
        files, 117
    transferring documents from
        computer to iOS device,
        124–125
    transferring documents to
        iWork.com, 119–120
Microsoft Office 365
    accessing Office Web apps, 178
    alternatives to iCloud,
        175–176
    benefits of, 177–178
    compared with Google
        Docs, 184
    e-mail account for, 182
    Excel or PowerPoint Web
        apps, 180–181
    features of, 176–177
    overview of, 176
    Word Web app, 178–179
Microsoft Outlook
    accessing contacts, calendars,
        and reminders, 200–201
    backing up data, 51
    configuring Contacts app to
        work with iCloud, 197
    Notes app syncing with, 195
    in Office 365, 176

setting up iCloud-related
    e-mail account on
    Windows PC, 193–194
viewing schedules online, 199
Microsoft PowerPoint
    apps, 180–181
    Keynote compatibility with, 26
    in Office 365, 176
    sharing document and
        files, 117
    transferring documents from
        computer to iOS device,
        124–125
    transferring presentations to
        iPad, 148–150
Microsoft Word
    importing Word documents
        into iPhone or iPad, 155
    in Office 365, 176
    Pages compatibility with, 26
    sharing document and
        files, 117
    transferring documents from
        computer to iOS device,
        124–125
    transferring Word document
        to iPad, 147–150
    Word Web app, 178–179
MMS (Multimedia Message
    Service), 7
mobile devices. *See also* iOS
    devices
    benefits of iCloud, 6
    finding/locating lost or
        stolen, 11–12
    linking to new iCloud
        account, 54–55
    requiring Wi-FI, 14
mobile documents, 28
MobileMe
    backing up during transition
        process, 48–52
    customizing new iCloud
        account, 52–53
    email account transferred to
        iCloud, 189
    features no longer supported,
        46–47
    iCloud replacing, 8
    initiating conversion to
        iCloud, 43–45
    linking mobile devices to
        new iCloud account, 54–55
    managing transition to
        iCloud, 41–42
    migrating to iCloud from, 31
    requirements for
        transitioning to iCloud,
        42–43
    services offered in, 39–40
    services that can be transferred
        to iCloud, 40–41

software requirements for
    using iCloud with Macs, 11
transferring mail and
    calendar information,
    44–46
transferring photos, 46–48
upgrading to iOS 5 as part
    of transition process, 46,
    48, 49
movies
    accessing past purchases, 230
    accessing rented movies
        from other computer or
        iOS devices, 231–232
    Apple TV options, 230
    limitations on rentals, 61
    purchasing, 60
    renting, 227
    transferring to Apple TV
        from iOS devices, 225–226
MP3s
    Amazon Cloud Player, 165–166
    benefits of cloud-based
        storage, 159
    converting AAC files to, 82
    listening on iOS devices, 165
    listening to music on
        Amazon Cloud Drive
        account, 164
    purchasing from Amazon
        MP3 Store, 167
    purchasing/managing music
        not bought from iTunes, 81
Multimedia Message Service
    (MMS), 7
music
    accessing from iCloud, 73–75
    accessing previous
        purchases, 19
    automatic sync, 205–207
    benefits of iCloud, 6–7
    configuring iCloud to
        synchronize among
        devices, 203
    downloading to multiple
        devices, 72–73
    Google Music service, 169–172
    learning about before
        purchasing, 64–65
    Music Unlimited service, 173
    purchasing music videos, 60
    purchasing/managing music
        not bought from iTunes, 81
    sharing, 9
    sharing content with/without
        iCloud, 36–37
    shopping for on iTunes
        Store, 62
    tasks iCloud can perform
        in conjunction with iOS
        devices, 29
    viewing on Macs or PCs, 73

Music app
  downloading songs from
    iCloud account, 91
  managing music with, 59
music library
  accessing music from iCloud,
    73–75
  accessing previous iTunes
    purchases on iPhone, iPad,
    or iPod Touch, 77–80
  accessing previous iTunes
    purchases on Macs and
    PCs, 75–77
  Apple ID required, 68–69
  browsing iTunes Store by
    genre, 66
  cloud-based services for, 140
  Complete My Album feature,
    66–68
  downloading purchased
    music to multiple devices,
    72–73
  installing and using iTunes
    on Mac computers, 70–72
  installing and using iTunes
    on Windows PCs, 72
  iTunes Match analyzing,
    83–84
  learning about music before
    purchasing, 64–65
  making purchases from
    iTunes Store, 60–61
  managing with iTunes, 69
  overview of, 59–60
  shopping for music from
    iTunes Store, 62
  viewing music accessible on
    Macs or PCs, 73
Music service, Google, 169–172
music services, cloud-based
  alternatives to iCloud,
    157–158
  Amazon.com. *See* Amazon.
    com
  benefits of, 159
  Google Music service, 169–172
  iCloud music library.
    *See* music library
  Music Unlimited, 173
  other options, 174
  Spotify, 172–173
Music Unlimited, 173
music videos, purchasing, 60

**N**
NAT-PMP (NAT Port Mapping
  Protocol), 25
Netflix, 230
newspapers, purchasing digital
  editions, 61
Newsstand, 68–69

Notes app, 194–195
Numbers app (spreadsheets).
  *See also* iWork
  avoiding file overwrites, 243
  iCloud compatibility of, 4
  importing/exporting files and
    documents, 218
  sharing files and documents
    from iPhone or iPad to, 156
  sharing files and documents
    to iCloud, 117
  software requirements for
    using iCloud with Mac
    computers, 11
  turning on iCloud
    functionality for specific
    apps, 35
  using iCloud as virtual drop
    box for file sharing, 26–28
  WebDAV compatibility
    of, 154
  when to share content with/
    without iCloud, 37

**O**
Office. *See* Microsoft Office
OffSiteBox.com, signing up for
  WebDAV, 154
OneNote, in Office 365, 176
online music services, 81
online storage. *See also* storage
  costs of, 9–10
  services offered in
    MobileMe, 39
  tracking use of, 211
OS X Lion
  Back to My Mac feature
    and, 25
  benefits of managing music
    with iCloud, 158
  requirements for using
    iCloud with Macs, 60
  transferring from MobileMe
    to iCloud, 42
Outlook. *See* Microsoft Outlook

**P**
Pages app (word processing).
  *See also* iWork
  avoiding file overwrites, 243
  backing up to iCloud,
    217–218
  iCloud compatibility of, 4
  importing documents into
    iPhone or iPad, 155
  importing/exporting files and
    documents, 218
  sharing document and files
    with iCloud, 117
  sharing documents and files
    from iPhone or iPad to, 156

software requirements for
  using iCloud with Mac
  computers, 11
turning on iCloud
  functionality for specific
  apps, 35
using iCloud as virtual drop
  box for file sharing, 26–28
WebDAV compatibility, 154
when to share content with/
  without iCloud, 37
passwords
  adding to iWork documents,
    120–123
  Apple ID and, 15
  installing and using iTunes
    and, 70, 72
  troubleshooting iCloud, 241
  what to do if you forget
    account info, 243–244
PCs. *See* Windows PCs
PDFs, QuickLook feature for
  viewing, 146
periodicals, purchasing, 61
personalization, of iCloud
  features, 4
photo galleries, Dropbox for
  creating/sharing, 142
Photo Stream, 6
  accessing on iCloud, 236–237
  accessing using Apple TV, 225
  adding images manually, 108
  adding images to, 96
  deleting all images, 110–111
  deleting images from iOS
    devices, 111
  deleting images from
    Macs, 112
  deleting images from
    Windows PCs, 112–113
  editing photos in, 108–109
  image resolution and, 96
  overview of, 95
  pros/cons of, 97
  setting up screen savers,
    238–240
  sharing images, 113–114
  sharing photos via iCloud, 18
  tasks iCloud can perform
    in conjunction with iOS
    devices, 30
  turn off without deleting
    photos, 113
  turning on for iPhones, iPads,
    and iPod Touch, 102–103
  turning on for Macs, 98–101
  turning on for Windows
    PCs, 102
  viewing images, 238
  viewing images on HD TV, 107
  viewing images on iOS
    devices, 104–106

viewing images on Macs, 104
viewing images on Windows
    PCs, 106
photos
    accessing on iCloud, 236–237
    adding images manually, 108
    benefits of iCloud, 6–7
    deleting entire Photo Stream,
        110–111
    deleting from iOS devices, 111
    deleting from Mac
        computers, 112
    deleting from Windows PCs,
        112–113
    downloading iPhoto or
        Aperture, 98
    editing, 108–109
    MobileMe services for, 39
    overview of, 95–96
    Photo Stream pros/cons, 97
    setting up screen savers,
        238–240
    sharing, 113–114
    sharing via iCloud account, 9
    sharing/storing with
        Dropbox, 150
    tasks iCloud can perform
        in conjunction with iOS
        devices, 30
    transferring from MobileMe
        to iCloud, 41, 46–48
    turn off Photo Stream without
        deleting photos, 113
    turning on Photo Stream on
        iPhones, iPads, or iPod
        Touch, 102–103
    turning on Photo Stream on
        Macs, 98–101
    turning on Photo Stream
        Windows PCs, 102
    viewing on Apple TV, 238
    viewing on HD TV, 107
    viewing on iOS devices,
        104–106
    viewing on Macs, 104
    viewing on Windows PCs, 106
    when to share content with/
        without iCloud, 36–37
Photos app
    Camera Roll Album, 96
    saving images, 105–106
    viewing images, 104–106
PNG image format, 107
podcasts, purchasing, 60
presentations. *See also* Keynote
    app (presentations/slide shows)
    embedding into web site or
        blog, 27
    importing/exporting, 218
    sharing, 117
    transferring to iPad using
        Dropbox, 148–150

using iCloud as virtual drop
    box for file sharing, 26–28
previewing, music selections,
    64–65
privacy, Apple ID and, 15
Purchased option, iTunes Store
    accessing previous purchases
        on iPhone, iPad, or iPod
        Touch, 77–78
    accessing previous purchases
        on Macs and PCs, 75–77

**Q**

QuickLook feature, in iOS 5, 146

**R**

ratings
    iTunes View options, 92
    for music, 64
RAW image format, 107
reminders
    activating iCloud for, 188
    configuring Calendar and
        Reminders app to work
        with iCloud, 198–200
    Windows PCs, 200
resolution, of Photo Stream
    images, 107
restores
    benefits of iCloud, 7
    of iOS devices, 218–220
ringtones, 61
ripping CDs, 74, 81

**S**

Safari
    activating iCloud for, 188
    backing up bookmarks, 50
    configuring to work with
        iCloud, 201–202
    setting up computer to use
        Safari bookmarks and
        reading list data, 202–203
    syncing bookmarks, 30
scheduling, in Office 365, 176
screen savers, 238–240
shared folders, in Dropbox,
    151–152
sharing
    Photo Stream images,
        113–114
    videos and photos using
        Dropbox, 150
sharing documents and files. *See
    also* cloud-based file-sharing
    e-mail for, 132–135
    exporting files to iTunes,
        iDisk, or WebDAV from
        iWork, 136
    exporting files to iWork.com
        from iWork, 135

manually exporting
    documents from iWork,
    131–132
Office 365 and, 180, 182
overview of, 117
password-protecting files
    uploaded files, 120–123
setting up iWork.com
    account, 117–118
third-party apps with iCloud
    compatibility, 136–137
transferring iWork files to
    iWork.com, 125–126
transferring Office and iWork
    documents to iWork.com,
    119–120
transferring Office
    documents to iOS devices,
    124–125
turning on iCloud
    functionality for iWork apps
    on iOS devices, 126–129
using iWork for iOS apps with
    iCloud, 129–131
Short Message Service (SMS), 172
slide shows, 107. *See also* Keynote
    app (presentations/slide shows)
SMS (Short Message Service), 172
software
    deactivating Backup
        Software, 55
    third-party iCloud options for
        Macs, 28
    updates, 10–11
song titles, shopping for music
    by, 62
Sony Music Unlimited, 173–174
Spotify, 172–173
spreadsheets, 148–150. *See also*
    Numbers app (spreadsheets)
star-based rating system, for
    music, 64
storage
    addressing files stored on
        Dropbox, 141
    Amazon Cloud Drive, 160–161
    benefits of cloud-based
        storage for music files, 159
    costs of online storage, 9–10
    of photos and videos with
        Dropbox, 142
    purchasing additional
        storage space from
        Amazon.com, 164
    services offered in
        MobileMe, 39
    tracking use of online
        storage, 211
streaming content, from iOS device
    to Apple TV, 227, 232–233
subscription, iTunes Match
    canceling, 86–87
    purchasing, 82

syncing
  app-specific syncing, 34–35
  avoiding file overwrites,
    242–243
  as backup option, 210
  benefits of iCloud, 207
  combining iTunes Sync and
    iCloud Backup, 222–223
  contacts and calendars, 8
  creating wireless backup,
    221–222
  ebooks, 203
  e-mail, 190–191
  files, 6
  iCloud vs. iTunes Sync,
    18, 196
  iCloud vs. USB cable, 7
  Internet connection for, 187
  iOS linked devices, 4
  iWork, 175
  music to all devices with
    auto-update service, 93
  notes, 194–195
  restoring from, 218–221
  setting up automatic sync,
    205–207
system preferences
  iTunes Store, 70–72
  launching MobileMe to
    iCloud transition from,
    43–44
  turning on mail
    synchronization for iCloud
    email accounts, 191–192
  turning on Photo Stream
    feature on Macs, 99

**T**

text editors, Notes app as,
  194–195
third-party apps
  with iCloud compatibility,
    136–137
  supporting Dropbox, 147
  supporting Google Docs, 183
third-party software, iCloud
  options for Macs, 28
TIFF image format, 107
time zones, creating iCloud
  accounts and, 52–53
TiVo, 226
Top Charts feature, iTunes, 62
troubleshooting
  avoiding file overwrites,
    242–243
  overview of, 241
  what to do if iCloud doesn't
    work, 241–242
  what to do if you forget
    account info, 243–244

TV (television), viewing Photo
  Stream images on HDTV, 107
TV shows
  accessing past purchases,
    19–20, 231
  accessing purchased shows
    on iCloud, 233–235
  Apple TV options, 230
  purchasing, 60
  purchasing season series, 226
Twitter
  sharing content from iOS 5
    apps, 37
  Spotify integration with, 172

**U**

Universal Plug and Play (UPnP), 25
updates
  Apple TV OS, 229
  iOS 5, 13
  iTunes, 82
  when using iCloud with Mac
    computers, 10
upgrades, to iOS 5 during
  transition from MobileMe, 46,
  48–49
UPnP (Universal Plug and Play), 25
USB cable, 209

**V**

videos
  purchasing music videos, 60
  sharing/storing with
    Dropbox, 150

**W**

web browsers
  apps. *See* Web-based apps
  configuring to work with
    iCloud, 201–202
  setting bookmarks and
    reading list data,
    202–203
  viewing popular songs
    with, 62
web pages, MobileMe and, 46
web sites, embedding presentation
  into, 27
Web-based apps
  accessing Office, 178
  benefits of, 184
  Excel or PowerPoint Web
    apps, 180–181
  Google Docs, 182–184
  Word Web app, 178–179
WebDAV (Web-based Distributed
  Authoring and Versioning)
    for collaboration or
    sharing, 140

copying files/documents
  from computer to iPhone
    or iPad, 154–155
  exporting to from iWork app
    on iOS devices, 135
  importing/exporting files and
    documents, 218
  overview of, 153–154
  transferring/sharing files or
    documents from iPhone or
    iPad to, 156
Wi-Fi
  backing up via, 209–212
  Find My Mac feature and,
    21–23
  hotspots, 209
  iOS mobile devices
    requiring, 14
  Photo Stream requirements, 96
Windows Mobile, Dropbox apps
  for, 141
Windows PCs
  accessing Photo Stream from,
    113–114
  accessing previous iTunes
    purchases, 75–77
  activating iTunes Match
    service, 91–93
  adding images manually to
    Photo Stream, 108
  addressing files stored on
    Dropbox, 141
  deleting all Photo Stream
    images, 110–111
  deleting Photo Stream
    images, 112–113
  iCloud use by, 21
  installing and using iTunes
    on, 72
  requirements for using
    iCloud with, 60
  setting up iCloud-related
    e-mail account, 193–194
  turning on Photo
    Stream, 102
  viewing Photo Stream
    images, 106
  what to do if you forget
    account info, 244
wireless backup, 210
Wireless iTunes Sync backup,
  221–222
word processing
  with Google Docs, 182
  with Pages. *See* Pages app
    (word processing)
word processors
  text editors compared
    with, 194